Foundations of English 9

SUE HARPER
ANITA GRIFFITH

NELSON

Australia   Canada   Mexico   Singapore   Spain   United Kingdom   United States

Foundations of English 9

Sue Harper, Literacy Resource Teacher, Peel District School Board, Mississauga, ON
Anita Griffith, English Teacher, Rick Hansen Secondary School, Peel District School Board, Mississauga, ON

Director of Publishing
Beverley Buxton

Director of Publishing, Literacy and Reference
Joe Banel

Executive Managing Editor, Development
Darleen Rotozinski

Project Manager
Ian Nussbaum

Developmental Editor
Sasha Patton

Executive Managing Editor, Production
Nicola Balfour

Senior Production Editor
Lisa Dimson

Indexer
Noeline Bridge

Production Coordinator
Ferial Suleman

Creative Director
Ken Phipps

Interior Design
Sharon Foster
Eugene Lo

Cover Design
Sonya Thursby, Opus House Incorporated
Eugene Lo

Art Management
Cheri Westra
Suzanne Peden

Cover Images
Top left: Ryan McVay/Photodisc Red/Getty Images; top right: Photodisc/Getty Images; bottom left: Eyewire Images; bottom right: Photodisc/Getty Images

Compositor
Pamela Clayton

Photo Researchers
Krista Alexander
Vicki Gould

Permissions
Linda Tanaka

Printer
Transcontinental Printing Inc.

Reviewers
The authors and publisher gratefully acknowledge the contributions of the following educators:

Leanne Bergeron, Ottawa-Carleton Catholic DSB
Rick Carter, Sudbury Catholic DSB
Inge Coates, Region 14, Sherwood Park, AB
Adrian Flynn, Dufferin-Peel Catholic DSB
JoAnne Folville, Halton Catholic DSB
Paul Frawley, Durham Catholic DSB
Gayleen Garvin, Limestone DSB
Donna Giacalone-Miller, Hamilton-Wentworth Catholic DSB
Debbie Green, Avon Maitland DSB
Myra Junyk, Toronto Catholic DSB
Helen LaCroix, York Region Catholic DSB
Noël Lim, Peel DSB
Jennifer McGilchrist, Hamilton-Wentworth DSB
Patricia Remmer, Upper Canada DSB
Tamar Stein, York Region DSB
Penny Vail Dunbar, Toronto DSB

COPYRIGHT © 2006 by Nelson, a division of Thomson Canada Limited.

Printed and bound in Canada
1 2 3 4   08 07 06 05

For more information contact Nelson, 1120 Birchmount Road, Toronto, Ontario, M1K 5G4. Or you can visit our Internet site at http://www.nelson.com

ALL RIGHTS RESERVED. No part of this work covered by the copyright herein, except for any reproducible pages included in this work, may be reproduced, transcribed, or used in any form or by any means—graphic, electronic, or mechanical, including photocopying, recording, taping, Web distribution, or information storage and retrieval systems—without the written permission of the publisher.

For permission to use material from this text or product, submit a request online at www.thomsonrights.com

Every effort has been made to trace ownership of all copyrighted material and to secure permission from copyright holders. In the event of any question arising as to the use of any material, we will be pleased to make the necessary corrections in future printings.

National Library of Canada Cataloguing in Publication Data

Harper, Sue, 1952–
Foundations of English 9 / Sue Harper, Anita Griffith.

Includes index.

ISBN 0-7747-1827-7

1. Readers (Secondary) 2. English language—Problems, exercises, etc. I. Griffith, Anita II. Title. III. Title: Foundations of English nine.

PE1121.H386 2005   428.6
C2004-906675-7

Table of Contents

Alternative Table of Contents   vi
Introduction   x

> Unit 1: Connections   1

Talk Before They Run *by Child Find Ontario* (Informational Text)   3
Dream Variation *by Langston Hughes* (Poem)   9
TWO SELECTIONS ON BREAKING DOWN THE BARRIERS
  Mother Goose & Grimm *by Mike Peters* (Cartoon)   11
  All Ears *by Gena K. Gorrell* (Informational Text)   12
The Blind Hunter *by Irene N. Watts* (Drama)   16
Coming Out of a Canadian Winter *by Lakshmi Gill* (Poem)   22
You Never Know (Tish) *by Wendy A. Lewis* (Short Story)   24
Unit 1 Activity   37

> Unit 2: Sports   39

Fix That Flat! *by Chris Hayhurst* (Informational Text)   41
Chew on This *by Jaclyn Law* (Magazine Article)   43
Is Skateboarding a Crime? *by L.M. Burke* (Informational Text)   46
Foul Shot *by Edwin A. Hoey* (Poem)   49
TWO SELECTIONS ON OVERCOMING OBSTACLES
  Kendra Ohama *by Laura Robinson and Maija Robinson* (Biography)   52
  Wheelchair Rugby (Informational Text)   57
Can Girls Really Play with Boys? *by Oakland Ross* (Newspaper Article)   60
A Fly in a Pail of Milk *by Herb Carnegie* (Autobiography)   66
The Hockey Game *by Wes Fineday* (Short Story)   72
Unit 2 Activity   79

> ## Unit 3: What …? 81

Superpoopers *by Nancy Finton* (Magazine Article)   83
🍁 Tiny Bubbles? *by Anne McIlroy* (Newspaper Article)   85
The Praying Mantis *by Dick King-Smith* (Poem)   88
🍁 Why Do People Yawn, and Why Are Yawns Contagious? *by Kathy Wollard* (Informational Text)   90
Two Selections on Bones
    Bones *by Walter de la Mare* (Poem)   93
    Gross Out? *by Britt Norlander* (Magazine Article)   94
Tallest Man Feels Lowly at the Top *by Anna Menlichuk* (Newspaper Article)   96
🍁 Blue Eyes *by Meghan Wafer* (Short Story)   99
🍁 The Magic Sieve *by Irene N. Watts* (Drama/Folktale)   102
mirrors dot com *by Lesley Howarth* (Short Story)   108
Unit 3 Activity   117

> ## Unit 4: Investigations 119

🍁 Fingerprinting the Dead *by David Owen* (Informational Text)   121
🍁 You Have the Right to Remain … Informed *by the Department of Justice Canada* (Informational Text)   125
🍁 The Gift That Could Not Be Stolen *by Burt Konzak* (Short Story)   132
🍁 Spittin' Mad? That'll Be $155 *by Robin MacLennan* (Newspaper Article)   136
Unbalanced *by William Sleator* (Short Story)   141
Guilt *by Steve Barlow and Steve Skidmore* (Drama)   150
Unit 4 Activity   155

> ## Unit 5: Empowerment 157

🍁 State of the Teen Nation *by Youth Culture Research: Trendscan* (Magazine Article)   159
🍁 Helping Kids Make Sense of the Media *by Terry Price* (Newspaper Article)   163
🍁 What Dreams May Come *by Jody Roach* (Poem)   168
🍁 Looking Like a Kid *by André Mayer* (Magazine Article)   170
🍁 What Are You Waiting For? (Quiz)   175
Two Selections on Our Roots
    🍁 slang tongue twist *by Vera Wabegijig* (Poem)   179
    🍁 Mother Tongue *by Susan Lee* (Poem)   180
The Ravine *by Graham Salisbury* (Short Story)   182
Unit 5 Activity   193

> **Unit 6: Tech Talk**   195

Future World *by Michael N. Smith* (Magazine Article)   197
🍁 Bubble Chamber *by Tania Nepveu* (Short Story)   201
New Science of Body Measurement (Graphic Text)   205
TWO SELECTIONS ON TEXT MESSAGING
     🍁 Tech Talk *by Ted Kritsonis* (Magazine Article)   207
     🍁 Zits *by Jerry Scott and Jim Borgman* (Cartoon)   209
🍁 Best Advice: Handle with Care (Graphic Text)   211
The Toynbee Convector *by Ray Bradbury (adapted by Ray Zone and
      Chuck Roblin)* (Graphic Fiction)   214
Unit 6 Activity   229

> **The Reference Shelf**   231

Section 1: The English Language   232
Section 2: Reading and Researching   239
Section 3: Writing   258
Section 4: Oral Communication Skills   277
Section 5: The Media   282

Glossary   290
Index   297
Acknowledgements   305

>>> Alternative Groupings of the Selections

> Genres

Informational Texts
(Including Magazine and Newspaper Articles, Instructions, Graphic Texts, and Quizzes)

Talk Before They Run   3
All Ears   12
Fix That Flat!   41
Chew on This   43
Is Skateboarding a Crime?   46
Wheelchair Rugby   57
Can Girls Really Play with Boys?   57
Superpoopers   83
Tiny Bubbles?   85
Why Do People Yawn, and Why Are Yawns Contagious?   90
Gross Out?   94
Tallest Man Feels Lowly at the Top   96
Fingerprinting the Dead   121
You Have the Right to Remain … Informed   125
Spittin' Mad? That'll be $155   136
State of the Teen Nation   159
Helping Kids Make Sense of the Media   163
Looking Like a Kid   170
What Are You Waiting For?   175
Future World   197
New Science of Body Measurement   205
Tech Talk   207
Best Advice: Handle with Care   211

Fiction
You Never Know (Tish)   24
The Hockey Game   72
Blue Eyes   99
mirrors dot com   108
The Gift That Could Not Be Stolen   132
Unbalanced   141
The Ravine   182
Bubble Chamber   201
The Toynbee Convector   214

Poetry
Dream Variation   9
Coming Out of a Canadian Winter   22
Foul Shot   49
The Praying Mantis   88
Bones   93
What Dreams May Come   168
slang tongue twist   179
Mother Tongue   180

Drama
The Blind Hunter   16
The Magic Sieve   102
Guilt   150

Biography/Autobiography
Kendra Ohama   52
A Fly in a Pail of Milk   66

Cartoons/Graphic Fiction
Mother Goose & Grimm   11
Zits   209
The Toynbee Convector   214

vi | FOUNDATIONS OF ENGLISH 9

> Authors According to Country

Canadian

Talk Before They Run—*Child Find Ontario* 3
All Ears—*Gena K. Gorrell* 12
The Blind Hunter—*Irene N. Watts* 16
Coming Out of a Canadian Winter—*Lakshmi Gill* 22
You Never Know (Tish)—*Wendy A. Lewis* 24
Chew on This—*Jaclyn Law* 43
Is Skateboarding a Crime?—*L.M. Burke* 46
Kendra Ohama—*Laura Robinson and Maija Robinson* 52
Wheelchair Rugby 57
Can Girls Really Play with Boys?—*Oakland Ross* 60
A Fly in a Pail of Milk—*Herb Carnegie* 66
The Hockey Game—*Wes Fineday* 72
Tiny Bubbles?—*Anne McIlroy* 85
Why Do People Yawn, and Why Are Yawns Contagious?—*Kathy Wollard* 90
Blue Eyes—*Meghan Wafer* 99
The Magic Sieve—*Irene N. Watts* 102
Fingerprinting the Dead—*David Owen* 121
You Have the Right to Remain ... Informed—*Department of Justice Canada* 125
The Gift That Could Not Be Stolen—*Burt Konzak* 132
Spittin' Mad? That'll be $155—*Robin MacLennan* 136
State of the Teen Nation—*Youth Culture Research* 159
Helping Kids Make Sense of the Media—*Terry Price* 163
What Dreams May Come—*Jody Roach* 168
Looking Like a Kid—*André Mayer* 170
What Are You Waiting For? 175
slang tongue twist—*Vera Wabegijig* 179
Mother Tongue—*Susan Lee* 180
Bubble Chamber—*Tania Nepveu* 201
Tech Talk—*Ted Kritsonis* 208
Best Advice: Handle With Care 211

American

Dream Variation—*Langston Hughes* 9
Mother Goose & Grimm—*Mike Peters* 11
Fix That Flat!—*Chris Hayhurst* 41
Foul Shot—*Edwin A. Hoey* 49
Superpoopers—*Nancy Finton* 83
Gross Out?—*Britt Norlander* 94
Unbalanced—*William Sleator* 141
The Ravine—*Graham Salisbury* 182
Future World—*Michael N. Smith* 197
New Science of Body Measurement 205
Zits—*Jerry Scott and Jim Borgman* 209
The Toynbee Convector—*Ray Bradbury* 214

Alternative Groupings of the Selections | vii

International

The Praying Mantis—*Dick King-Smith* (Britain) 88
Bones—*Walter de la Mare* (Britain) 93
Tallest Man Feels Lowly at the Top—*Anna Menlichuk* (Ukraine) 96
mirrors dot com—*Lesley Howarth* (Britain) 108
Guilt—*Steve Barlow and Steve Skidmore* (Britain) 150

> Themes

Identity

Dream Variation 9
Coming Out of a Canadian Winter 22
You Never Know (Tish) 24
A Fly in a Pail of Milk 66
The Hockey Game 72
Tallest Man Feels Lowly at the Top 96
Unbalanced 141
Guilt 150
State of the Teen Nation 159
What Dreams May Come 168
Looking Like a Kid 170
slang tongue twist 179
Mother Tongue 180

Diversity

Dream Variation 9
A Fly in a Pail of Milk 66
The Hockey Game 72
slang tongue twist 179
Mother Tongue 180

Science and Technology

Chew on This 43
Superpoopers 83
Tiny Bubbles? 85
Why Do People Yawn, and Why Are Yawns Contagious? 90
Gross Out? 94
Fingerprinting the Dead 121
Guilt 150
Looking Like a Kid 170
Future World 197
Bubble Chamber 201
New Science of Body Measurement 205
Tech Talk 207
Zits 209
The Toynbee Convector 214

Humour

Mother Goose and Grimm 11
Superpoopers 83
Tiny Bubbles? 85
Zits 209

Being a Teenager

Talk Before They Run 3
You Never Know (Tish) 24
Is Skateboarding a Crime? 46
You Have the Right to Remain … Informed 125
Unbalanced 141
State of the Teen Nation 159
Helping Kids Make Sense of the Media 163
Looking Like a Kid 170
The Ravine 182

Everyday Heroes

All Ears 12
The Blind Hunter 16
Kendra Ohama 52
A Fly in a Pail of Milk 66
Looking Like a Kid 170

FOUNDATIONS OF ENGLISH 9

Family and Friends

Talk Before They Run   3
The Blind Hunter   16
You Never Know (Tish)   24
The Magic Sieve   102
mirrors dot com   108
The Gift That Could Not Be Stolen   132
Unbalanced   141
The Ravine   182

Social Issues

Talk Before They Run   3
Is Skateboarding a Crime?   46
Can Girls Really Play with Boys?   60
A Fly in a Pail of Milk   66
You Have the Right to Remain ... Informed   125
The Gift That Could Not Be Stolen   132
Spittin' Mad? That'll be $155   136
Guilt   150
State of the Teen Nation   159
Helping Kids Make Sense of the Media   163
Bubble Chamber   201
New Science of Body Measurement   205
The Toynbee Convector   214

Overcoming Barriers

Mother Goose and Grimm   11
All Ears   12
Kendra Ohama   52
Wheelchair Rugby   57
Can Girls Really Play With Boys?   60
A Fly in a Pail of Milk   66

Practical Matters

Fix That Flat!   41
Chew on This   43
Why Do People Yawn, and Why Are Yawns Contagious?   90
You Have the Right to Remain ... Informed   125
State of the Teen Nation   159
Helping Kids Make Sense of the Media   163
What Are You Waiting For?   175
Best Advice: Handle With Care   211

Nature and the Environment

The Blind Hunter   16
Coming Out of a Canadian Winter   22
The Magic Sieve   102

Introduction to Students

Welcome to *Foundations of English 9*. Even if you don't usually read introductions to textbooks, we hope you will read this one. This book was written for you, and we hope you enjoy reading it. We've chosen subjects that we hope will interest you, and we've included a variety of types of reading.

Foundations of English 9 is about strategies: reading strategies, writing strategies, and strategies for listening and speaking. These strategies will have an effect on the way you read, write, and speak in your other subjects, at home, and at work.

The **Purpose** section before each selection will tell you about the types of things you're going to be asked to do as you read each selection.

The Before Reading questions before each selection will allow you to begin thinking about what the selections are about and the work you will be doing.

As you read each selection, you will see notes in the margins, under the heading "As You Read." These notes might give you information, ask you questions, or request that you do something while you are reading. The purpose of these notes is to make you think about and react to what you're reading.

After you have read the selections, the After Reading questions will allow you to check that you have understood what you have read and the strategies you have been working on. These activities will also extend your understanding of what you've read. Many activities are done with a partner or a small group. You are often given examples, and longer activities are broken into smaller steps to help you complete your work successfully.

Next to many of the After Reading activities, you will see icons. These icons tell you if you are reading, writing, using language skills, or learning about the media.

Media   Reading   Writing   Language

At the end of each unit are some suggestions for evaluating what you've learned. These activities relate to the questions that you read on the opening page of the unit.

Reading

Good readers use many "tricks," or strategies, to understand a text they're seeing for the first time. They don't often think about these strategies; in fact, they may not even realize they are using them.

Foundations of English 9 will show you how to use these reading strategies. Some of them, like **rereading** when you don't understand, will be ones you have used before. Others, like **thinking aloud**, may be ones you haven't used before. Being a good reader is about knowing the strategies, knowing when to use them, and practising them in English and in all the subjects you study in high school. The goal is to make these strategies automatic so that you don't always have to think about them.

You will see these strategies in a **coloured font**. These strategies will be explained in The Reference Shelf (on pages 239 to 245)

One very important strategy you should use every time you start a new text is to **preview** it. **Ask yourself** questions about the text.
- What's in this text?
- How is it laid out?
- What features have the writers included to help me understand the texts?
- Are there features that make it hard for me?

In a textbook, there are many features that can help you as you read!
- Table of contents
- Use of colour
- Illustrations, pictures, charts, and graphs
- Type features like bolding, *italics*, and underlining
- Titles and **subtitles**
- Margin notes
- Glossary (Words defined in the glossary are shown in **bold** throughout the text.)

Take a "text tour" of Foundations of English 9. *Look through the book. Make a list of the features that will help you read and learn more easily. As a class, combine your ideas, discussing why each feature should help make your reading easier.*

AFTER Reading

CHECKING FOR UNDERSTANDING

On your own, think about how previewing, asking questions, and knowing text features can help you read and understand what you have read.

Share your ideas with a partner. Be prepared to present your ideas to the rest of the class.

Writing

Just as there are reading strategies, there are strategies that good writers use. These strategies take place before, during, and after writing. Here are some examples.

Before Writing	During Writing
• understanding instructions • making connections to what you already know • thinking about **purpose** and **audience** • **brainstorming** • mind mapping, webbing, or drawing • discussing • questioning • rapid or **quick writing** • researching • deciding on purpose and audience	• keeping purpose and audience in mind • choosing a form • choosing a voice (**first person, third person**) • organizing • making connections between ideas • choosing the right words (formal, informal) • staying on topic • thinking of ways to emphasize the ideas

After Writing

Your Own Writing	Others' Writing

• checking to make sure you have followed directions
• questioning what you have written
• rereading
• reordering ideas
• adding ideas
• deleting unnecessary ideas
• substituting a better idea for an existing idea
• checking spelling and grammar
• rewriting
	• asking questions about
	  • ideas
	  • organization
	  • voice
	  • word choice
	  • sentences
	  • grammar and spelling

FOUNDATIONS OF ENGLISH 9

AFTER Reading

CHECKING FOR UNDERSTANDING

1. Use the strategy of **quick writing** and write for two minutes about what you do when you are asked to write something for a class. This class could be English, History, Art, or any other subject area. You will talk about your quick writing when you have finished.

2. Compare your ideas to the ideas in the chart on page xii. How many of the strategies do you recognize? How many of them do you actively use?

Oral Communication

Listening and speaking are oral communication skills. Did you know that you spend about 80 percent of the time you are awake listening? Think about how much time you spend listening to your teachers, your parents, your bosses, and your friends. With cell phones, we listen and speak to each other at all hours of the day and night.

We talk and listen for many reasons:
- gossiping
- getting information
- getting help with problems
- giving advice
- doing homework
- following procedures
- complaining

You can probably think of many more reasons to talk and listen.

In school and in the workplace, good listening and speaking skills are essential. Poor listening or poor speaking skills can lead to miscommunication, incorrect work, and even safety hazards. Poor listening is one of the main reasons companies lose money.

In *Foundations of English 9*, you will use speaking and listening, especially in pairs and small groups, to think about your ideas aloud and to listen to the ideas of others in order to expand your own understanding. You will learn how to organize ideas and information, and to pass those ideas and that information on to others in logical and interesting ways. You will dramatize and read as a group to hear the wonder of the sounds and **rhythms** of oral language. Finally, you will develop your confidence when speaking in front of small and large groups.

*With a partner, **brainstorm** a list of reasons why you talk and listen. Combine your ideas with those of your classmates.*

Introduction to Students

AFTER Reading

CHECKING FOR UNDERSTANDING

1. Using pictures and words, show how you feel when you are asked to speak in class.
2. List some strategies you've heard about that you could use to make speaking in front of the class more fun.

No matter how well you read, write, speak, and listen, the purpose of *Foundations of English 9* is to help you learn to talk about the strategies that you already use and learn some new ones. These reading, writing, and communications strategies will help you become more successful in your personal lives, in school, and at work.

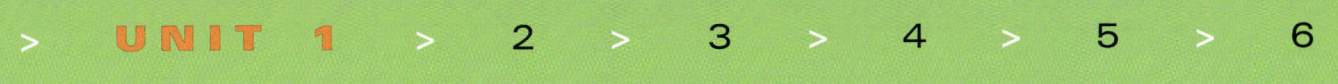

UNIT 1 > 2 > 3 > 4 > 5 > 6
CONNECTIONS

Talk Before They Run, **page 3**

Coming Out of a Canadian Winter, **page 22**

"I replay those five minutes over and over again, thinking of ways I could have saved Alex, by running downstairs and pushing her out of the way or at least by yelling out the window."

from "You Never Know (Tish),"
page 25

Think About It

THINK

- How does connecting with who and what is around us help us make it through difficult times?
- How do we create connections with who and what is around us?
- How do we build and maintain the connections we create?
- Why is it important to connect with ourselves?

> > > 🍁 **Talk Before They Run** by *Child Find Ontario* (informational text) ... 3

Dream Variation by *Langston Hughes* (poem) ... 9

Two Selections on Breaking Down the Barriers
    Mother Goose & Grimm by *Mike Peters* (cartoon) ... 11
    🍁 **All Ears** by *Gena K. Gorrell* (informational text) ... 12

🍁 **The Blind Hunter** by *Irene N. Watts* (drama) ... 16

🍁 **Coming Out of a Canadian Winter** by *Lakshmi Gill* (poem) ... 22

🍁 **You Never Know (Tish)** by *Wendy A. Lewis* (short story) ... 24

Unit 1 Activity ... 37

UNIT 1
Connections

Look at the titles above. What do you think each selection is about? What connections are being made?

UNIT 1 | CONNECTIONS

informational text

PURPOSE
- To look at how design helps the reader understand the messages
- To notice the vocabulary and **tone** a writer uses when writing for an adult **audience**

CHILD FIND ONTARIO

TALK Before THEY RUN

Tips for Parents of Teens

BEFORE Reading

With a partner, create a **T-chart** from the **point of view** of a young person who is thinking of running away.

Positive Things About Running Away	Negative Things About Running Away

Share your ideas with the class.

AS YOU READ

- Ask a question: What would make me want to pick up this brochure?

- Ask a question: Why would this brochure appeal to parents of teens?

Our Vision

(1) Child Find Ontario is dedicated to reducing the incidence of missing, runaway, and exploited children throughout Ontario. We work proactively to educate the public to prevent the occurrence of missing children, whether caused by parental abduction, stranger abduction, by running away, or by injury or becoming lost. Affiliated with Child Find Canada, we are a registered charitable organization that for over 15 years has been assisting families with the trauma of a missing or runaway child or teenager.

AS YOU READ

Ask a question: What is the meaning of *component*? Is it important for me to know it right now?

(2) In 2000, over 48,000 cases of runaway teens were reported to police in Canada (over 1,100 cases in Peel Region). Teen runaways are the largest <u>component</u> of missing children nationally. Over 90% of runaways were successfully located.

How Parents Should Respond to Signs

(3) Immediately tell your teen you are concerned he/she may leave home. Invite him/her to discuss their problems with you or someone else. Be calm, understanding, and supportive. Suggest positive ways of handling stress. Tell your teen you want him/her to stay and you are committed to help the family work things out.

How to Prevent Your Teenager from Running Away

(4) • Regularly spend quality time with each of your teens. Listen to them attentively in a non-judgmental way. Praise appropriate behaviour.

(5) • Take their concerns seriously. Do not dismiss their worries and fears.

(6) • Pay attention when they ask you for help. Make your teen your priority.

(7) • Confront trouble signs directly, firmly and calmly. Discuss your concerns and the consequences of continued unacceptable behaviour. Avoid lectures.

(8) • Talk with others. Your teen's friends, their parents or their teachers may have helpful suggestions.

(9) • Speak with professional counsellors about your situation.

In 2000, over 48,000 cases of runaway teens were reported to police in Canada.

What to Do if Your Teenager Runs Away from Home

Ask a question: Did I know this *fact* before I read this?

(10) Remember: No matter what you have been told, there is no law requiring a waiting period before reporting a missing child to the police or before entering the data into the CPIC (Canadian Police Information Centre). The first 48 hours following the runaway episode are the most important in locating the teen.

(11) While many runaway teens return home during this 48-hour period, it is critical to take every action available to you to help locate and safeguard your child. To help locate your runaway teen, immediately follow these steps.

(12) • Remain calm and logical. Ask yourself why and where your child may have run. Check his/her room, desk and/or clothes for clues. Check local spots your child may frequent, as well as area hospitals and treatment centres if you suspect your child of drug use. Call your child's employer or coworkers, if any.

(13) • Contact your child's friends and their parents, school, neighbours, relatives and others who may know where your child is. Ask them to call if they hear from your child. If your child has a computer, check it for leads such as online contacts and details of a planned meeting.

(14) • Report the runaway to the police. Have an officer take the report at your home. Give him/her a recent photo of your child and a description of his/her clothes, including jacket, shoes and knapsack colour. Record the officer's name, badge number, telephone, fax and report numbers. Ask who will follow up the initial investigation.

(15) • Ensure police enter your child's name and description at the Canadian Police Information Centre (CPIC) and National Crime Info Center (NCIC). This will not give your child a police record, but it may help find him/her.

(16) • Report your missing child to Child Find Ontario (CFO) at 1-800-387-7962. Have the police-report information (as mentioned above) handy.

(17) • Child Find Ontario will help produce posters or fliers if it becomes necessary. Place them in store windows and hand them out at truck stops, youth-oriented businesses, hospitals, treatment centres, and law enforcement agencies. Request permission first. Keep track of all posters and remove them once your child has returned.

(18) • Keep a notebook by the phone. Record all information about the investigation, including all conversations and people you've spoken with.

(19) Research shows that the typical runaway will likely not stay away for long, typically 48 hours to 14 days. Also, very few leave their immediate community; they will usually stay with friends. Most runaways come home of their own accord.

(20) NOTE: If you have reason to believe that your child may have been abducted or lured away by a non-family member or non-custodial family member, do not disturb or remove any of your child's items before the police arrive. Doing so could destroy key clues about the disappearance and/or evidence at a potential crime scene. In the

AS YOU READ

Stop and ask a question about what you've just read.

... there is no law requiring a waiting period before reporting a missing child to the police ...

Talk Before They Run | INFORMATIONAL TEXT

AS YOU READ

case of a non-family abduction, the first three hours are the most critical in recovering a child safely. Thus, do not delay in contacting the police and explaining all of the facts leading to the belief that your child is an abduction victim.

What to Do When Your Teenager Returns Home

(21) • Be happy. Many teens fear the initial meeting with their parents. Remain calm. Express relief and tell your child you love him/her and that together you will solve any problems.

(22) • Make follow-up phone calls. Let all your contacts, including the police, know your child has returned home. Police may need to speak or meet with your child.

(23) • Allow time to settle in. Your child may need a shower, a meal, clean clothes, or sleep.

(24) • Get medical attention. Visit your family doctor to address any medical concerns.

(25) • Talk with your teen. Discuss how you can work together to prevent him/her from leaving again. Acknowledge some problems take time and effort to solve. Be sure you resolve the problems safely and reasonably.

(26) • Look for assistance. People and organizations in your community can help counsel your family. Child Find Ontario can refer you to an appropriate agency. Asking for help is a sign of strength and shows you are taking the issue seriously.

Stop and ask a question about what you've just read.

(27) Improve communication and the quality of your relationship with your teen so that running away ceases to be an option.

Operation Go Home

(28) Child Find Ontario may be able to help you with transportation if your teen wants to come home. Operation Go Home reunites runaway youth (under 18 years of age) with their families. The youth must contact Operation Go Home at **1 (888) 644-1261** (*Ontario only*), **1 (800) 668-4663** (*Canada-wide*) and ask how they can return home safely.

Basic Truths About Teenagers Who Run Away

Teens who run away are not bad

(29) They made the bad decision to run. We need to teach them ways of facing and solving problems, even when we are their problem.

UNIT 1 | CONNECTIONS

Most teens know of a teen who has run away

(30) This can lead to romantic ideas of life on the streets considering most teens glamorize the experience.

Parents cannot lock teenagers in

(31) Teens can choose to walk out the door against your wishes.

Parents of teens who run away are not bad parents

(32) Parents are also under a lot of pressure.

Signs Your Son or Daughter Is Thinking About Running Away From Home

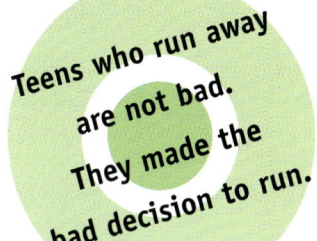

Teens who run away are not bad. They made the bad decision to run.

(33) While no one knows which teens will run and which won't, here are signs to look for:

Changes in behaviour patterns:

(34) Teens may stop eating or overeat; never sleep or oversleep; over socialize or under socialize; have falling grades; suffer from depression and sudden mood swings.

Rebellious behaviour:

(35) Some runaways will skip school, break rules at home, pick fights with the family.

Disclosure of intention to run:

(36) Some runaways hint or threaten they will run. Friends, school personnel/staff, or other parents may be aware that your child wants to leave home.

Accumulation of money and possessions:

(37) Some runaways will slowly withdraw cash from their savings accounts and/or keep a bag of clothes in their closet.

Preoccupation:

(38) Some runaways are preoccupied with bullying, suspension, poor grades, peer pressure anxiety, sexual orientation, pregnancy, alcohol, and/or drug problems.

Problems at home:

(39) Some runaways may be dealing with abuse, a difficult step-parent, and/or the breakup of their parents' marriage.

Transition:

(40) Teens who have moved to a new community or school may fantasize about their previous community or school.

AFTER Reading

CHECKING FOR UNDERSTANDING

1. Make **jot notes** to explain how asking yourself questions helps you better understand what you read.

PURPOSE / AUDIENCE / FORM

2. **Reread** the "Basic Truths About Teenagers Who Run Away" section through to the end of the selection. Copy out a sentence that sounds like it was written for an adult. In your notebook, underline the words, phrases, and/or punctuation that made you think this. Be prepared to read your sentence and explanation aloud.

STYLE AND CONVENTIONS

3. List the **graphic features** (for example, **subtitles**, font) that help the reader understand the message of this brochure. State each feature's **purpose**.

CRITICAL THINKING

4. a) As a class, create a T-chart with the headings "Yes, this is an effective brochure for parents" and "No, this is not an effective brochure for parents." Collect and record ideas for both sides.

   b) Determine your own **opinion** of whether or not the brochure is effective for parents, and find a partner who agrees with you. With your partner, create a **tree organizer** like the one below to support your opinion.

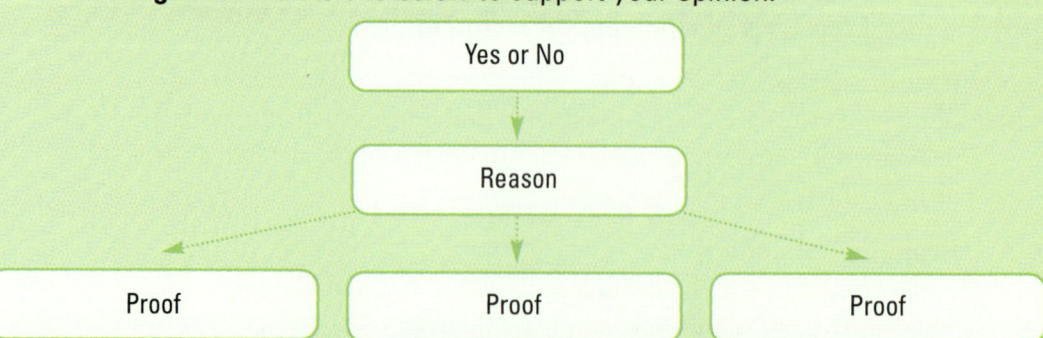

   c) Write an opinion paragraph (see The Reference Shelf, page 259) using the reason and proofs from your tree organizer.

UNIT 1 | CONNECTIONS

poem

Dream Variation

LANGSTON HUGHES

PURPOSE
- To understand how a poet uses words to create **style** and **tone**
- To understand that poetry can be fun

BEFORE Reading

Fold a piece of paper in half. With a partner, **brainstorm** a list of your reactions to or feelings about poetry (what you think about it). Record your list on the left-hand side of your page. Title your list "Before Reading."

    To fling my arms wide
    In some place of the sun,
    To whirl and to dance
    Till the white day is done.
5   Then rest at cool evening
    Beneath a tall tree
    While night comes on gently,
        Dark like me —
    That is my dream!

10 To fling my arms wide
    In the face of the sun,
    Dance! Whirl! Whirl!
    Till the quick day is done.
    Rest at pale evening …
15 A tall, slim tree …
    Night coming tenderly
        Black like me.

AFTER Reading

CHECKING FOR UNDERSTANDING

1. With your partner, return to the list you brainstormed before reading. On the right-hand side of your page, record what you have observed about the structure of "Dream Variation" and your reactions to the poem (what you think about it). Title your list "About Dream Variation." Compare your two lists. Place a check mark beside the items that are different. Share your check-marked items with another pair of students.

PURPOSE / AUDIENCE / FORM

2. This poem seems to be written for a certain type of audience. As a class, make a list of words to describe the audience for this poem. Think about items such as age, gender, level of education, and personal interests. Give support from the poem for each item on your list.

STYLE AND CONVENTIONS

3. a) This poem repeats different words. Count and record how many times the poet uses the following words: *fling, whirl, sun, me, dance.* Suggest a reason why the poet would repeat words.
   b) **Scan** the poem and notice how similar the stanzas are to each other. Suggest reasons why the poet would make the stanzas so much alike.
   c) Form a group of four students. Together, **reread** your answers for questions #3(a) and (b), taking special notice of which words are repeated. Next, reread the title of the poem and explain why it is a good title for this poem.

CRITICAL THINKING

4. Poetry is meant to be read out loud. Together in your group of four, prepare a **reader's theatre** oral reading of "Dream Variation." Each person must read out loud. Decide who will read which parts, what volume of voice you will use, and what actions you will use. You might also like to put a **rhythm** to the poem. Practise your performance and be prepared to share it with the class.

UNIT 1 | CONNECTIONS

[cartoon + informational text]

PURPOSE
- To understand the importance of the relationship between hearing dogs and their owners
- To write a paragraph about hearing dogs

Breaking Down the Barriers

BEFORE Reading

1. a) Read *Mother Goose & Grimm*. What is Grimm signalling in the first panel of the cartoon? How does Mother Goose misinterpret his signal?
   b) Grimm's signal is shown by actions. Does the action make his message easy or difficult to understand? Explain.

2. Before you read "All Ears" (page 12), read the facts from the selection across the bottom of pages 11 to 13. Sort the facts into at least three different categories. Give each category a title. Keep your sorted facts because you will need them for another activity.

MOTHER GOOSE & GRIMM — BY MIKE PETERS

facts

1) People who are deaf have a barrier between themselves and the hearing world.
2) Dogs who are alert, curious, and have a lot of energy make good hearing dogs.
3) Since the 1970s, dogs have been learning to become hearing dogs.
4) Hearing dogs alert their owners to unusual noises.
5) The lives of people who are deaf can be frustrating or dangerous.

All Ears

GENA K. GORRELL

(1) Since the 1970s, dogs have been going to school to learn to help people who are almost or entirely deaf. Their lack of hearing puts a barrier between them and most other people, and it can make life frustrating and even dangerous. Imagine caring for a baby when you can't hear the child fall or cry. Imagine not being able to hear a smoke alarm or fire alarm, a burglar breaking a window, or an ambulance racing down the street.

Imagine not being able to hear a smoke alarm or fire alarm, a burglar breaking a window, or an ambulance racing down the street.

(2) Hearing dogs—also called hearing-ear or signal dogs—stay close to their owners, ears pricked for every noise. They learn to alert to many specific noises—the phone or doorbell; alarms of all kinds; the whistle of a boiling kettle, the ping of a microwave, or the sound of someone calling the person's name. They also alert to unusual sounds such as breaking glass. When they hear something significant, they paw or lick to get their partners' attention, and lead the way to the source of the noise.

(3) This is one line of work where alertness, curiosity, and energy matter more than size. Terriers, miniature poodles, even Chihuahuas work as hearing dogs. But they need to be bright enough to learn many hand

facts

6) The company and friendship given by a hearing dog is helpful to a person who is deaf.

7) People who are deaf are able to relax knowing danger won't sneak up on them when they have a hearing dog.

8) Terriers, miniature poodles, and Chihuahuas can be hearing dogs.

9) Some dogs can learn American Sign Language (ASL).

10) Hearing dogs take their jobs very seriously.

12 UNIT 1 | CONNECTIONS

> **AS YOU READ**

(4) signals, and perhaps some American Sign Language (ASL). They also need confidence and initiative, because, unlike many service dogs, they don't wait for a command. It's up to them to take action, using their own judgment and experience to decide which sounds matter (a knock at the door) and which ones don't (a knock at the neighbour's door). One dog even tells his owner when the cat is scratching to come in.

(4) Viva is a slim, dainty, sweet-natured black standard poodle. She works as a hearing dog for Cheryl Osten, and understands all the basic doggy words in ASL. When Cheryl babysits her young grandsons, Viva tells her if the children are fighting or making a racket. Several times Viva has used her body to block Cheryl's path so she couldn't cross the street when a car or motorcycle out of sight around a corner was racing toward them. "I feel much more comfortable when she's with me," says Cheryl.

"I feel much more comfortable when she's with me," says Cheryl.

(5) After her early training, Viva almost failed the test to be a hearing dog. Petting is the reward she gets for doing her job, and the family was giving her lots of attention and affection without making her earn it. When they cut back on the praise, Viva got down to work and passed her test with flying colours. But she sometimes gets a little jealous of the other animals in Cheryl's house—two dogs and three cats who hardly lift a paw to earn *their* keep.

(6) "Viva really understands the fact that I hear and my mom doesn't," says Cheryl's daughter Ruth. "Sometimes she comes to me first, if she thinks I'll get the message faster. And she'll do whatever's necessary to get Mom's attention—even jump up on her back, if she's facing away." In her spare time, Viva pays friendly visits to a nursing home for the elderly deaf people.

(7) Hearing dogs take their duties very seriously. Although Viva is terrified of fireworks and thunderstorms, she always comes and tells Cheryl about them—and then runs away and hides. Another woman, Roxanne, found out how determined her dog Star was the first time she took Star to stay at her mother's.

◀ *What is one signal Viva uses to alert her owner to danger?*

facts

11) People who are deaf can relate to hearing people better if they have a hearing dog.
12) Some hearing dogs can tell the difference between a hearing person and a person who is deaf.
13) Hearing dogs alert their owners to many specific noises often heard in a house.
14) Hearing dogs get their owners' attention by pawing or licking them.
15) Hearing dogs can help with dangerous traffic situations.

AS YOU READ

What is one signal Star used to alert her owner's mother that it was time to get up?

(8) Star responded to my mother's alarm clock, rushing down the hall to wake [Mom] up. But Mom wasn't ready to get up and used the snooze alarm. Ten minutes later Star responded to the alarm again, and again mom rolled over and went back to sleep. On the third ring, Star ran down the hall and bit my mother's nose.

(9) Hearing dogs keep their partners safe on the rare occasions when there really is danger. Maybe just as important, they enable their partners to relax, day in and day out, in the knowledge that danger *isn't* sneaking up on them. The dogs also help their partners relate to hearing people. On top of that, they offer full-time company and friendship in a world that can be lonely and sometimes hostile.

AFTER Reading

CHECKING FOR UNDERSTANDING

1. Return to the categories you created in question #2 of the Before Reading activities. Review the way you sorted your facts and the titles you gave each category. Make revisions to your categories to reflect what you learned by reading this text. Share your categories and facts with a partner. Discuss the similarities and differences in your categories.

PURPOSE / AUDIENCE / FORM

2. Turn to page 258 of The Reference Shelf and review the eight different types of writing. Decide which type of writing "All Ears" is. Give two reasons from "All Ears" to support your answer.

14   UNIT 1 | CONNECTIONS

STYLE AND CONVENTIONS

3. a) Working together in a group of four students, **brainstorm** a list of adjectives (see The Reference Shelf, page 233) to describe the relationship between hearing dogs and their owners. Be prepared to share your list with the class.

   b) Still in your group of four, brainstorm a list of adjectives to describe the emotions a person who is deaf would feel about having a hearing dog. You can use information from the text to help you get started. Be prepared to share your list with the class.

   c) With your same group of four, imagine that you are a person who is deaf who has been offered a hearing dog. Decide whether or not you will accept the dog, and give three reasons to support your decision. Share your decision and supporting reasons with another group of four students.

CRITICAL THINKING

4. a) Return to your categories from question #2 of the Before Reading activities (revised if necessary). Individually, you will be writing a paragraph based on "All Ears." Choose one category to write about. Next, choose the three most important facts in that category. Write your paragraph in your own words. Remember to include an interesting title for your paragraph, a topic sentence for each of your three facts, and a conclusion.

   b) Trade your paragraph with a partner, and edit each other's writing. Remember to give constructive feedback by using the questions for editing (see The Reference Shelf, page 273). Put "Edited by: Your Name" at the top of your partner's paper.

   c) Return the paragraph to your partner. You should carefully consider the questions or suggestions made by your partner. Revise your paragraph.

[drama]

PURPOSE
- To understand the elements of **subject** and **theme**
- To understand **point of view, plot, language, atmosphere, character,** and **setting**

The Blind Hunter

Based on a Legend of the Inuit

IRENE N. WATTS

BEFORE Reading

1. Form a group of three students. Review the elements of a **narrative** (see The Reference Shelf, page 246). Sort these words:

   > strange, hunter, mother, hate, appease, lied, loon, igloo, blind, truth, wickedness, son

   into these categories:

   > characters, setting, problem, **outcomes**, unknown words

2. Develop a **gist statement** for this play. Look at how you sorted the words, and make a logical guess about what is going to happen in this story.

 The setting is the Arctic, inside and outside an igloo.

The sounds of the Arctic begin the play: an Arctic loon calling, the wind moaning. The hunter and his mother sit motionless beside a stone lamp.

NARRATOR: When I was a boy, my father would tell me all the old stories of animals, of the spirits, of good and bad shamans.

As the narrator begins the story, the mother and the young hunter come to life in their places at the kudlik (seal-oil lamp).

16   UNIT 1 | CONNECTIONS

NARRATOR: There was a young hunter and his mother, who lived on the edge of our settlement a long time ago. They say she was not one of the settlement, her ways were strange, she came from elsewhere. Her son was a good hunter: seal, fox, and ptarmigan returned to his spear, and he had already killed his first bear.

Hunter mimes stalking the animals, spearing a seal through a hole in the ice, cutting up meat with his knife, and piling more and more animals on the platforms around the igloo.

MOTHER: The mother cleaned and scraped, and dried and cooked, and there was no rest for her from sewing and mending.

The hunter brings her his parka to patch.

HUNTER: I am tired from the day's hunt, I will sleep now.
MOTHER: She had no rest and she began to hate him, and so she made a magic song …

She waits until her son is asleep and then begins her preparations.

> And mixed up the brains of the Arctic fox, and of a hunter sealed in ice, with whale blubber, and smeared her son's sleeping eyelids with the ointment.

When she has finished pounding the mixture, she speaks softly:

> Seal the light,
> Close off his sight,
> Blind, blind, blind.

She returns to her place at the lamp. The hunter wakes up and slowly discovers that he cannot see. The mother watches him.

HUNTER: What spirit did I offend yesterday? Whom must I now appease? Mother, you will have to bring me food now, for I am blind and helpless.
MOTHER: "What there is, you will share." And she threw him only scraps, but she ate well.
NARRATOR: It was a long winter, and the woman had rest and time enough, and plenty to eat. The hunter had provided well for them. But she lied to him:

AS YOU READ

◀ Stop reading. In a group of three, record in your notebook a Q1 and Q2 question using the Q-chart (see The Reference Shelf, page 242).

The Blind Hunter | DRAMA | 17

> **AS YOU READ**

MOTHER: The food is almost gone.
NARRATOR: One day a polar bear stood outside the ice window of the igloo, and tried to get in.

Bear (optional) stands outside.

HUNTER: Mother, I hear the bear's hot breath, and smell his wet fur. Bring me my bow and guide my arm, so that I may shoot to kill.

The mother stands beside him and guides his arm. He shoots, there is the sound of a great weight falling.

HUNTER: Mother, I heard the ground tremble, the bear fell. Now we will have fresh meat at last.

He tries to move to the igloo opening, but she pushes him aside.

MOTHER: "You missed him, poor blind creature. Sit in your corner." And she did not share the meat with him.
NARRATOR: And so the winter drew on, and the hunter grew weaker.

A loon cries. The hunter hears it and crawls to the door of the igloo.

Stop reading. In a group of three, record in your notebook a Q1 and Q3 question using the Q-chart (see The Reference Shelf, page 242).

HUNTER: I can smell the warm air; the voice of the loon tells me that winter has passed. Ice break-up. The world I cannot see is beautiful. I will get to the water.

Slowly he makes his way to the water's edge. His mother is nowhere in sight. A loon appears.

LOON: I can help you find your sight. We will dive under the water and wash away the bad magic.
HUNTER: You are a powerful helper, but how can you carry me on your small wings, even though I am weak after the long winter, and how will I not choke in the icy water?
LOON: You must trust me! Climb on my back and hold on to my neck.
NARRATOR: Then the hunter put his arms around the loon's neck and the loon, whose spirit strength could make him lift kayaks, dove under the water and rose again.
LOON: What do you see?
HUNTER: I see light, bright and white as ice.

UNIT 1 | CONNECTIONS

LOON: Then your eyes do not see enough.
NARRATOR: A second time the loon and the boy dove beneath the water and came back up for air.
LOON: What do you see now?
HUNTER: I see the whole world and all that is in it.
LOON: Then you see too much.
NARRATOR: One more time they disappeared under the water, and this time when they returned to land, the hunter said:
HUNTER: I see as I did before, and I fear I will die of joy and of cold!
LOON: You will not die, and you will live to be a great hunter, and they will sing songs for you and me, the loon and the boy who was blind.
NARRATOR: And the loon flew off, calling the coming of spring.

The hunter returns home, where his mother is scraping a skin with her ulu.

HUNTER: Tell me, Mother, is that the skin from the bear that I killed when I was blind?
MOTHER: "No, my son," said his mother, "it was left for pity for me by a passing hunter."
NARRATOR: They looked into each other's eyes, and each knew the truth.
HUNTER: I need to become strong again. Come with me to catch whale; the ice is breaking.
MOTHER: The woman dared not refuse, now that she knew her son could see.

◀ Stop reading. In a group of three, record in your notebook a Q1 and Q2 question using the Q-chart (see The Reference Shelf, page 242).

The Blind Hunter | DRAMA

AS YOU READ

Stop reading. In a group of three, record in your notebook a Q1 and Q4 question using the Q-chart (see The Reference Shelf, page 242).

NARRATOR: They walked to the shore and climbed into their kayak, and the hunter threw his harpoon into the fat side of a whale, and tied the other end of the line around his mother's arm.

HUNTER: Help me drag in the whale!

NARRATOR: But the whale began to drag and twist to free himself from the harpoon, and the mother called to her son.

MOTHER: Help me, my son.

HUNTER: I cannot help you, Mother. *(looks away)*

NARRATOR: The whale dragged the woman into the water and under the waves. Her cries became one with the whale, and she was never seen again. They say that she became a Narwhale. If you listen to the voices of the whales you can hear the cry of the woman dragged forever through the water for her wickedness.

The play ends with the loon flying around the hunter and the kayak. There is a moment of stillness, and then the cry of the whales is heard again.

AFTER Reading

CHECKING FOR UNDERSTANDING

1. a) Return to your responses to the Before Reading activities. Evaluate the accuracy of the gist statement your group made. Join another group of three students, and compare your gist statement to theirs.
   b) Return to your original group of three. Share the questions you recorded during reading with the other group members. Answer each other's questions orally. If someone disagrees with an answer, work together to come to an agreement. (See The Reference Shelf, page 280 for tips on working together in a group.)

PURPOSE / AUDIENCE / FORM

2. Review the difference between subject and theme in The Reference Shelf, page 251. As a class, **brainstorm** different subjects for this play. Next, choose one of the subjects and develop a theme statement for *The Blind Hunter*.

20 UNIT 1 | CONNECTIONS

STYLE AND CONVENTIONS

3. a) The author of this play uses fairly formal language. Rewrite the following passage using less formal language: "I can smell the warm air; the voice of the loon tells me that winter has passed. Ice break-up. The world I cannot see is beautiful. I will get to the water." Share your rewrite with two other students.

   b) Copy and complete the chart below in your notebook. Be prepared to share your answers with the class.

Advantages of Formal Language	Disadvantages of Formal Language
Advantages of Informal Language	Disadvantages of Informal Language

   c) As a class, make a list of when it is appropriate to use formal language and when it is appropriate to use informal language.

CRITICAL THINKING

4. a) Plays are written to be performed. As a class, divide *The Blind Hunter* into smaller parts by creating divisions when there is a change in setting, time of day, or action (see The Reference Shelf, page 251). Give each of the smaller parts a **subtitle** that describes what happens in that section.

   b) Form a group of five students. Each person in the group must take a role: the **narrator**, the mother, the son, the loon, and the director. Choose a section of the play to perform. The director will help the others determine how to say their lines, where to stand, and what actions to make. Practise your section of the play until you have a polished performance. Include sound effects where possible.

   c) Each group will perform their section of the play for the rest of the class.

[poem

Coming Out of a Canadian Winter

LAKSHMI GILL

PURPOSE
- To understand how a poet uses words to create **style** and **tone**
- To understand that poetry can help express feelings

BEFORE Reading

Think for a few moments about which season is your favourite, and why (be specific). When your teacher tells you to do so, move to the corner of the room that represents your favourite season. Each person will explain to the rest of the group why he or she likes that season the best.

AS YOU READ

You will be asked to stop and **infer** the meaning of a word. To infer meaning, use the words around the underlined word to help you figure out its meaning.

The process is slow.
The snow comes and goes
teasing the earth,
the birth of blossoms
5   brutalized by the wind.

The winter won't let go.
It's a <u>perverse</u> devil
disguised in light—
don't let that sun
10 <u>deceive</u> you.

◀ Infer the meaning of perverse.

◀ Infer the meaning of deceive.

Thawing out is our <u>a-Maying</u>.
After the drip, drip,
suddenly the skin unlocks,
pale and <u>withered</u>.
15 Spring is a shock.

◀ Infer the meaning of a-Maying.

◀ Infer the meaning of withered.

UNIT 1 | CONNECTIONS

AFTER Reading

CHECKING FOR UNDERSTANDING

1. a) As a class, discuss your answers for the words *perverse, deceive, a-Maying,* and *withered*. Make up guidelines about when to stop reading to check the meaning of a word, and when it's okay to keep reading.

   b) With a partner, decide whether this poet likes or dislikes winter. Copy and complete this graphic organizer in your notebook.

   The poet likes/dislikes winter because ...
   — The poem says ... → Support 1
   — The poem says ... → Support 2

PURPOSE / AUDIENCE / FORM

2. Poets use a variety of word combinations to add meaning to their poems. Look at each of the following phrases from the poem. Decide if each underlined part helps you see a picture in your mind, understand the meaning of the poem, or both.
   a) <u>b</u>irth of <u>b</u>lossoms <u>b</u>rutalized
   b) <u>d</u>isguised in light—
      <u>d</u>on't let that sun <u>d</u>eceive you
   c) <u>drip</u>, <u>drip</u>

STYLE AND CONVENTIONS

3. a) For each **stanza**, look at the types of sentences used (see The Reference Shelf, page 235) and decide how these stanzas are alike in structure.

   b) On a scale of 1 to 10, where 1 means you hate it, 5 means it's okay, and 10 means you love it, decide how much you like or dislike the structure of the poem. Decide on at least one reason why you feel that way.

CRITICAL THINKING

4. a) Write a poem about your favourite season using the style and form of "Coming Out of a Canadian Winter."
   b) Create and complete a word web (see The Reference Shelf, page 270).
   c) Use your word web to write your poem.
   d) Post your poem in the classroom.

short story

YOU NEVER KNOW (TISH)

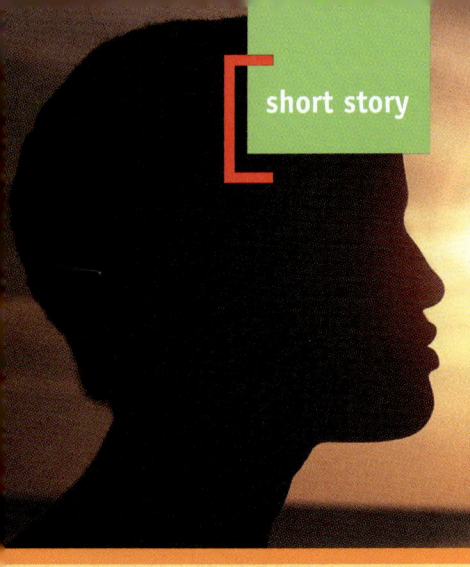

WENDY A. LEWIS

PURPOSE
- To understand the complexity of teenage relationships
- To *infer* the *theme* of a story

BEFORE Reading

Copy the chart below into your notebook, and complete the "Before Reading" columns only.

Before Reading		Statement	After Reading		What in the story changed my mind, or kept my opinion the same?
Agree	Disagree		Agree	Disagree	
		Friendships should last forever.			
		Boyfriends or girlfriends should not harm a friendship.			
		Confessing to a friend that you like him or her more than a friend should not affect your friendship.			
		Time heals all wounds.			

AS YOU READ

Predict what Baba knows. (Baba means grandmother.)

Predict what happened to Alex.

Predict what is wrong with Baba's brain.

(1) Baba knew.

(2) The newspapers said Alex was in the wrong place at the wrong time. They said no one could have saved her because no one could have known. But Baba knew.

(3) Five whole minutes before the bullet left the gun, Baba knew what was going to happen, and, what's more, she told me. Somehow, somewhere in her poor tangled brain, she found the words to warn me, but I didn't understand what she said.

24 UNIT 1 | CONNECTIONS

(4) I replay those five minutes over and over again, thinking of ways I could have saved Alex, by running downstairs and pushing her out of the way or at least by yelling out the window. She might have pretended not to hear me and walked away, but at least she'd be gone from the path of the bullet.

> **I replay those five minutes over and over again, thinking of ways I could have saved Alex ...**

(5) Instead I did nothing, and because of that she is dead. My ex-best friend, Alex, is dead.

(6) Alex saved *me* the day I met her.

(7) It was my first day at a new school in a new town, and I was petrified. I leaned against the chain link fence wishing I could ooze through it and run home to Baba. Already I thought of her house as home. Money was tight after my parents' divorce, and Mom was holding down two jobs, so Baba was the one who got me ready for school, who braided my hair and stuffed me with pancakes for breakfast. Food meant love to Baba, and she gave me lots of both. That first day, she packed enough lunch for me to share with the whole class if I got up the nerve to offer it. So there I was at recess with a package of Baba's special Hairy Cookies in my pocket, gripping them so tightly some snapped between my fingers.

(8) The playground was packed with kids who ignored me, so I ignored them and watched the one girl my age who wasn't skipping rope or playing tag. She was sitting farther down the fence, pretending to read, but really she was watching the other kids over the top of her book. Then she spotted me staring and came running over. Her dark curls bounced as she ran, and she grinned at me with perfectly small white teeth.

(9) *Snap!* Another Hairy Cookie turned to dust in my pocket, but Alex didn't mind. She liked them, and she liked me, too. By the end of recess, she had declared Hairy Cookies her favourite food and me her best friend. It turned out that she was new, too, and said it was "density" that we found each other. She was in the other Grade Two class, but we played together at recess and after school. Baba let us hang around the kitchen while she made dinner, as long as we helped out.

AS YOU READ

◀ Predict what the **narrator** did instead of saving Alex.

◀ Predict how the narrator will deal with the death of Alex.

◀ This reminds me of ...

(10)   "Many hands make light work!" she'd say, using one of the many sayings that were passed down like recipes from *her* grandmother, Baba Rose. That's who she got her sixth sense from, too. She used to amaze Alex by knowing who was calling when the phone rang, or what her Christmas presents were, even when we had disguised them with oddly shaped boxes. Alex and Mom both said she was psychic, but I had my doubts. Until now that is—and that time Alex fell off her bike.

(11)   We were riding home with our arms full of pussy willows, when Alex hit a stone and went flying. The whole length of her leg was scraped and bloody. She was crying and shaking and breathing funny.

(12)   "Tish, help me!" she whimpered.

(13)   I didn't know what to do except get her home fast to Baba, who was waiting for us at the door with a bowl of warm water and bandages as if she'd known Alex was hurt. She fixed up Alex's leg, and then wrapped her pillowy arms around her and rocked her back and forth, humming and patting her hair until Alex calmed down. We were getting too big for sitting on laps, but it seemed to be just what Alex needed.

(14)   Sometimes we went to Alex's house. It was enormous and new although it was made to look a hundred years old, with Victorian gingerbread dripping off the eaves and a round turret on one corner. Alex slept in the turret bedroom like a princess in a fairy-tale castle. We'd stretch out on her queen-size bed and talk for hours at a time about everyone and everything. We'd gossip about our teachers, pick apart our classmates and dream out loud. Her mom would bring us fancy store-bought cookies on a tray, and her dad, Dr. Meyers, would call me their Kid Number Two.

(15)   Alex had all twenty of her Barbies displayed in a glass cabinet. She said she got her first Barbie when she was three and insisted on getting a Ken so they could have weddings. I was glad she was past playing with Barbies. I never liked the way they had to totter around on high heels because their feet were shaped that way. The most fun I had with my Barbie was feeding her to my toy crocodile. Not that I told Alex about that.

UNIT 1 | CONNECTIONS

(16)   In Grade Seven, Alex started plastering her walls with posters of guys who had square jaws and smoldering eyes and locks of hair drooping down their foreheads. Every few months she'd fall in love with a different movie star and describe to me in detail her fantasies, which always ended with a crushing passionate kiss. She never understood why I didn't love those guys, too. They're not real, I'd tell her. They look like they're molded from plastic, like Barbie's Ken.

(17)   In high school, the posters came down, but the crushes continued, on real guys this time. Grade Thirteen guys who were on the football team. Alex would get all flustered and silly if one of them walked by or held a door open for us.

(18)   She worried that someday she'd get asked out and not be ready.

> **She worried that someday she'd get asked out and not be ready.**

(19)   "Ready for what?" I wanted to know.
(20)   "For kissing," said Alex. "I need to practice."
(21)   "You mean like on the back of your hand or something?"
(22)   "No …." She giggled. "What if *we* practiced, you and me? Then we'll both be ready."
(23)   I didn't want to, but I couldn't tell her why.
(24)   Alex shrugged. "Okay, it's no big deal."
(25)   But it *was* a big deal, for me. I told her I'd think about it.
(26)   Two days later, we were in her turret bedroom when I said I'd do it. I've never been so nervous. Alex just laughed, as if it meant nothing to her.
(27)   "Close your eyes so you can pretend I'm a guy," she said. "And tilt to the right, okay?"
(28)   They were little kisses, tilted to the right at first, then straight on, then to the left. Her lips were soft as feathers. Our noses rubbed. I felt like a blind person discovering for the first time what my best friend looked like. We kissed some more. In her mind, Alex was probably seeing a Grade Thirteen football stud or maybe a square-jawed movie star. But I was thinking, *Wow! This is Alex! Beautiful, special, amazing Alex!*
(29)   She jerked her head back. Her face was flushed pink.
(30)   "Alex, what's wrong?"
(31)   "I can't do it!" she said. "I pretended at first but then … ew-w-w-w!

◀ Kissing each other is a good/bad idea because …

It was too gross!" She made a face, wiped her mouth and laughed. "Let's forget we did that, okay, Tish?"

(32)   "Sure," I said.

(33)   I stayed a bit longer. We looked at some magazines, and then I went home. Same as always, except now it was different. Now I knew I loved Alex, and she knew it, too.

(34)   That was two years ago, when we were fifteen. That spring, Keenan Jones asked Alex to go to the formal. He wasn't in Grade Thirteen, but he did play football and Alex said he was the best-looking guy in Grade Twelve. I didn't go. I hated the dances, where people would either make out in the corners of the gym or stand by the stage like zombies and watch the band.

(35)   But all Alex talked about was going to the formal. And after the formal, all she talked about was Keenan. Keenan this and Keenan that. When we talked in the hall at school, she'd always be glancing over my shoulder to see if he was coming. Soon she was busy all the time with Keenan and his friends, a tight little group of cheerleader girls and jock guys. They even let Alex onto the cheerleading team as a spare, even though the tryouts had been months before.

(36)   The worst part was that she seemed to love it, love *them*, the same people we used to pick apart in her room, the same people we used to call shallow, boring, snobbish airheads. To be fair, she did try to include me. She'd try to coax me to go with them to movies or to their field parties, but I kept making excuses not to go.

> **The worst part was that she seemed to love it, love *them*, the same people we used to pick apart in her room, the same people we used to call shallow, boring, snobbish airheads.**

(37)   The one thing I did agree to do was the mock royal wedding at school last year. Alex was Princess Anne, and she got me the part of a bridesmaid. I did it because I wanted to be with Alex, but I hated the itchy dress and the way they pulled my hair back so I looked like a horse and the way everyone acted like someone they weren't. I didn't get to be much with Alex anyway. I was stuck helping Mandy Solesby,

AS YOU READ

If I were Tish, to fix the friendship I would ...

(38) the other bridesmaid, arrange Jewel's train and stopping the flower girls from rolling all over it. I should have backed out and let someone else have the part, but I didn't, and my scowling face is recorded forever in the official royal wedding portrait in the '82 yearbook. A horse among beauty queens. The troll at Ken and Barbie's wedding.

Things were never the same after that kiss in her bedroom. We never talked about it, but I thought about it all the time. It used to be Alex always daydreaming, and now it was me. My daydream about Alex started the same way it had in real life, in her turret bedroom, a smile on her lips, her head tilted to the right, but instead of ending in revulsion and rejection, it ended with acceptance and understanding. I've dreamed this scene so many times that I can almost believe it's a real memory.

(39) A few months ago, in May, I wrote Alex a letter and mailed it to her gingerbread house. I remember every word.

> *Dear Alex,*
> *Every time I try to talk to you, I turn into a witch. I'm sorry. Maybe I can say what needs to be said better on paper. I'll try anyway.*
>
> *I've been feeling so many things lately. Anger, confusion, but mostly sadness. I miss you. Can you say that to a friend, a girl friend? Well, I do miss you. I miss the friendship we had, and I'm sorry if I did something to destroy it.*
>
> *I'm glad you've found Keenan. It seems for as long as I've known you, you've longed to fall in love. I hope he's everything you wished for.*
>
> *You're probably wondering what the point of this letter is. I guess it's this ... that I've watched our friendship fade during the past year or so and yet we've never talked about it. Maybe if we stop pretending we're still friends, I'll stop being mad at you and myself. I want you to remember me as I used to be, and not like the witch I've become. So I'm writing to say good-bye. Our friendship deserves at least that—a decent burial.*
>
> *So farewell, my best and dearest friend,*
> *Tish*

(40) I mailed the letter on a Friday afternoon and spent the whole weekend wondering how to break into the mailbox so I could get it back. What had I been thinking? I didn't want to end our friendship! If it was possible at all to save it, I was willing.

(41) I couldn't face her. I faked the flu on Monday and Tuesday, and by the time I went back to school on Wednesday, Alex had received the letter. I knew it as soon as I saw her face. She was in the bathroom putting on lipstick and nearly dropped the tube when she saw me.

AS YOU READ

(42) "Tish! Hi ... how are you feeling?"

(43) *Like I've made the biggest mistake of my life.* "Better, thanks."

(44) "You had that flu that's going around, eh?"

(45) I nodded.

(46) "I was going to call ...." said Alex.

(47) *But you didn't.*

(48) "I ... uh," she glanced around and crouched down to look under the stall doors to make sure we were alone, "I got your letter."

(49) "Alex—"

(50) "It was amazing, Tish. I'm so glad you sent it."

(51) "You are?"

(52) "I've been feeling bad about what's happened, too. Things aren't the same as they used to be, are they?"

(53) "Well, no ...."

(54) "So I was thinking, maybe you're right. Maybe we should take a break for a while."

(55) "Oh ..." What was wrong with me? I wanted to grab her by the shoulders and say, *Forget the stupid letter! I take it back! I'll be nice, I'll play along, I'll go to those stupid parties and find a boyfriend if that's what you want!* But I didn't really want those things. I wanted Alex and our friendship back, the way it used to be.

> **I'd been *dumped*. *Dumped* where people *dump*.**

Tish agrees with Alex because ...

(56) "Okay, I guess that's best," I said.

(57) Alex smiled, and I remembered her perfect small white teeth on the playground that first day.

(58) "See ya around, Tish."

(59) "Yeah, see ya."

(60) Alex dropped the lipstick tube into her purse, walked out of the bathroom and out of my life. The bell rang. History class was starting, but I didn't care. I sat in a stall and thought about the word *dump*. I'd been *dumped*. *Dumped* where people *dump*.

(61) It stank in the bathroom. I hadn't noticed it before, but I sure noticed it now, a rotten, wet, putrid smell that reached into my stomach, churned up my breakfast and made me throw up. Again and again, I retched in the toilet until my eyes watered and my throat burned and there was nothing left inside me.

UNIT 1 | CONNECTIONS

> **AS YOU READ**
>
> If I were Tish, I would …

(62) When the trembling stopped, I rinsed my mouth, splashed cold water on my face, and walked to class, convinced that I'd ended what had already been ending and that now I could get over Alex and let the place inside where I kept my feelings for her grow cold and hard.

(63) In October, a film crew descended on our town to shoot some scenes for a suspense thriller called *You Never Know*. All everyone talked about that week was the star, Oksana Riker—where she'd been seen around town, how nice she was to the groupies who followed her everywhere. We were let out of school early on Friday to watch the filming. It was a foot-chase scene down Main Street, so Baba and I had front-row seats upstairs in her enclosed sun porch, where Alex and I used to watch the Santa Claus parade every year.

(64) I could see Alex on the sidewalk below, pressing against the traffic barriers, laughing and tossing her hair the way she used to when she was trying to catch a guy's eye. Maybe she was hoping to get discovered by someone on the film crew. She'd always wanted to be an actress.

(65) Margaret, Baba's lady-sitter, came in to say good-bye, and Baba gave her a long tight hug. Sometimes Baba thinks Margaret is her mother and cries when she has to go.

(66) Baba had arranged my old stuffed animals beside her on the couch so they could watch TV with us. She had her feet on the coffee table, and I was painting her toenails bubblegum pink. The colour wasn't my choice.

(67) "Are you sure, Baba?" I asked when she pointed to the pink bottle. "That one's kind of gaudy."

(68) "Yup," she said. That's all she said anymore—"yup," "nope," or she'd shrug her shoulders to say, "I don't know." I hadn't heard a full sentence cross her lips in ages.

(69) I chattered away as I painted her nails, telling her about the film shoot and glancing out the window now and then.

(70) "Alex is down there," I said.

(71) Baba's foot jerked suddenly and wound up with a pink stripe painted down her big toe. She sat up straight as a board, eyes wide

You Never Know (Tish) | SHORT STORY | 31

AS YOU READ

(72) with panic, her mouth opening and closing like a fish gasping for air.
"Baba! What is it?"

(73) I wished I had her sixth sense so I could read her mind. She was trying so hard to tell me something. Finally the words came out, croaky and small, but lined up in the right order, a real sentence: "You … never know … from where you sit … where the man … in the balcony … will spit."

(74) It was a miracle! I glanced up at the picture of Jesus that hangs over Baba's TV. Over the years, I'd heard dozens of Baba's proverbs and sayings, but I'd never heard that one.

(75) "Can you say it again, Baba?"

(76) She shook her head, and tears filled her eyes as she rocked back and forth on the couch. The stuffed animals wedged around her tumbled to the floor. I wrapped my arms around her and rocked with her, humming the tuneless song she used to sing to me. When she calmed down, she said it again. "You never know, you never know, from where you sit … where the man in the balcony will spit!"

> **Right on, Baba, I thought. Spit happens.**

(77) "Are you talking about yourself, Baba?" I thought maybe she meant God, up in heaven, was spitting on her by giving her Alzheimer's. But she shook her head.

(78) "About *me* then? Are you talking about *me*?" I had told her about my feelings for Alex, but mostly because I thought she couldn't understand.

(79) "Nope," said Baba.

(80) "Well, *who* then?"

What do you think Baba is trying to say?

(81) "You never know!" she said. Then she clamped her mouth shut and began rocking again. I held her and hummed and thought about what she had said.

(82) *You never know from where you sit where the man in the balcony will spit.*

(83) Right on, Baba, I thought. Spit happens. Spit rains down on you. Alex was my best friend, and now she's lined up with the other spitters, her stupid quarterback boyfriend and her airhead cheerleader friends, spitting. Give me a T! Give me an I! Give me an S! Give me an H! What does that spell? FREAK!

(84) The word echoed in my head like a gunshot. *Freak! Freak!* But it wasn't an echo. It *was* a gunshot. Baba whimpered.

(85) "It's okay. It's just the film shoot," I told her, but I looked out the

32 UNIT 1 | CONNECTIONS

window to make sure. There was an awful lot of screaming suddenly, right outside our house.

(86) If I'd been down in the crowd, I never would have seen Alex on the ground with all those people pressing around her. But high up as I was, I could see her eyes flutter open and shut. I could see her lips moving, trying to speak. I could see the patch of pavement beneath her head become a dark wet halo.

(87) I had a front-row balcony seat for The Death of Alex.

(88) Beautiful, special, amazing Alex.

(89) My ex-best friend, Alex.

(90) I read about Timothy Horn in the newspapers. Age nineteen, author of eight hundred love letters to Oksana Riker. He had hitchhiked all the way from his home near Detroit to see her. In Levis and a navy coat, he looked like everyone else in the crowd, and that's why no one noticed him until he climbed to the roof of the Sub Shop across from our house, pulled a gun from his pocket and fired three shots at Oksana. The first two hit the pavement. The third one hit Alex.

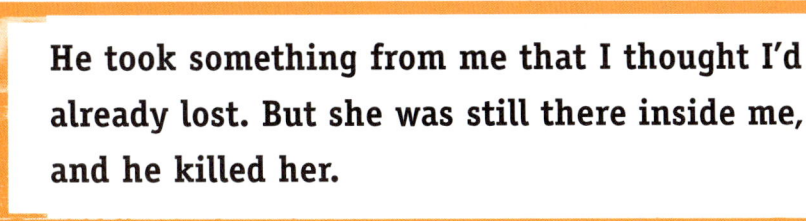

> **He took something from me that I thought I'd already lost. But she was still there inside me, and he killed her.**

(91) I watched her die as one last shot rang out. I didn't hear, notice or care about it, but I read about it after. Just before the police rushed out on the roof to grab him, Timothy Horn shot himself. *Freak*.

(92) I spend a lot of time hating Timothy Horn. I hate that he was born. I hate that his father had a gun that was easy to steal. I hate that he was a bad shot. I hate his obsession, which reminds me of mine.

(93) If Baba were herself, she'd say, "Let go of the hate. Forgive him." I can't. He took something from me that I thought I'd already lost. But she was still there inside me, and he killed her. The cold hard place inside me ached. There was a hole in it now, with bloody ragged edges, as if a bullet had torn its way through.

(94) Mom couldn't get time off work, so I went by myself to Alex's funeral. The church was packed. I sat in the back pew beside Ginger Byam,

who's in my Family Studies class. I wondered what she was doing there. She was a loner and had never been Alex's friend as far as I knew.

(95) "What's in the basket?" she whispered.

(96) "Babka," I whispered back. When she looked confused, I added, "Cake for the reception. Alex liked it."

(97) Then we stopped talking because Mandy Solesby had stood up at the front. I remembered that she was the minister's daughter. I'd always thought of her as just one of the cheerleaders in a tight sweater and short skirt, giggling about nothing. But this was a Mandy I'd never seen in school. She read a poem about friendship and talked about what Alex's friendship had meant to her. Mandy's voice quavered, but she never lost it. I glanced at Ginger. I could tell she was impressed, too.

(98) At the reception afterward, I placed the babka on the food table with one of Baba's embroidered napkins fanned beneath it. "Presentation is important," Alex used to say. I wanted to talk to her parents, but they were always surrounded by family or Keenan and his friends, and I just couldn't face them.

(99) I wandered over to the picture wall, where there were snapshots of Alex. I was in some of them, swimming in their pool, roasting hot dogs at their family barbecues, lying beside Alex in a pile of leaves with only our faces showing.

(100) There were some recent pictures of Alex that were beautiful. Sweaty and smiling after a cheerleading practice, soft and serious against a backdrop of pussy willows, and a close-up that showed her laughing eyes and perfect white teeth.

(101) "I guess you knew she wanted to be a model, eh?" Ginger had come up beside me to look at the pictures, too.

(102) I nodded. "She could have been one easily. Look at these."

(103) "I don't have to," said Ginger. "I took them."

(104) "Really?" Then I remembered it was Ginger who took the royal wedding portraits, where we all look so stiff, but Alex looked so natural in these photos. So alive. "Could I get a copy of this one?" I asked.

(105) "Sure," she said. "You guys were best friends, weren't you?"

(106) "Once upon a time we were."

(107) "She talked about you the day I took these by the pussy willows. She told me about falling off her bike … when you helped her."

(108) "She was always helping Alex, weren't you Tish?" I turned to see Alex's parents, holding hands behind me. The mascara was smudged beneath her mother's eyes. Her dad winked at me like he used to. "Hi, Number Two," he said.

(109) I didn't know if Alex had told them why we drifted apart. I didn't know if they'd seen the letter.

(110) "I miss her so much," I whispered.

(111) Mrs. Meyers nodded and put her hand to her lips. "Here I go crying all over again."

(112) "I'm sorry," I said. What I meant was, I'm sorry I didn't understand Baba's warning. I'm sorry I didn't save your daughter. I'm so sorry.

(113) I left quickly so I wouldn't have to talk to anyone else, ran down the church steps and headed up the street, cursing my stupid dress shoes. I felt like kicking them off so I could run faster and let the sidewalk rip open the soles of my feet. I wanted to bleed, and I wanted Baba to fix it. I wanted her to wrap her pillowy arms around me and rock and hum and pat my hair. I wanted her to tell me something, anything, even another cryptic proverb that might help me get through this.

(114) "Tish! Wait up!" Keenan ran up beside me. "I tried to find you in there, but you got away."

(115) *It's called avoiding you*, I thought. Then I saw he'd been crying. Poor Keenan. I'd spent a lot of time hating him before I started hating Timothy Horn. *Say something*, I told myself. *Be polite. He just lost his girlfriend.*

(116) "Keenan … I'm sorry about Alex." How many times had I said that today or had it said to me?

(117) "Thanks, Tish. Same to you. I—uh—wanted to ask you …" He looked as awkward as I felt.

(118) "A few of us are getting together at my place after this, to talk about Alex and stuff. Would you come?"

(119) "Oh, I don't think so … but thanks for asking."

(120) "Tish? Please come. You were Alex's … best friend."

(121) I looked him right in the eye then, and I saw something there. He *knew*. Alex must have told him about the kiss and the letter, about my feelings for her. Oh God. I wanted to sink through the sidewalk.

(122) But then I realized something else. He knew, but he still wanted me to come. And I realized that of all the people in the world, maybe only Keenan could understand how I felt, because he had loved her, too.

(123) Margaret was home with Baba making Hairy Cookies for tonight's dessert. Baba was probably fine, happy with the woman she thought was her mother. There would be time later to sit with her and hum and rock and tell her about Alex's funeral.

(124) "Okay," I said to Keenan. "I'll come."

◀ Tish agrees to meet up with Keenan because …

You Never Know (Tish) | SHORT STORY

AFTER Reading

CHECKING FOR UNDERSTANDING

1. a) Complete the chart you created in the Before Reading activity. Share your answers for one of the statements with a partner.
   b) While you were reading the beginning of the story, you were asked to stop and **predict** what would happen. Discuss your predictions with the rest of the class. Decide why predicting is a useful tool to help you understand a text.

PURPOSE / AUDIENCE / FORM

2. Review the difference between **subject** and theme in The Reference Shelf, page 251. As a class, **brainstorm** different subjects for this story. Next, choose one of the subjects and develop a theme statement for the story. Your theme statement can start by saying, "In 'You Never Know (Tish),' the author is saying …"

STYLE AND CONVENTIONS

3. a) **Scan** the story and find the places where the author uses italics. In your notebook, make **jot notes** summarizing the reasons the author uses italics.
   b) On a scale of 1 to 5, where 1 means "it didn't help my understanding," 3 means "it helped my understanding a bit," and 5 means "it really helped my understanding," decide how much the author's use of italics helped you better understand what the author wanted to emphasize.
   c) Share your rankings with the class.

CRITICAL THINKING

4. a) Copy the following chart into your notebook. **Reread** the story and fill in each column. An example has been done for you.

The character	wanted	but	so
Tish	a friend at her new school,	all the kids ignored her and Tish was shy,	Alex, who was also new, made friends with her.

   b) As a class, use your charts to write a **summary** (see The Reference Shelf, page 260) of the story.

UNIT 1 | CONNECTIONS

UNIT 1 Activity

For your project for this unit, you will be evaluated using a rubric your teacher will discuss with you before you start. You will be expected to keep any process work and submit it with your final product.

Choose one of the following activities to complete. Details of each of the assignments will be given below.
1. two-paragraph **supported opinion** piece
2. **script** for a skit
3. brochure

If you want to use a selection that doesn't have a specific character, you can create a character, such as a teen or parent who would read "Talk Before They Run."

1. **Supported opinion paragraph**
   Think about the following question from the Think About It box on page 1: *How do we build and maintain the connections we create?* Choose two characters from any selection in this unit. You will write a supported opinion paragraph about each character to answer this question: "Did the character successfully build and/or maintain connections with others?"

   Here are the steps you should follow:
   1) Choose two characters from any selection in this unit.
   2) Make two **T-charts** like this one.

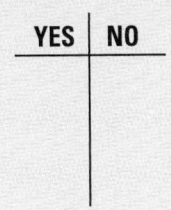

YES	NO

   3) Fill in one of the **T-charts** with **jot-note** supports that answer the question, "Did the character successfully build and/or maintain connections with others?" Repeat this step using your second character and second T-chart.
   4) Decide if you will argue yes or no for each character based on the supports you have in each column of your T-charts.
   5) Write your supported opinion paragraph for each character.
   6) Edit your work using the guidelines in The Reference Shelf on page 273.
   7) Create a polished copy of your supported opinion paragraphs.

2. **Script for a skit**

   Write a script about two characters from this unit. Your script will take place five years after the end of the story. The characters should talk about what they have done since their story ended, what they have learned, and how their lives have changed because of the connections they made or lost.

   Follow these steps:
   1) Choose two characters.
   2) **Reread** and **scan** the selections from which you chose the characters.
   3) Make **jot notes** of each character's connections with others, and what they learned from these connections.
   4) Imagine what might have happened to each character after their story ended.
   5) Choose a setting for the encounter.
   6) Start writing your script following this outline:
      - two people meet after five years
      - they both tell what happened to them in their story
      - they tell what they learned, and how those lessons influenced the next five years of their life
   7) Practise your script until it is polished.

3. **Brochure**

   "Talk Before They Run" (page 3) talks about the problem of not making or not maintaining connections. In a small group, create a brochure for Grade 6 students that explains how to improve communication in families.

   Follow these steps:
   1) In your group, **brainstorm** and record what good communication is.
   2) Organize your ideas into topics such as body language and tone of voice.
   3) Decide which of your ideas are the most important.
   4) Write tips for Grade 6 students on how to communicate with parents.
   5) Design your brochure.
   6) Edit your brochure.
   7) Create a final version of your brochure.

> 1 > UNIT 2 > 3 > 4 > 5 > 6

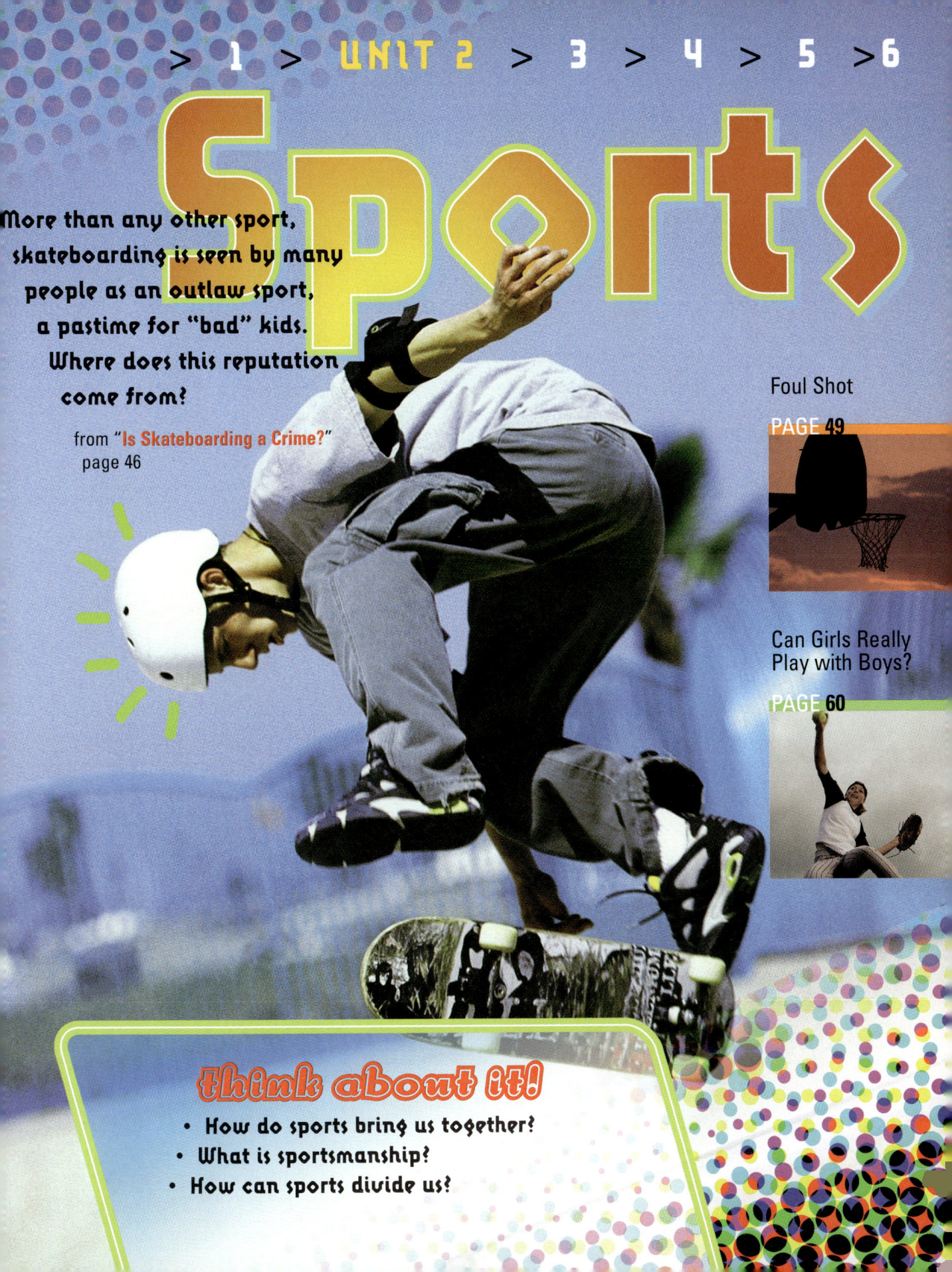

Sports

More than any other sport, skateboarding is seen by many people as an outlaw sport, a pastime for "bad" kids. Where does this reputation come from?

from "**Is Skateboarding a Crime?**"
page 46

Foul Shot
PAGE 49

Can Girls Really Play with Boys?
PAGE 60

think about it!

- How do sports bring us together?
- What is sportsmanship?
- How can sports divide us?

> > > **Fix That Flat!** by Chris Hayhurst (informational text) ... 41

🍁 **Chew on This** by Jaclyn Law (magazine article) ... 43

🍁 **Is Skateboarding a Crime?** by L.M. Burke (informational text) ... 46

Foul Shot by Edwin A. Hoey (poem) ... 49

Two Selections on Overcoming Obstacles
  🍁 **Kendra Ohama** by Laura Robinson and Maija Robinson (biography) ... 52
  🍁 **Wheelchair Rugby** (informational text) ... 57

🍁 **Can Girls Really Play with Boys?** by Oakland Ross (newspaper article) ... 60

🍁 **A Fly in a Pail of Milk** by Herb Carnegie (autobiography) ... 66

🍁 **The Hockey Game** by Wes Fineday (short story) ... 72

Unit 2 Activity ... 79

UNIT 2
Sports

> You're hitting the court in a few hours for a game of hoops against a rival high school. Your stomach is rumbling. What's your game plan? If your answer is "chocolate bar and pop," park yourself on the bench, buddy. You won't get very far with a meal like that.
> *from "Chew on This," page 43*

informational text

PURPOSE
- To think about how the **audience** determines the **language** and details included in a set of directions
- To create clear directions for a procedure

Fix That Flat!

CHRIS HAYHURST

BEFORE Reading

1. Write directions or draw a map from the school to your home. Imagine that your directions or map will be used by someone new to your area.
2. Trade your directions or map with a partner. Based on your partner's directions or map, draw a map or write directions from the school to your partner's home. Use the opposite **format** that your partner used (for example, if your partner wrote directions, you will draw a map). Return the map or directions to your partner. How closely have you translated their work?

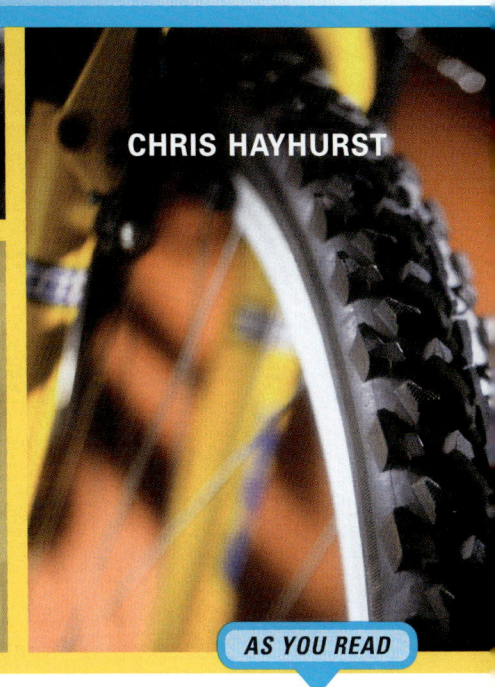

AS YOU READ

When you see, "Are these directions clear?" **reread** the instructions. If unclear, tell how to make them clearer by writing "I need to know..."

Fixing a flat tire on a bicycle is simple. Just follow these steps:

1. Take the wheel off of your bike.
2. Lever the tire off of the rim with tire irons. This is the tricky part. Slide a tire iron under the lip of the tire and pry the tire's edge over the rim. Take another tire iron and do the same thing a few inches farther down the rim. Soon you'll be able to slide the tire off of the rim with your fingers or with a third tire iron.

◀ Are these directions clear?

3. Pull out the popped tube and either patch it or get a new one.
4. Inspect the inside of the tire for anything sharp that might pop your new tube.

◀ Are these directions clear?

5. Pump some air into the new or repaired tube, then place it on the rim beneath the lifted tire. Make sure that the valve goes through the hole in the rim, and be careful not to pinch or bunch up the tube!

◀ Are these directions clear?

6. Using your fingers, push the edge of the tire back beneath the lip of the rim.
7. Finally, pump up the tire and put it back on your bike.

AFTER Reading

CHECKING FOR UNDERSTANDING

1. Survey the class to find out who has and has not changed a bicycle tire. Find out which students found the directions in "Fix That Flat!" clear or unclear. How does familiarity with a topic affect the way directions need to be written?

PURPOSE / AUDIENCE / FORM

2. Based on the survey results from question #1, how does an audience's experience affect the details needed in the directions and the type of vocabulary used? What conclusions can you make? Develop rules based on these conclusions.

STYLE AND CONVENTIONS

3. a) Write on the board some different ways the directions in "Fix That Flat!" could be given.
   b) With a partner, put the directions from "Fix That Flat!" into a different form. Post the directions around the classroom. Take a tour of the different formats and decide which ones work best for you. Be prepared to explain why.

CRITICAL THINKING

4. a) Create directions for a procedure you know well (for example, how to make a certain recipe or how to set an electronic watch). Decide on the best format for your directions (for example, sentences, point form, diagrams, or in a rhyme). Assume the audience will have no experience with your procedure.
   b) Create a feedback sheet like the one below, and attach it to your directions.

   My name: _____   Procedure: _____

Name	Vocabulary/Visuals	Details	Order/Clarity

   c) In a group of four, sit in a circle and pass your directions to the person on your right. Read the directions you have, and fill in the chart. When you have finished, pass the directions around until three readers have commented on the directions.
   d) Read the comments on your feedback sheet. Write down what you would change in your directions to make them even better.

magazine article

JACLYN LAW

CHEW on THIS

PURPOSE
- To infer why this article would appear in a magazine for teenagers
- To think about the way the author has captured the reader's attention with her writing

BEFORE Reading

Copy the letter of each of the four statements below into your notebook. Decide if you agree or disagree with each statement, and write "true" or "false" beside each letter.

A. A chocolate bar is the best energy food for an athlete before or during a game or event.

B. It's important for an athlete to eat pasta right before a game or event.

C. Eating a big meal before a game will keep an athlete from getting hungry.

D. During a game or event, drinking a sports drink is a good idea.

As you read, look for more information on these statements.

(1) You're hitting the court in a few hours for a game of hoops against a rival high school. Your stomach is rumbling. What's your game plan? If your answer is "chocolate bar and a pop," park yourself on the bench, buddy. You won't get very far with a meal like that. Here's what will happen: first the sugar is absorbed quickly into your bloodstream forcing your body to release insulin to deal with it. Then, once you get moving, you could actually trigger hypoglycemia (low blood sugar). The result? Shaking, chills, and loss of coordination, not to mention hunger that would impress the critters in *Jeepers Creepers*. If you want to improve your athletic performance by making better food choices, read on.

AS YOU READ

◂ A

AS YOU READ

(2) In the past, to power up for an event, athletes shovelled down as much pasta as humanly possible a couple of hours before the coin toss. Now, fitness and nutrition research shows that eating healthy meals all the time is the most effective approach. According to the Center for Human Nutrition in the U.S.: "Now we know that the foods you eat every day to support your training do far more to enhance performance than the foods you eat right before you compete. From a nutrition standpoint, there is little you can do in the few hours before an event that will drastically improve your performance."

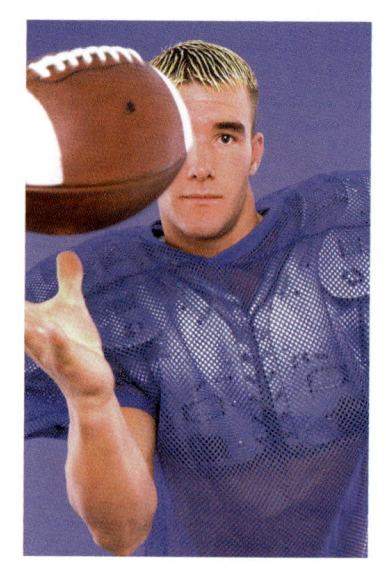

B ▶

(3) So what's a ravenous right winger to do? Basically, you need to choose foods that will prevent you from feeling hungry, keep you hydrated, and make you feel comfortable so you can focus all your attention on the game. Here's a plan to get you game-ready:

- Try not to eat within three hours before the event.
- Avoid heavy meals the day before and the day of competition.

C ▶

- Choose complex carbohydrates (whole-grain cereals, vegetables, and fruit)—they'll keep you feeling full.
- Avoid foods high in fat, protein, and fibre, as they're tougher to digest and make you feel sluggish. Take a pass on anything greasy, spicy or unfamiliar—this is not the time to experiment with new foods. And hey, eat foods you actually like!
- Every athlete is different—eventually you'll figure out which foods work best for you.
- Nothing saps energy faster than dehydration, so load up on liquids. The day before the game, drink an extra four to eight glasses of fluid. Continue drinking extra fluid up to two hours before the game, then take a drink during every break (ideally, every 15 to 20 minutes). Be aware that sports drinks and fruit juices can be high in sugar—the insulin surge that follows could leave you feeling drained rather than pumped.

D ▶

BREAKFAST OF CHAMPIONS: Whole-grain breads or cereals, fresh fruit, low-fat milk

BETWEEN-GAME SNACKS: Bagel with peanut butter, banana and low-fat yogurt, small apple, low-fat granola bars

44 UNIT 2 | SPORTS

AFTER Reading

CHECKING FOR UNDERSTANDING

1. a) Go back to the lettered list in your notebook. If you have changed your mind about any of your answers, change your answer.
   b) Find the letters in the margin of your text that match the statements from Before Reading, and **reread** the information. Make brief **jot notes** on the correct information in your notebook. Be ready to read your jot notes to the class.

PURPOSE / AUDIENCE / FORM

2. a) This article was written for teenagers. In a single sentence, record in your notebook the **purpose** of this article. You may be able to think of more than one purpose. As a teenager reading this article, do you think it fulfills its purpose? With the class, give a thumbs up or a thumbs down to show your opinion.
   b) Add at least two more sentences to the one you have already written, explaining why you believe the article does or does not fulfill its purpose. Make sure you refer to examples from the article to support your **opinion**. Be prepared to read your paragraph out loud.

STYLE AND CONVENTIONS

3. a) The author uses **direct address** in this article. That means she talks directly to the reader (you). Think about why she might have written the article this way. Be ready to share your thoughts with the class.
   b) As a class, draw some conclusions about when you might want to use direct address in your own writing, and record your conclusions in your notebook.

CRITICAL THINKING

4. Based on the information in the article, plan a menu for a healthy breakfast and mid-morning snack that will keep you alert and feeling satisfied. Below the menu, explain your choices. Be sure to refer to the article in your explanation.

Chew on This | MAGAZINE ARTICLE | 45

informational text

PURPOSE
- To identify the writer's **opinion** and decide whether or not you agree with it
- To look at the way the writer has supported the opinion

L.M. BURKE

Is Skateboarding a Crime?

BEFORE Reading

Create an effect-and-cause chart in your notebook like the one below. The "effect" on the left is what many people feel about skateboarders. Individually, fill in the chart with as many causes (reasons) as you can think of for people feeling this way. As a class, discuss your ideas. As class members contribute ideas, add these to your chart.

Effect	Cause
People think skateboarders are bad kids.	1. 2. 3. 4. 5.

AS YOU READ

Infer why companies won't insure people involved with dangerous sports.

Infer why music might be called "aggressive."

(1) More than any other sport, skateboarding is seen by many people as an outlaw sport, a pastime for "bad" kids. Where does this reputation come from? It's not completely clear, but it may have something to do with the risks and potential dangers of the sport. Street skaters in particular risk injuring not only themselves but also passersby, and skate parks often have trouble finding insurance because of the fear that skaters might seriously injure themselves or others. It's true that skaters can get hurt, sometimes seriously or even fatally, but several other sports, including football and bicycling, have greater percentages of injuries per year than skateboarding does.

(2) Then there's the music. For years many skaters have listened to punk and ska, which lots of people consider too loud and aggressive. The

outrageously baggy clothes that some skaters wear make them stand out in a crowd and add to skateboarding's reputation as a sport for rebels. And in lots of cities and towns, skating on public streets is illegal, so skaters in those places may literally be lawbreakers.

(3) Fortunately more and more cities across the United States and Canada are beginning to view skating as a sport rather than a criminal act. Many are allowing skate parks, where people can skate without worrying about cars, pedestrians, or uneven, skin-eating pavement. That's all most skaters want: a place to thrash hard, skate safely, and have fun.

AS YOU READ

◀ Agree or disagree with the author about what skaters want.

After Reading

CHECKING FOR UNDERSTANDING

1. a) Add any new ideas from this text to the effect-and-cause chart you created before you read the text.
   b) The writer seems to sympathize with skaters. Find two words, phrases, or sentences that prove this.

PURPOSE / AUDIENCE / FORM

2. Create and fill in a chart like this one. The intended audience is the group of people the writer thought would be most interested in his or her topic.

Intended Audience/Reader	How I Know
Age	
Interests	
Gender	

Compare answers with your classmates.

Is Skateboarding a Crime? | INFORMATIONAL TEXT

STYLE AND CONVENTIONS

3. If you were a parent reading this article, you could probably find several reasons not to let your son or daughter be a skateboarder or hang around with skateboarders. Find three words or phrases that describe skaters negatively.

CRITICAL THINKING

4. a) How well has the writer convinced you that skateboarding is not a crime? Choose one of the following to reflect your opinion: "not convincing," "a little convincing," "fairly convincing," "very convincing." Explain your choice to the class.
   b) Find two other students in the class who share your opinion. Together, make a list of reasons why you felt the way you did about the author's ability to convince you. Report to the class.
   c) After all groups have reported, survey the class to see if people have changed their minds while listening to another group's ideas.
   d) Make a class list of "rules" you should follow if you want to convince someone else that your opinion is the right one. To help you make this list, think about what this author did, or did not do.

poem

Foul Shot

EDWIN A. HOEY

PURPOSE
- To appreciate the way the poet has used description and action verbs
- To understand that not all poems rhyme or have a regular **rhythm**

BEFORE Reading

Using the expertise from the class, talk about what happens when a basketball player takes a foul shot.

AS YOU READ

Good readers talk to themselves as they are reading. As you are reading the poem, stop when you get to a question in the margin. Try to answer the question.

With two 60's stuck on the scoreboard
And two seconds hanging on the clock,
The solemn boy in the center of eyes,
Squeezed by silence,
5   Seeks out the line with his feet,
Soothes his hands along his uniform,
Gently drums the ball against the floor,
Then measures the waiting net,
Raises the ball on his right hand,
10 Balances it with his left,
Calms it with fingertips,
Breathes,
Crouches,
Waits,
15 And then through a stretching of stillness,
Nudges it upward.

◀ Why did the poet included 10 "s" sounding words in the first 6 lines?

◀ How do these verbs help me see what the player is doing?

(continued) ▶▶

Foul Shot | POEM   49

AS YOU READ

The ball
Slides up and out,
Lands,
20 Leans,
Wobbles,
Wavers,
Hesitates,
Exasperates,
25 Plays it coy

How can screams be "unsounding"?

Until every face begs with <u>unsounding</u> screams—
And then

And then

And then,

30 Right before ROAR-UP,
Dives down and through.

AFTER Reading

CHECKING FOR UNDERSTANDING

1. Retelling a story helps you remember what has happened. With a partner, **retell** the story in your own words. Your partner will add more details to what you said.

PURPOSE / AUDIENCE / FORM

2. a) Imagine that "Foul Shot" has been entered into a poetry contest and you are one of the 20 judges. **Reread** the poem several times. Make **jot notes** or a **graphic organizer** to organize your thoughts. Make at least one comment on the content, the way the poem looks on the page, and the words that the poet uses.

50 UNIT 2 | SPORTS

b) Rate the poem using a scale of 1 to 4, where 1 means you don't like it at all, and 4 means you really like it.

c) Form a group of three with classmates who gave the poem the same rating as you did. Discuss why you gave the poem the rating you did. Add any new ideas to your notes. Present your ideas to the class.

STYLE AND CONVENTIONS

3. Make one list of verbs (see The Reference Shelf, page 233) the poet has used to describe the player and a second list of verbs used to describe the flight of the ball. Next to each verb, write another verb the poet could have used instead. Try to create the same feeling as the poet did with his choice of verbs. As a class, decide whether the poet used the best verbs for the poem.

CRITICAL THINKING

4. a) Reread the notes you created for question #2. Write a paragraph supporting your **opinion** of the poem (see The Reference Shelf, page 259). Be sure to include comments on the way the poem looks and the poet's word choices.

   b) Form a group of three. Exchange paragraphs with another group. Number yourselves one to three. Each group member is responsible for making sure the paragraph he or she is reading has enough information on these topics:
   - Number one—look for comments on content.
   - Number two—look for comments on the look of the poem.
   - Number three—look for comments on the poet's word choices.

   If you do not find information on your topic, record that fact on the bottom of the writer's page. Suggest what the writer could include in his or her second draft.

   c) Continue until you have commented on each paragraph. Return the paragraphs to the writers.

   d) Write a second draft of your own paragraph using RADS (Reorder, Add, Delete, and Substitute) (see The Reference Shelf, page 272) and your editors' comments to help you improve it.

Foul Shot | POEM

biography + informational text

PURPOSE
- To practise separating what is important to know from what is interesting to know
- To write a **news report**

OVERCOMING OBSTACLES

BEFORE Reading

Imagine you have been in an accident and you are told you will not be able to walk again. Do a **quick write** (see The Reference Shelf, page 269) in which you write your immediate reactions to the news. Write for two minutes without stopping.

Kendra Ohama

Wheeling and Shooting Her Way Around the World

LAURA ROBINSON AND MAIJA ROBINSON

AS YOU READ

When you are asked to stop and take a note, **reread** the section and decide what is important enough to write down.

(1) Kendra always loved sports, but it wasn't until she found out how exciting wheelchair basketball was that she took herself seriously as an athlete. One day she was shopping, and a man—who would later become her coach—came up to her and asked if she would be interested in playing wheelchair basketball. It took her by surprise, but he told her they were practising at Calgary General Hospital, and she decided to see what the sport was about.

(2) "It was the first time I had been in a chair that was so moveable and I thought, 'Wow, this is great! I'm going to use this as an everyday chair.' I had so much coordination to wheel and dribble." So began Kendra's amazing career in wheelchair basketball, though the journey towards her career had started many years earlier.

STOP. Take a note. ▸

(3) Kendra's family had a potato farm near Ranier, Alberta, a small town outside Calgary, and like most farm kids, the six children in her family all had plenty of chores. They would have to grade potatoes, make sure the sprinkler was running properly, and sometimes even change the sprinkler's pipes. Everyone worked hard, but her family had always worked hard. Kendra's grandparents had come to Canada from Japan, but still had family and friends there. During harvest time, Japanese friends of the family would make the long trip to Canada and help out. Kendra and her siblings were young at the time, and they didn't grow up speaking Japanese and couldn't communicate too well with their visitors.

(4) Kendra says both her mom and dad were born in Canada and they ran into racism when they were kids. "Our parents didn't want us to learn Japanese," she says. "They had a hard time when they were growing up and so they wanted us to fit in. Unfortunately I didn't learn the language. Except," she says with a laugh, "all the bad words." Years later in her career as an international athlete, Kendra realized how much she would have loved to speak Japanese.

AS YOU READ

◀ STOP. Take a note.

> "Our parents didn't want us to learn Japanese," she says. "They had a hard time when they were growing up and so they wanted us to fit in. Unfortunately I didn't learn the language. Except," she says with a laugh, "all the bad words."

(5) In Ranier, even though she had plenty of chores at home, Kendra played many sports at school. Because she often stayed late to practise, when she was a teenager, she would sometimes drive to school instead of taking the school bus. One winter day while Kendra was in high school, she was driving to school when she hit black ice. The car spun out of control and Kendra flew out the windshield. "I was a typical sixteen-year-old," she comments. "I thought seat belts were for other people."

(6) "Just after the accident when they flew me to Foothills Hospital, I was in and out of consciousness, but I remember asking the doctor if I was ever going to walk again," she says. "I think that may have helped me, that my subconscious was already trying to accept that I wouldn't walk again."

Overcoming Obstacles | BIOGRAPHY + INFORMATIONAL TEXT

AS YOU READ

(7) Indeed, her doctor told her she wouldn't walk, but her physiotherapist thought she could, and they set about to see if this was possible. With the help of many months of strenuous exercise and practice, Kendra was able to walk with braces from her feet to her hips, and a set of crutches. Her physiotherapist told her it was thanks to her healthy active body that she was able to make quick and amazing progress in her rehabilitation. Kendra had always loved volleyball, baseball, and badminton, and participated in judo and track and field, too. "My doctor came in and he was really surprised. But I thought the braces were too slow and I had to use both hands with the crutches, so I decided to use a chair." Kendra was so intent on learning how to go with the flow of her new life that she thinks that is why she didn't experience any depression. And she began to realize how important her sports background was.

> **After her first workout, Kendra knew she'd found her sport.**

(8) Five years later she showed up at Calgary General Hospital and started to play basketball—the one sport she hadn't played seriously in high school. After her first workout, Kendra knew she'd found her sport. She dedicated herself to being the best she could possibly be. "I went all summer and winter to the gym," she says. "I didn't miss a practice and I trained with the men's and women's teams. We played in Edmonton and in the United States. I did a lot of wheeling too—10 kilometres, three times a week."

(9) In the summer of 1990 Kendra was invited to her first national team camp in Vancouver, as a guard. She didn't make the team, but the experience was really important for her because she learned what skills she had to work on. She came home and worked on the accuracy of her shot, and on rebounds. Kendra trained as hard as she could for the next ten months, because if she made the team in 1991, she knew she'd have a good shot at making the team competing in 1992 at the Barcelona Paralympic Games. All her efforts paid off and Kendra played on the team that went to the World Stoke–Mandeville International Tournament in England. Canada took the gold at that tournament over ten teams, and started on a gold medal roll that would continue for more than ten years.

STOP. Take a note.

(10)   Kendra says one of the reasons the team has done so well for so many years is their mental training. Players from other countries may be faster or have better skills, and the U.S. athletes are much younger, most of them in their mid-twenties. The Canadians, meanwhile, are in their mid-thirties, but they visualize and imagine different scenarios—at the foul line, in layups, everything. In their imaginations they add all the distractions, the fans, the refs, the bad calls, anything that might make them overlook their task and take their focus off the moment. They just won't allow outside distractions to bother them.

(11)   "For all athletes, you have to know your routine before the game. Same thing goes with off the court," says Kendra. "You have to organize your personal life so you can focus on your sport and not worry too much about personal problems. They seem to melt away when you focus on the positive things.

(12)   "The other thing is, if you get too involved in personal problems, it will affect team cohesion. Our team gets along really well, and we respect our coach."

(13)   In the summer of 2002, the team's winning streak since 1991 was finally broken by the U.S. at a tournament in Brazil, but they only let it happen once. They arrived in Kitakyūshū, Japan, for the World Championships that fall, determined to get their streak back, and they did. But it wasn't winning the World Crown that most affected Kendra this time. It was visiting Japan, the country of her ancestors.

(14)   During these World Championships, the Canadian women were becoming superstars. They won game after game, eventually capturing yet another gold medal. Fans loved them, and with their bright red and white jackets and track pants, the team could go few places without being celebrities.

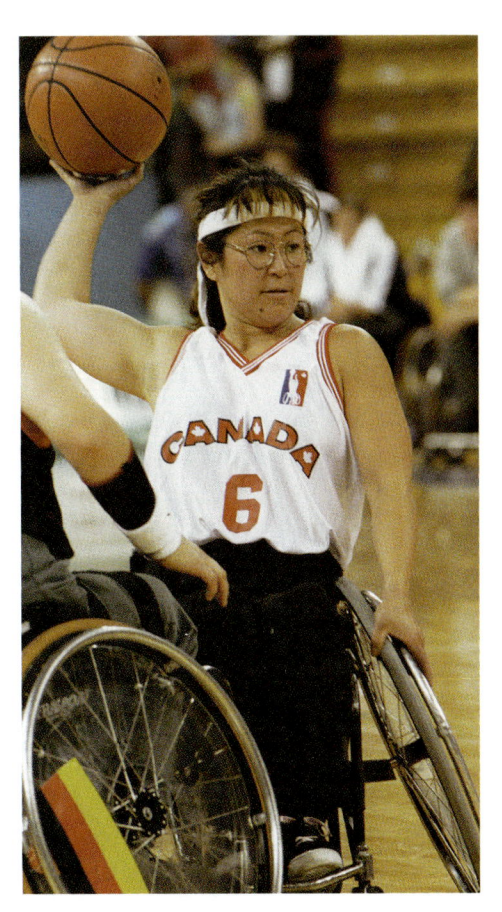

AS YOU READ

(15) "After one game I received a message that somebody was coming over to meet me. The team went down to dinner, and afterwards I noticed a couple were waiting near us. The man had worked for my parents all those years ago and he and his wife drove two hours just to see me. I was so moved by this. I don't know how they found out, but they knew I was playing on the Canadian team all these years later."

(16) After the final game, while Kendra celebrated in the change room with her teammates and took her time getting out to the stadium lobby, another family was waiting to see her. Yet another young man who had worked for her parents when he was in his teens had tracked her down. He brought his wife and daughter along to meet her.

(17) "His little girl had brought flowers for me. I was overwhelmed that they would wait so long to say hello. I wish I had known they were waiting and I wouldn't have celebrated for so long in the change room."

(18) "It was weird and exciting to be in Japan. I never expected it to be that way. I still see myself as a Canadian, but I felt like I had come home. Our coach sent me out to play at the end of the final, and he had tears in his eyes. He said, 'This one's for Gonzo'—that's my nickname. I realized he was crying because I was playing in the place of my heritage."

STOP. Take a note.

> "It was weird and exciting to be in Japan. I never expected it to be that way. I still see myself as a Canadian, but I felt like I had come home."

(19) But there was even more soul searching for Kendra in Japan. She found a piece of history there that has made her study the country in a much more detailed way. "I went to Hiroshima, and I was overwhelmed there too. I had heard about the bomb being dropped, but you can't imagine what the people must have gone through. It's so surreal when you think about some of the things that happen—it's your own heritage, not just history.

(20) "I wasn't expecting to have that connection at all," says Kendra. "I'm not sure exactly what I was feeling. People just seemed to be drawn to me, just because I was Japanese, and there I was, not understanding a word of what they were saying! I wish my parents had taught us the language, but I know they thought they were speaking English for our own good."

STOP. Take a note.

(21) Kendra looks towards the Paralympic Games in Athens, Greece, in September 2004 as her next big challenge. Today Canada has a junior women's wheelchair basketball team, and Kendra says there are around

56 UNIT 2 | SPORTS

five players who are starting to push for spots on the senior team, so she's training hard to maintain her position, and preparing for setbacks. It's been a long journey from the accident in Ranier to her World Championship golds and three Paralympic victories. Athens will be another big step in Kendra's journey.

◀ STOP. Take a note.

> In 2004, the Canadian women's wheelchair basketball team won a bronze medal at the Paralympic Games in Athens, Greece.

Wheelchair Rugby

(1) Wheelchair rugby began in Canada in 1977. Although it is a relatively new sport for people with a disability, it is developing rapidly throughout the world. Wheelchair rugby is a combination of the pace, regulations, and skills required in basketball and rugby. The games are held on a basketball ground, and the ball used is similar to the one used in volleyball.

> **Wheelchair rugby began in Canada in 1977. Although it is a relatively new sport for people with a disability, it is developing rapidly throughout the world.**

(2) Men and women athletes with a physical disability can participate in wheelchair rugby. The athletes are assessed as to their balance and the mobility of the upper part of their body (trunk), the handling of the ball (passing, receiving, dribbling), and the use of the competition wheelchair (fast-forward volition, stopping, changing direction). They are graded accordingly.

(3) The wheelchairs require constant maintenance during a game because of the hard collisions.

(4) Each game consists of four periods of eight minutes each, with intermissions in between. Each team consists of four players and eight substitutes. The objective of each team is to score a goal by touching or passing with the two wheels over the goal line of the opposing team while holding the ball. The team with the highest score at the end of the game is proclaimed winner. The teams consists of both men and women athletes.

AFTER Reading

CHECKING FOR UNDERSTANDING

1. Using the notes you took while reading about Kendra Ohama, **retell** Kendra's story to a partner. Your partner will listen for important details you may have left out. When you have finished, your partner will fill in any details that he or she thinks were important enough to be included. Then your partner will use his or her notes to retell Kendra's story to you. You will have a chance to point out any details you think he or she should have included.

PURPOSE / AUDIENCE / FORM

2. Instead of starting with Kendra's early childhood, the author chose to start with the story of Kendra meeting her future coach. Write two possible reasons for this unusual start.

STYLE AND CONVENTIONS

3. **Reread** the first paragraph of Kendra Ohama's story and the informational text on wheelchair rugby. What differences do you notice in the way the two texts sound? Why do you think they sound so different?

CRITICAL THINKING

4. a) Write a news report about Kendra Ohama. Look at the chart you created as you read Kendra's biography. Draw a **flow chart** (see The Reference Shelf, page 271) to organize your ideas into three paragraphs. Each paragraph should have a topic and ideas from the biography to support the topic. You may need to reread parts of the text to fill in some details you may have left out in your jot notes.
   b) Write the lead paragraph that introduces that topic of your report and grabs your reader's attention.
   c) Using your flow chart, write the rest of your report.
   d) Form a circle of four people. Pass your report to the person on your left. At the bottom of the report, ask the writer a question about <u>one</u> of these topics: ideas, **organization** of the article, content, style, word choice (see The Reference Shelf, pages 273 to 275). Keep passing the reports to the left until each person has asked one question about each report. When you get your report back, look at the questions and think about how you may use them to revise your writing.
   e) After writing your report, use a grammar and spell check computer program or a dictionary and an editor (a family member or a classmate) to ensure your writing is error-free.

Overcoming Obstacles | BIOGRAPHY + INFORMATIONAL TEXT

newspaper article

PURPOSE
- To separate **fact** from **opinion**
- To form an opinion in answer to the question, "Can girls really play with boys?"

Can Girls Really Play with Boys?

OAKLAND ROSS

BEFORE Reading

Draw an imaginary line across the board or create a real line with tape on the floor. Put four markers on the tape representing "Never," "Sometimes," "Often," and "Always." This line is called a values line. In your mind, answer the question, "Can girls compete equally with boys in sports?" Mark or stand on the line where your opinion falls.

AS YOU READ

You will be asked to decide whether a statement is fact, opinion, or both. Write the paragraph number and either "Fact," "Opinion," or "Both" in your notebook.

▶ Stop and decide—A.

▶ Stop and decide—B.

This article was first published on November 23, 2003.

(1) No sooner had Hayley Wickenheiser bade farewell to Finland than certain Canadian tongues started wagging.

(2) The top woman hockey player in Canada—and the world—Wickenheiser said she wasn't satisfied with her role this season with Salamat, the Finnish men's professional team she joined last year.

(3) The club won Finland's third-division championship in the spring and Wickenheiser was a not-inconsiderable factor in its success, with two goals and nine assists in fewer than two dozen games.

(4) But this season, Salamat was promoted to Finland's second division, where the level of play is both faster and more physical.

(5) Wickenheiser ventured onto the ice for no more than a few minutes per game and had no goals or assists this season so far.

(6) "I wasn't happy," the 25-year-old native of Shaunovon, Sask., said the other day before boarding a plane in Helsinki and heading home

UNIT 2 | SPORTS

(7) to Calgary. "I missed my family a lot. I finally came to this conclusion in the end, because I didn't get to show my skills in the kind of role that I wanted."

On hearing about Wickenheiser's decision, some Canadians will no doubt be settling back into their recliners and smiling with satisfaction—"gloating" might not be too strong a term.

(8) *I told you so*, they might be thinking. *Girls just cannot play hockey with boys.*

▸ Stop and decide—C.

▸ gloating: showing others how great you are

Girls just cannot play hockey with boys....

Or just maybe the issue is a tad more complicated.

(9) Some might go even further: *Girls cannot play* sports *with boys. Period.*
(10) And maybe they are right.
(11) Or just maybe the issue is a tad more complicated.
(12) Just ask Gail Greenough.
(13) Among the finest equestrians in Canada, the 43-year-old Edmontonian excels in show jumping, one of the few Olympic disciplines in which men and women compete as equals.
(14) "At this level, mentally, you have to be extremely tough, whether you're a woman or a man," says Greenough, who is the first woman in history to have won the individual world championships in her sport, competing against all comers, male or female.
(15) That was back in 1986.
(16) "Up to now, in sport, the difference between the sexes has been the focus," says Greg Malszecki, a professor of kinesiology at York University. "If skill level is the focus, then on any given day some women could be competitive against men."
(17) In disciplines that require both stamina and endurance, not to mention the divine virtue of buoyancy, the distaff sex already fare extremely well.
(18) Take long-distance swimming. Here, women rule.
(19) Eighty years ago, Gertrude Ederle swam the English Channel two hours faster than any man had ever done before.
(20) The first human to swim Lake Ontario? Marilyn Bell, in 1954.
(21) Back on dry land, men continue to outperform women in marathon running, but the gap is closing quickly.
(22) Last April, British runner Paula Radcliffe ran the London marathon

▸ Stop and decide—D.
▸ equestrians: horseback riders
▸ Stop and decide—E.

▸ Stop and decide—F.
▸ kinesiology: the study of muscles and human motion
▸ distaff: female

▸ Stop and decide—G.

AS YOU READ

disparity: being unequal

▶ (23) faster than any British male in the race, in a time that would have won her the men's Olympic gold medal in any year up to 1984.

(23) In many other sports, the <u>disparity</u> in performance between men and women, while dwindling, remains considerable.

(24) Still, an extraordinary female competitor—Swedish golfer Annika Sorenstam, for example—will occasionally surge to the top of the women's field and come oh so close to joining the best of the men.

(25) The Sorenstams and Wickenheisers of this world are the exceptions, certainly, but they are evidence that the barriers separating male and female athletes may not be as <u>impermeable</u> as some people may think.

impermeable: not allowing anything past
speculate: to think

(26) Many experts <u>speculate</u> that cultural odds are stacked against women when it comes to sports.

(27) In the first place, most of the athletic competitions now being contested anywhere in the world were originally devised by men, for men, with the purpose of testing physical and mental attributes that men possess and value. For the most part, female competitors have been obliged to adapt themselves to these sometimes awkward models.

(28) In the second place, males still tend to begin acquiring basic athletic skills at an earlier age, giving them an advantage that lasts a lifetime.

Stop and decide—H.

> **On average, boys were able to throw twice as far as girls of the same age, if they were all using their dominant arms.**

(29) From an early age, boys spend a disproportionate amount of their time running, jumping, tumbling, wrestling each other, and throwing things.

(30) Malszecki at York University cites a recent U.S. study of school-age children that measured their ability to throw a ball. On average, boys were able to throw twice as far as girls of the same age, *if* they were all using their dominant arms.

(31) But the study also measured throwing ability when the children used their non-dominant arms, and here the performance of the two sexes was almost exactly equal.

(32) Malszecki concludes from this that males aren't necessarily better equipped, physically, to fling a small round object through the air. They've just had more practice.

UNIT 2 | SPORTS

(33)   He believes that women might eventually be able to compete as equals with men in practically any sport.

(34)   Not everyone goes this far.

(35)   "I don't know if it's ever going to be the same because of the physical makeup," says Karen Lofstrom, executive director of the Canadian Association for the Advancement of Women and Sports. Still, certain exceptional women athletes will inevitably want to test their skills against the best of the men.

(36)   For all Wickenheiser's talent, it's unlikely she'll ever be a legitimate NHLer either, but she does have a young son and he might one day have a daughter.

(37)   Time passes, things change, and you just never know.

AS YOU READ

◂ Stop and decide—I.

◂ Stop and decide—J.

AFTER Reading

CHECKING FOR UNDERSTANDING

1. a) The class will number off, one, two, one, two, and so on. The number twos will form a circle with each person facing outward. The number ones will form a circle outside of the number twos, with each person facing toward a person in the inside circle.

   Number twos facing outward

   Number ones facing inward

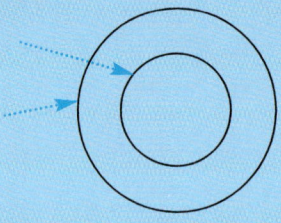

   You will need your textbooks or notebooks with you.

   The number ones will start, telling their partners one opinion, fact, or a statement that is both an opinion and a fact, that they found in the article. Number two will agree or disagree that it is a fact, an opinion, or both, and state the reason why.

   Number two will then state an opinion, fact, or a statement that is both, that they found in the article. Number one will agree or disagree that it is a fact, an opinion, or both, and state the reason why.

   The outside circle will move three spaces to the right to a new partner. The number ones will state another opinion, fact, or a statement that is both, that they found in the article, and the number twos will do the same. Repeat the activity rotating the outside circle one or more places until all 10 statements in the article have been discussed.

   As a class, make a rule about how to tell when a statement is a fact, an opinion, or both.

   b) Having read the article, reform the values line using the same question as in the Before Reading activity. You can change your opinion and stand in a different place or go back to where you were before reading the article. As a class, talk about why people moved or didn't move after they had read the article.

PURPOSE / AUDIENCE / FORM

2. This article has few graphic elements, which makes it look hard to read. Suggest four places the text could have been broken up by a **subheading**, and write a subheading for each section.

STYLE AND CONVENTIONS

3. A paragraph has an **introduction**, a body, and a conclusion. In several places, this writer has included paragraphs that have fewer than 10 words. **Scan** the article to find examples of these very short paragraphs. Make a list of reasons why a writer would write such short paragraphs. Find a partner. Taking turns, present one reason at a time and defend your reason. As a class, listen to several of the pairs' lists, adding ideas if possible.

CRITICAL THINKING

4. a) Think back to where you stood on the values line. Make a mind map using your answer to the question, "Can girls compete equally with boys in sports?" as the central idea, and your reasons branching out from it. (see The Reference Shelf, page 270). Choose your best three reasons, and be prepared to present them to the class.

   b) As a class, hold an informal debate. Organize the class into groups. Each group must support one of the opinions: Never, Sometimes, Often, Always, to answer the question, "Can girls compete equally with boys in sports?" Each person in each group will state one support for their opinion, starting with the "never" group and moving through "sometimes," "often," and "always."

autobiography

PURPOSE
- To write an interview using **facts** you have read
- To understand the difference between important and interesting facts

HERB CARNEGIE

A Fly in a Pail of Milk

The Herb Carnegie Story

Death of a Dream: New York Rangers' Training Camp, 1948

BEFORE Reading

1. Using the title, **subtitle**, and the following adjectives, **predict** what will happen to Herb Carnegie in the autobiography you are about to read. Defend your predictions to a partner.
   Adjectives: eager, happy, elated, surprised, angered, satisfied, hurt, frustrated

2. Everything you read is filled with facts. Some are interesting, but also important. They may be important because you will be tested on them or they are for research you are doing. Other facts you read are interesting but not important. Label one side of a page "Important" and the other side "Interesting." As you read, record four important facts you would need to know if you interviewed Herb Carnegie. Then record four interesting facts you would not need to know.

AS YOU READ

Herb Carnegie was a Canadian hockey player in the 1940s who dreamed of playing for the National Hockey League.

Euphoria *means extreme joy. Write a sentence using* euphoria.

(1) Of all the moments while playing in Sherbrooke, none matched the <u>euphoria</u> of being invited to the Rangers' training camp. I arrived at our home on Empress Avenue to find my wife Audrey sitting in the backyard. She seemed unusually nervous as she handed me an envelope with red, white, and blue trim and the name New York Rangers on it. This envelope could contain the invitation to the NHL which I had hoped for since childhood. I opened it with a mixture of anxiety and exhilaration while Audrey watched uneasily. The letter, dated August 20, 1948, read:

This is to advise you that you are to report on Tuesday, September 14, 1948 to the New York Rangers Hockey Club's training camp at the Eagle's Nest, Saranac Lake, N.Y.

You are instructed to obtain proof of your nationality in the form of a Birth Certificate, and to present same, along with the enclosed letter from this Corporation, to an office of the United States Immigration and Naturalization Service. These offices are located in most of the principal cities of Canada, notably Montreal, Toronto, Winnipeg, Windsor, Regina, Calgary, and Vancouver. By submitting your Birth Certificate and the enclosed letter to one of these offices you will be granted the necessary twenty-nine (29) day pass required to enter the United States. These instructions must be followed otherwise you will not be permitted to cross the border. The U.S. Immigration authorities are enforcing these regulations very strictly. You should start immediately to attend to these instructions and not wait until the last minute.

You will please bring your own skates, and any other equipment that might prove helpful to you. And if possible, have your skates sharpened so that you will not lose any time in getting on the ice.

Rail transportation from your home will be furnished you by your local Canadian Pacific Railway, or, Canadian National Railway, agent, as the case may be, in due course.

Trusting that you will read this letter carefully and comply with the instructions outlined, and looking forward to seeing you at our training camp, I remain,

Yours very truly
Frank Boucher, Manager
New York Rangers Hockey Club

(2) Although merely a form letter which the Rangers had sent to everyone they wanted in camp that fall, I could hardly read it and trembled as tears of joy blurred my vision. At last, or so it then seemed, my day had arrived.

(3) Nothing in the letter was of a personal nature. There was no mention of past successes or of the team's plans for me. The only specific reference to me was my name on the envelope. There was also a second letter, written by Boucher to the United States Immigration and Naturalization Service in Canada. In it, he confirmed Herbert

Carnegie was under agreement with the Rangers to report to training camp. Still, after all these years, I was getting a chance to demonstrate my talent and to take my rightful place on the top rung of hockey's ladder.

(4) I was ready. On a daily basis for ten years, I had been preparing myself both mentally and physically for this opportunity. My body was rock-hard, the result of lifting tons of concrete blocks during the summers. It gave me the legs, forearms, and shoulders needed to play in the NHL. I headed off to camp with one goal and one goal only—to show off the talent which had been ignored for so long. I was 29 years old. In those days professional hockey players were considered long in the tooth by that age. Regardless of that fact, I was as eager as I was ready.

(5) I had a superb training camp marked by both happy and sad memories. The former include the anticipation of meeting NHL greats such as Edgar Laprade, Don Raleigh, Sugar Jim Henry, Jack Evans, Buddy O'Connor, and other stars of the era. During the first week, I was with a group of about 80 nervous "NHL Dreamers"—players from across the country recommended by scouts to attend training camp.

(6) Each player was given a coloured jersey to wear during those first days. Thus, one played with the red line, the blue line, or whatever. The colours were assigned before camp began as a method for coaches to grade the talent on hand. Defencemen wore their own distinctive jerseys. On the second day, some players had their colour switched as decisions were made on their likely ranking within the Rangers' organization. There was, of course, the Rangers in the NHL, next came New Haven in the American League, then St. Paul, Minnesota, and, finally, Tacoma, Washington.

(7) Midway through the first week, Muzz Patrick talked with me. I was elated initially when

he described me as a great hockey player. But the feeling evaporated instantly when he revealed the team's intentions—the Rangers' Tacoma team, the bottom of the Rangers' barrel. Patrick offered me $2700, far less than what Sherbrooke was paying me. It was a dramatic indication of the calibre of players consigned to Tacoma. As an inducement, he offered to help me up the ladder to the Rangers. My response was instantaneous: "No, sir," I told him, "I don't think I want to do that."

> **I was elated intially when he described me as a great hockey player. But the feeling evaporated instantly when he revealed the team's intentions— the Rangers' Tacoma team, the bottom of the Rangers barrel.**

(8) The next day, Lynn Patrick, Muzz's brother, came up with a different offer—$3700 to play in St. Paul. It was still below my Sherbrooke pay cheque and far below my expectation to play in the NHL. Politely, I refused it as well. The following day, Phil Watson, the Rangers' coach, offered me $4700 to play in New Haven. I told Watson exactly what I had said to the Patricks, that I considered myself more than capable of cracking the NHL line-up. "Fine," he replied. "Stay 'till the big team arrives on Monday." The first week of training was reserved for rookies while the regulars arrived for the second week.

(9) The second week witnessed the arrival of Buddy O'Connor, Sugar Jim Henry, Edgar Laprade, all the big guns I'd heard about in newspapers and on radio. Camp started and I was having a great time. I was more than capable, after all those years, of measuring my own skills against those of others. And I skated well, checked well, taking the puck away from the stars, scored goals, and set up plays. In short, I played the game as I had always played it. Things seemed to be going superbly. I was sure, or so I thought, to make the team.

(10) On Wednesday of that week, Boucher called me into his office. "Herb," he said, "you're an excellent hockey player, but I'd like to make sure by sending you first to New Haven." I was surprised by his unexpected remark. I listed a few guys already playing for the team and wondered if my ability was any less than theirs. Boucher was caught off-guard. He thought for a moment, then he looked at me. "I just want to be sure," was all he said. The conversation was over and I left camp both satisfied and angered. In the first case, I had proven myself.

(11)   There was no doubt in my mind, then or now, that I was every bit as good as the most talented player on that team: Except, I had once more been stopped by the colour barrier. The Rangers and its management were unable to look beyond the colour of my skin. For their part, the Rangers' players could not believe that I was headed back to Sherbrooke. And their supportive comments only reinforced my conviction that I belonged with the Rangers or some other NHL club.

> **There was no doubt in my mind, then or now, that I was every bit as good as the most talented player on that team: Except, I had once more been stopped by the colour barrier.**

(12)   The scars of that experience mark my soul to this day. The Rangers' training camp was the end of my dream to play in the NHL. I was deeply hurt and frustrated by the realization of what had happened. Now I was certain that I had the talent, the skill, and the attitude to play in the NHL. The only thing I lacked, to the everlasting shame of the NHL, was white skin. I can scarcely do justice to the persistent hurt in the pit of my stomach.

(13)   I wasn't a coloured kid, I was a Canadian kid who dreamed just like other Canadian boys of playing hockey in the NHL. In spite of my father's warnings and the urging of others to go to university, I chose to follow my dream. My parents had taught me well, perhaps too well, to believe that I could attain whatever I desired. All I had to do was work as hard as I could and use my talent to the fullest. I had refused to accept the racism underlying Conn Smythe's early remark about turning Herbie Carnegie white. And yet it would take nothing less than that to get me into the NHL. My dream would not come true, not because of a lack of talent or a willingness to work hard, but because of racism. The pain has dulled somewhat over the years, but it has never disappeared.

AFTER Reading

CHECKING FOR UNDERSTANDING

1. With a partner, look at the four points each of you chose as most important. Explain to your partner how you decided on those four points. Be prepared to share your thinking with the class.

PURPOSE / AUDIENCE / FORM

2. Publishers receive thousands of manuscripts every year from people wanting to write a book. Most of them are rejected. Based on the excerpt you have just read, give four reasons why a publishing company would choose Herb Carnegie's autobiography to publish. Think about his **purpose** for writing it and the different **audiences** it might appeal to.

STYLE AND CONVENTIONS

3. State two ways the editor of this autobiography has made the letter from the Rangers' manager look different from the rest of the story. Why is making the letter look different helpful to the reader?

CRITICAL THINKING

4. a) With a partner, create four **open-ended** questions for Herb Carnegie that could be answered with information stated directly in the text, or information you can **infer** from the text. Refer back to the list of important points you created while you read.
   b) For each of the four questions, talk over the answers you think Carnegie would give. Prepare an interview with a partner in which one of you is Carnegie and one of you is the interviewer. Order the questions in a way that is logical and interesting. Be prepared to perform your interview when called upon.

A Fly in a Pail of Milk | AUTOBIOGRAPHY

short story

PURPOSE
- To practise asking different types of questions as you read
- To **infer** the "big idea" or **theme** of the story

WES FINEDAY

The Hockey Game

BEFORE Reading

Characters are a major part of a short story. Create a graphic organizer like the one below to show four ways writers reveal their characters. One example has been completed for you.

Writers reveal characters by → showing what other characters say about them

You will use your organizer again after you read the story.

AS YOU READ

You will see an asterisk (*) each time the character does something new. Use a Q-chart like the one on page 242 to write a question in your notebook about the events or actions that lead up to that point. Answer your questions.

(1) The knocking at my door woke me up. It was a Saturday morning, which meant that there was no school. I got out of bed, got dressed, then walked out of my bedroom and across the hallway to the bathroom. The door was closed. Someone was in there. I went back to the bedroom, made my bed, picked up my books, and put them on the dresser. I had been doing my homework just before I fell asleep. There was still quite a bit to do.

(2) Grade Nine sure wasn't easy, at least not as easy as Grade Eight. I had finished my Grade Eight at boarding school last year, had done quite well in fact. This year was different. The Department of Indian Affairs had sent me to live in Moose Jaw to do my Grade Nine. They had explained to me that they had found me a "good Christian boarding home" to live in. They also told me I should consider myself lucky to have this opportunity. At the time I wondered if it would be anything like the school I had left.

72 UNIT 2 | SPORTS

(3) I went back to the bathroom. It was vacant. I had a good wash and went back to the bedroom.

(4) They had driven me to Moose Jaw from the boarding school and with that move everything had changed. Now I was in a bedroom by myself instead of a dormitory with thirty other kids. The food eaten by these Christians was unlike anything I ever got at boarding school or at home. For breakfast they would eat dry cereal and pour milk over it to make it soggy. With this they ate toast that was also soggy with butter. For lunch and supper we would have meat and potatoes or rice. I'd eaten these before, but not the way this woman cooked it. She used tomatoes and stuff that looked like powder that she kept in small jars over the stove. She must have had twenty different kinds of powder. It was awful. My stomach would hurt for hours after and sometimes I would get ill and bring it all up.

When I tried to tell her that I couldn't eat the food she called me ungrateful and told me my parents would be glad to have something like this to eat. I doubted that.

(5) When I tried to tell her that I couldn't eat the food she called me ungrateful and told me my parents would be glad to have something like this to eat. I doubted that. My parents liked eating rabbit and bannock, berries and potatoes just fine. But I didn't tell her that. Arguing would just get me into more trouble.

(6) Another knock at the door. "Come and eat your breakfast," called a voice from the other side of the door. I got up and followed my landlady to the kitchen. There on the table was my breakfast—cereal, toast, and milk.

(7) While I was eating breakfast, the woman who was my landlady explained to me that they were going on a family outing. "Not too many more nice weekends before the snow comes," she said. "We're going to take advantage of this one." I could hear their two little boys playing downstairs in the basement. They were playing with the electric train set their father had set up down there. I was not allowed to go near it. I was also not allowed to play with their boys without permission. I wondered about that sometimes. I did not understand why they treated me so differently from the way they treated everyone else. I suspected they did not like me. The landlady's voice intruded on my thoughts.

(8) "Drink up your milk now, and don't bother coming back until nine o'clock this evening. The house will be locked." These Christians sure don't trust Indians, I thought as I got up and took my dishes to the sink.

AS YOU READ

(9) After breakfast, I wandered outside to the back yard. The landlord was already out there washing his car. I sat on the back steps and watched him. "Come over here and give me a hand with this," he called. So I did. When we were finished washing and waxing the car, he went back inside and soon they all came out. They seemed to be in a good mood, laughing and talking about the wild animal park. I got up and headed for the sidewalk and started walking down the street. I had nowhere to go, but I thought they would get mad if it looked like I was going to hang around the house all day. I was barely half a block from the house when they drove by. The parents were in front, looking straight ahead, the kids were sitting in the back, looking around. They waved as they went by. I waved back and smiled, trying to look happy.

(10) I watched until the car turned the corner two blocks down the street, then I turned around and walked back to the house. I went into the back yard and stood on the back step for awhile and finally sat down.

(11) The back yard was separated by a tall picket fence from the yards on either side of it. There was also a garden at the back.

(12) The neighbour's back door opened. A man and a woman followed by a little boy stepped outside. They did not see me. The man was dressed in shorts and a tee shirt, the woman in a bathing suit. They sat down on a couple of lawn chairs, which were placed around a small table. The little boy ran to the end of the yard, where there was a swing and slide and a sandbox full of toys. I looked back at the parents. They had been joined by a small black dog with short curly hair. He was sprawled on the ground between the two people, soaking up the sun. I got up from the steps and went a little closer to the fence so I would be out of sight. They might get mad at me. From where I now sat, I could hear them talking about a new car they were planning to buy. The man talked about a contract for playing hockey. This meant they could get a new car. He also had another job. This would take care of their other bills.

* ▶ (13) I thought about my parents and family at home. My dad had more than two jobs. He had to catch horses before he could do anything. This was a job in itself. Our horses could run very fast and jump fences. Then he had to drive them out to the bush so he could chop wood and haul it home, where he sawed it into small pieces so it would fit into our

> The parents were in front, looking straight ahead, the kids were sitting in the back, looking around. They waved as they went by. I waved back and smiled, trying to look happy.

UNIT 2 | SPORTS

cookstove. He also had to haul water. And hunt. He usually did this when he was out in the bush chopping wood. I could see him standing on top of a load of wood on a sleigh, or maybe walking beside it if it was really cold. It was better to keep moving on very cold days. There would usually be a rabbit or two and sometimes even three if he was lucky. We used to run outside to meet him and fight about who would carry the rabbits into the house to give to my mom. She was very good at cleaning and skinning rabbits. She had been doing it for years.

(14) Too bad my dad couldn't get a job playing hockey, I thought. I was sure the folks back home who played hockey didn't get paid to do it. They just did it to be together and have fun. I had heard my dad telling a story to some people about a hockey game. They had cleared the ice on a section of the creek that runs through our reserve. A group of young fellows had got together to have a game. There were just about enough of them for two teams, but one of the teams was minus a goaltender. They managed to talk Leo, who didn't know how to skate, into putting on a pair of skates and being their goalie. Leo shoved some newspapers up each pantleg and wrapped them around his ankles and tied them up with twine. Two of his teammates supported him on either side and pulled him out to his goal. He managed, barely, to stay on his feet by propping himself up with the crude goalie stick someone had hastily nailed together for him. For a puck, they were using a freshly frozen piece of horse dropping they had picked up in someone's barn. Dad said these really smarted if they hit an unprotected spot. The other boys had chopped down suitably curved willow trees for hockey sticks.

> For a puck, they were using a freshly frozen piece of horse dropping they had picked up in someone's barn. Dad said these really smarted if they hit an unprotected spot.

(15) Leo's team won the game. Ecstatic over their victory, they all rushed off to the fire, which was roaring beside the creek. They didn't notice Leo until someone started laughing and pointing at the rink. There was Leo, crawling across the ice on his hands and knees toward the fire, dragging his stick behind him.

(16) I smiled remembering the story. Suddenly, I heard a car starting. I had forgotten about the people next door. While I had been thinking, or daydreaming as my teachers called it, the neighbours had moved back inside. Now they had come back out and were about to drive off in their car. I looked up at the sun and realized I had been sitting there daydreaming all morning. And now I was hungry.

AS YOU READ

(17) Back home if you were hungry you just went somewhere to visit at mealtime and you would be sure to get fed. I decided to give it a try. I tried to think of someone I could go and visit. There was Allen, who lived across the street and was in my class at school. But he hadn't been very friendly to me. I decided not to go over there. A few houses down lived another kid who was in my class. His name was Robert. He had asked me if I wanted to come to the field beside their place and play football. I had wanted to but I didn't know how to play football, so I had declined the invitation.

(18) I got up and walked down the street. When I reached their house I almost turned around, but I was hungry. I thought it was a funny thing that no one ever used their front door since it was closer to the street. They all used the back door. Our house at home only had one door so we had no choice.

(19) I stood there trying to muster the courage to knock on the door. The screen door was the only obstacle between me and the food I could smell cooking inside. That spurred me on. I knocked and waited. I could hear voices and finally a very tall lady came to the door.

(20) "Is Robert home?" I asked, hoping she would invite me in.

(21) "Yes, he's in," she replied. "But he's having his dinner. Why don't you come back in half an hour or so? He should be finished by then." With that she closed the door and walked away. I felt embarrassed, thinking she must have known why I was there. Well I wouldn't try that again. I turned around and retraced my steps to the back yard of the house where I lived. It was then that I noticed the carrots in the garden. Too dangerous, I decided; my landlady would notice if I took even one. I sat down by the fence and immediately fell asleep. I must have slept most of the afternoon, because when I awoke the neighbours were back. I could hear them talking on the other side of the fence. I got up and went over to the fence. There was an outside tap sticking out of the wall of the house. The landlady ran a hose from it to the garden to water those carrots. I thought of them again. My hunger had returned. It was more urgent now. I turned on the tap and let the water run over my arms and hands. It felt cool and refreshing. I cupped my hands and filled them

> Back home if you were hungry you just went somewhere to visit at mealtime and you would be sure to get fed.

76 UNIT 2 | SPORTS

up, stuck my face in the water and felt a tingle go all the way down to my toes. I was awake again. I dried myself off with my shirt sleeves. Then I went and sat back down in my spot. There I felt safe.

(22) "Make mine kind of rare, I like it like that," said the woman. Suddenly I was blasted by the aroma of meat cooking over the fire. I knew the smell, having often eaten meat cooked over a fire. I was just drifting off on memories of home when the man next door yelled, "That damn dog!" Just then the dog came bounding around the corner of the fence and into the yard I was in. It was carrying a steak in its mouth. The man was not far behind. He came running around the fence, still carrying the huge fork he must have been using to turn the meat. So preoccupied with what was behind it that it totally ignored anything in front of it, the dog ran right into me. The dog and the man came to a dead stop.

(23) "Well, hello there. I didn't think there was anyone home here," the man said to me.

(24) "There isn't," I answered. "They went somewhere for the day. They're not going to be home until around nine o'clock."

(25) "Do you live here?" he asked, seeming to have forgotten about the steak.

(26) "Yes," I answered.

(27) "Have you eaten yet?"

(28) "No," I replied, not daring to look at the man.

(29) "We were just going to eat. You could join us if you wanted to. Come on," he urged. I did not need much urging. He speared the steak the dog had dropped, turned around and started to walk back into his yard, his dog and me close behind.

(30) I did not leave any of the huge steak they served me. I could barely move, but I somehow managed to put away a large helping of ice cream for dessert. It was the best meal I had eaten in a long time.

(31) The man's name was Jake. It turned out that he played hockey for the Moose Jaw Canucks. He gave me a couple of tickets to the next game against the Regina Pats. I didn't go to the game but I hope they won.

The Hockey Game | SHORT STORY | 77

AFTER Reading

CHECKING FOR UNDERSTANDING

1. a) With a partner, number yourselves one and two. Number one will ask a question he or she has created while reading, and number two will try to answer it. The questioner will compare his or her own answer to the one that was given by his or her partner, and the pair will talk about all possible answers. The partners will then reverse roles, with number two asking the question and number one trying to answer it. Repeat the process until all the questions have been asked. Choose the best question from the partnership. Your teacher will write the best questions on the board.
   b) As a class, talk about how asking questions helped you understand the story.

PURPOSE / AUDIENCE / FORM

2. One important element of a short story is **character**. Create a two-column chart in your notebook with the titles "What is he like?" and "How do I know?" Fill in the chart about the main character who is telling the story. Refer to the graphic organizer you created before reading to remind you what to look for in the story.

STYLE AND CONVENTIONS

3. a) Work with a partner. One of you will take on the role of the landlady. The other one will take on the role of Jake, the man next door. Starting with the landlady, retell the story from her point of view. Next have Jake tell the story from his point of view. Be prepared to perform your retelling for the class.
   b) The main character in this story is also the narrator. Why is the main character the best person to tell this story? Before answering, think about the stories that were told by the landlady and Jake.

CRITICAL THINKING

4. a) Theme is the "big idea" of the story. It can't be summarized in a word; it must be put into a sentence. A good way to start a theme statement is, "In this story the author is saying …" Create a theme statement for "The Hockey Game." (See The Reference Shelf, page 251.)
   b) With a partner, compare your statements and explain how you came up with them. Remember, there can be more than one "big idea" in a story.
   c) As a class, make a list of theme statements on the board and talk about the strengths of each one.

Unit 2 Activity

For your project for this unit, you will be evaluated using a rubric your teacher will discuss with you before you start. You will be expected to keep any process work and submit it with your final product.

Choose one of the following activities to complete.

1. How do sports bring us together? Answer this question using one or more readings from this unit. (Some suggestions are "The Hockey Game," "Kendra Ohama," and "Wheelchair Rugby.")

   Follow these steps:
   1) Gather ideas from the reading to answer the question. Create a **graphic organizer** to organize your ideas. Decide on the answer to the question based on the facts and information you've gathered.
   2) Choose one of the following forms to present your answer: a series of paragraphs supporting your opinion, a report, a narrative, or a poem.
   3) Highlight the ideas you would like to use and organize them so you are ready to write your first draft.
   4) Write your draft.
   5) Use questions from The Reference Shelf, page 273, to help you edit your work, or ask someone in the class to edit your work for you.
   6) Revise your work and prepare to hand it in. Make sure you have included all your rough work.

2. What is sportsmanship? Write a report that answers this question. Use ideas or characters (real or fictional) from the readings in the unit. Include graphic elements in your report that will help others read and understand it.

   Follow these steps:
   1) Form your answer using ideas from the readings.
   2) Create a graphic organizer that includes information and ideas from the readings that support your answer.
   3) Highlight the ideas you would like to use, and organize them so you are ready to write your first draft.
   4) Write your report.
   5) Use questions from The Reference Shelf, page 273, to help you edit your work, or ask someone in the class to edit your work for you.
   6) Revise your work and add graphic elements, using technology or creating them by hand.
   7) Prepare to hand in your work. Make sure you have included all your rough work.

3. How can sports divide us? Create an interview with either Hayley Wickenheiser ("Can Girls Really Play with Boys?," page 60) or Herb Carnegie ("A Fly in a Pail of Milk," page 66). Through your questions and their answers, show how sports have excluded certain people. You may need to do some more research to help you write their answers.

Follow these steps:
1) Create a chart like the one below: Put a quotation or a piece of information from your reading in the left column. In the right column, put a question you could ask to allow the person to talk about those experiences. An example has been done for you. If you do additional research, make sure you write down the source of your information.

Hayley Wickenheiser

Information that shows the sport excluded the person	Question I could ask the person in the interview
"The club won Finland's third-division championship in the spring and Wickenheiser was a not-inconsiderable factor in its success, with two goals and nine assists in fewer than two dozen games" (paragraph 3). When Salamat was promoted to second division "Wickenheiser ventured onto the ice for no more than a few minutes per game and had no goals or assists this season so far" (paragraph 5).	What was it like playing with Finland's Salamat team the past two years?

2) Organize your questions and answers in the most logical order for an interview. Remember to start with something that is going to grab your audience's attention.
3) Either tape your interview or write your interview.
4) Use questions from The Reference Shelf (page 273) to help you edit your work, or ask someone in the class to edit your work for you.
5) Revise your interview and prepare to hand it in by re-recording or re-writing it. Make sure you also hand in all your rough work.

‹ 1 › 2 › UNiT 3 › 4 › 5 › 6

WHAT...?

Tiny Bubbles?
PAGE **85**

Gross Out?
PAGE **94**

At age 33, **LEONID STADNIK** wishes he would stop growing. He's already 8 feet, 4 inches (2.54 m) tall.

from *"Tallest Man Feels Lowly at the Top,"* page 96

Think about it!

› What is normal?

› How does where we live and who we know help us define "normal"?

› How does the unexplained influence the way we define "normal"?

› Why are people drawn to the unexplained?

Superpoopers by *Nancy Finton* (magazine article) ... 83

🍁 **Tiny Bubbles?** by *Anne McIlroy* (newspaper article) ... 85

The Praying Mantis by *Dick King-Smith* (poem) ... 88

🍁 **Why Do People Yawn, and Why Are Yawns Contagious?** by *Kathy Wollard* (informational text) ... 90

Two Selections on Bones
  Bones by *Walter de la Mare* (poem) ... 93
  Gross Out? by *Britt Norlander* (magazine article) ... 94

Tallest Man Feels Lowly at the Top by *Anna Menlichuk* (newspaper article) ... 96

🍁 **Blue Eyes** by *Meghan Wafer* (short story) ... 99

🍁 **The Magic Sieve** by *Irene N. Watts* (drama/folktale) ... 102

mirrors dot com by *Lesley Howarth* (short story) ... 108

Unit 3 Activity ... 117

UNIT 3

What ...?

Look at the titles above. What do you think each selection is about?

82 UNIT 3 | WHAT ...?

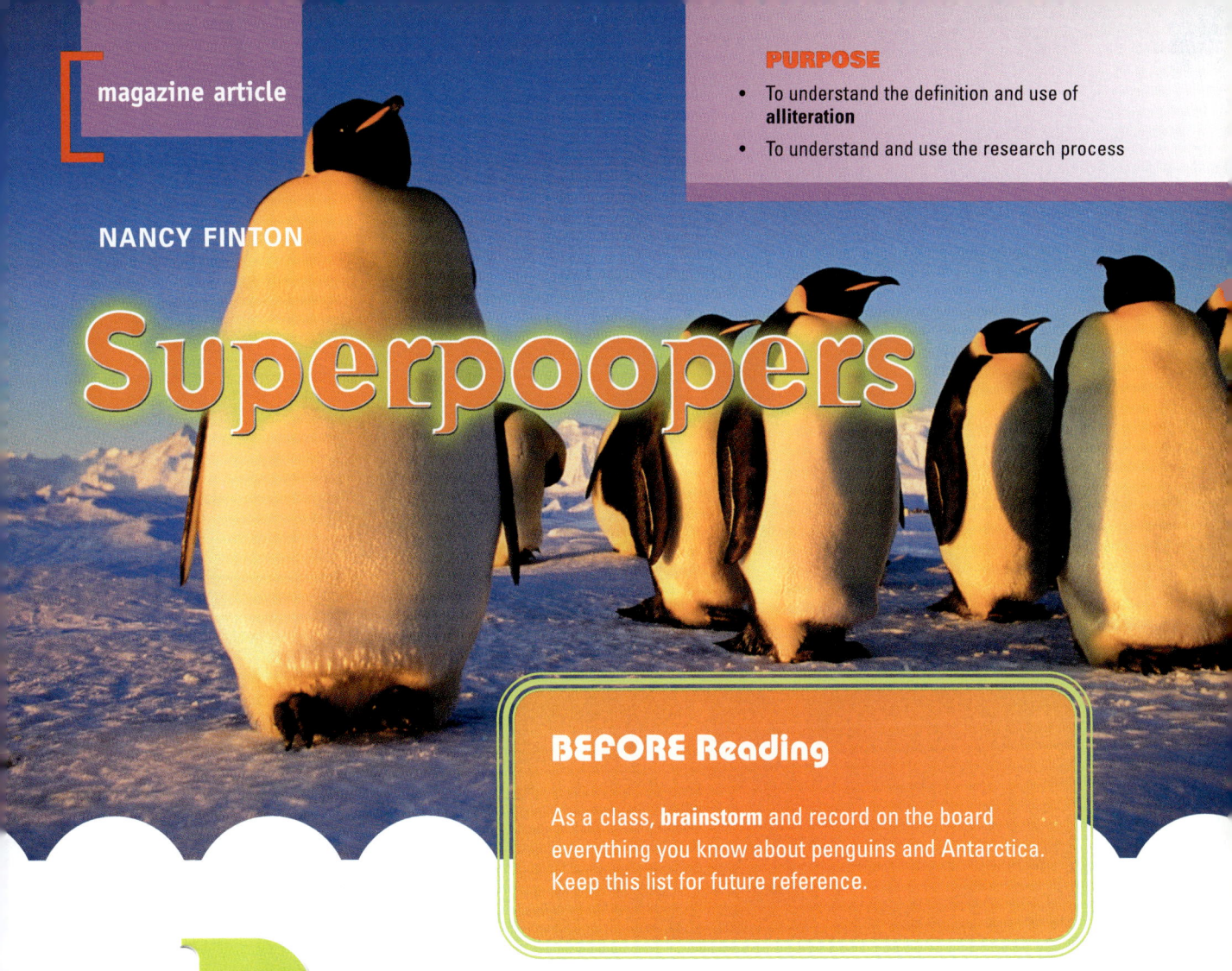

magazine article

PURPOSE
- To understand the definition and use of **alliteration**
- To understand and use the research process

NANCY FINTON

Superpoopers

BEFORE Reading

As a class, **brainstorm** and record on the board everything you know about penguins and Antarctica. Keep this list for future reference.

(1) Penguin parents never leave their nests—not even for a bathroom break. They must stay home to protect thin-feathered chicks from Antarctic temperatures. So what's a penguin to do when nature calls? "A penguin stands up, moves to the edge of its nest, turns around, bends a little forward, lifts its tail, and shoots," says biologist Victor Benno Meyer-Rechow from the International University of Bremen in Germany.

(2) He discovered that a penguin uses enough *force* (push or pull) to send its poop flying a whopping 40 centimeters (16 inches) from its clean nest! During research trips to Antarctica, Meyer-Rechow saw penguin nests ringed by streaks of feces. He decided to calculate the pressure inside a penguin's intestines needed for top propulsion. So, he measured the waste's *density* (mass per given volume), its *viscosity* (how easily a liquid flows), and the height of launch. Turns out a penguin's intestines exert about four times more force than those of humans.

AS YOU READ

◀ What is the most surprising thing you've read in this article so far?

AFTER Reading

CHECKING FOR UNDERSTANDING

1. Return to the brainstormed list the class created before reading. **Reread** the article. In your notebook, make **jot notes** of the **facts** you learn.

PURPOSE / AUDIENCE / FORM

2. With a partner, determine what **audience** this article is written for. Find three reasons in the text to support your answer. Copy and complete the **graphic organizer** below to record your answer.

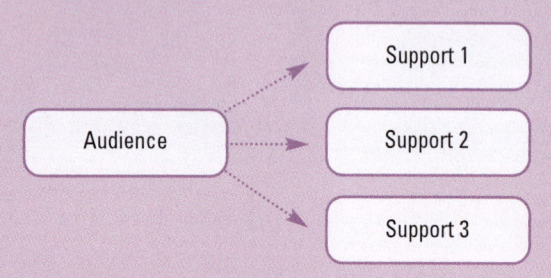

```
              ┌──────────┐
          ┌──▶│ Support 1│
┌────────┐│   └──────────┘
│Audience│├──▶┌──────────┐
└────────┘│   │ Support 2│
          │   └──────────┘
          │   ┌──────────┐
          └──▶│ Support 3│
              └──────────┘
```

STYLE AND CONVENTIONS

3. a) Alliteration is created when two or more words in a series begin with the same letter or sound (for example, dazzling dogs, chewy chocolate). Find two examples of alliteration in the text, and record them in your notebook.
   b) Think up two alternative titles for this article that use alliteration.

CRITICAL THINKING

4. a) As a class, brainstorm a new list of questions you would like to ask about penguins or Antarctica. Record the list on the board.
   b) With a partner, choose four things from the new brainstormed list.
   c) Research your topic (see the Reference Shelf, page 253). Record all notes in your own words and keep all process work to hand in.
   d) On your own, write a rough draft of a report (see The Reference Shelf, page 259) on your findings. Use your research questions as **subheadings** in your report.
   e) Trade your report with your partner, and edit each other's work.
   f) Create a final copy of your report (see The Reference Shelf, page 272).

newspaper article

Tiny Bubbles?

Fish May Be Talking

ANNE MCILROY

PURPOSE
- To understand the concept of **alliteration**
- To *infer* meaning while reading

BEFORE Reading

In your notebook, create a word web (see The Reference Shelf, page 270) that shows ways that humans and animals communicate with each other. Group your answers according to these pairings: human to human, human to animal, animal to animal. Share your web with two other people. As a class, decide on the advantages and disadvantages of being able to communicate with others, and record your ideas on the board.

As you read, you will be asked to stop and make inferences about the article using sentence starters.

---

(1) The sound was unmistakably rude. University of British Columbia biologist Ben Wilson was alone in his lab late one night with a tank full of herring when he heard what he thought was somebody blowing a raspberry.

(2) He worried his equipment was acting up or that his friends were playing a joke on him. He had an underwater microphone in the herring tank, part of an experiment to see how they reacted to killer whale sounds, and he turned up the volume on his speaker. The farting sound came again, and then again over the next few nights. It was so loud that his colleagues down the hall complained.

(3) "They said I was being rude."

(4) Little did they know that Dr. Wilson was in the midst of discovering what may turn out to be a new form of communication between fish, one that will have immense appeal to 10-year-old boys.

(5) Careful observation showed the farting noises were coming from the herring at the same time as a steady stream of air bubbles was coming

AS YOU READ

◀ So far, this article is ... because ...

◀ 10-year-old boys would like the fish sounds because ...

Tiny Bubbles? | NEWSPAPER ARTICLE | 85

AS YOU READ

(6) out of their hind ends. His team dubbed the noise Fast Repetitive Tick, or FRT, and found signs the herring may use it to communicate. They make the noises more frequently when there are other fish in the tank, and only at night, when they can't see each other.

(6) Yesterday, Dr. Wilson headed off for a month at sea off the coast of Alaska to monitor the sounds of herring in the wild. Herring are social, in that they travel in vast schools with hundreds of thousands of other fish.

(7) "I want to know if they are making these sounds in the wild, and what on Earth it sounds like," Dr. Wilson says.

(8) What would it smell like? Fish farts probably aren't stinky, Dr. Wilson says. The air bubbles come from the swim bladder, which herring use for buoyancy. There is, however, some debate about how herring get gas into their swim bladders. Some researchers believe it may come from their digestive systems.

(9) Most fish can't hear at the frequency the herring use for their FRTs, which means they can signal each other without alerting salmon or other fish that find herring delicious. But humans can hear it.

(10) "If you put your ear up against the tank, you would have heard it," says Dr. Wilson, who has a link to the sound on his Web site, http://www.zoology.ubc.ca/~bwilson/herring.html.

▶ Dr. Wilson needs to use synonyms for fish sounds because …

(11) He tries to find polite synonyms for fart—including "digestive system venting" and "burst pulse sounds." A paper published by the Royal Society in Britain on his discovery avoided the f-word altogether.

▶ Noise pollution would affect the health of the herring because …

(12) This means that noise pollution caused by humans could have an impact on the health of herring populations.

(13) Other species of fish have been known to use their swim bladders to create grunting or buzzing sounds to attract potential sexual partners. But this is the first time scientists have caught fish farting, says Dennis Higgs, a biologist at the University of Windsor. "No one thought these fish made any noise at all."

(14) Do other fish also make farting noises? "I just don't know," Dr. Wilson says.

86 UNIT 3 | WHAT …?

AFTER Reading

CHECKING FOR UNDERSTANDING

1. As a class, discuss the inferences you made while reading. Next discuss why it is important to make inferences while you are reading.

PURPOSE / AUDIENCE / FORM

2. This article is about a topic that, according to the article, would "appeal to 10-year-old boys." Yet, this article was originally published in *The Globe and Mail*, which is a newspaper for adults. Decide who you think the **audience** for this article really is. Find three things from the article that support your answer. Share your ideas with the class.

STYLE AND CONVENTIONS

3. Alliteration is created when two or more words in a series begin with the same alphabet letter or sound (for example, cute cuddly kittens; shiny shoes; hip hop). Think up two alternative titles for this article that use alliteration.

CRITICAL THINKING

4. Create a **graphic organizer** (see The Reference Shelf, page 269) to sort the following list of words into at least three different categories. Give each category a title, and be prepared to explain why you sorted the words the way you did.

Words to sort:
- biologist
- killer whale
- schools of fish
- survive
- herring
- FRT
- wild
- evolution
- Ben Wilson
- nighttime
- swim bladder
- salmon
- experiment
- communication
- sound frequency
- Alaska

poem

PURPOSE
- To understand the concept of **homophones**
- To convert text from one form to another

The Praying Mantis

DICK KING-SMITH

BEFORE Reading

1. Think of some of the things you have seen or heard people do when flirting with a person they like. As a class, record your ideas on the board.

2. Read this poem twice. The first time, read without stopping. The second time, stop each time you are told to do so, and **visualize** in your head what you think is happening in the poem. If you need to have words defined to help you understand what is happening, you can **infer** the meaning, ask another student, or look the meaning up in the dictionary.

AS YOU READ

Stop reading and visualize. ▶	The praying mantis seems to be
	Intent on its devotions,
Stop reading and visualize. ▶	And yet its intellect is free
	Of all religious notions.
Stop reading and visualize. ▶	5 The mantis male thinks, in a daze
	Of love, 'I'll court and win her!'
	But when he has, the female preys.
Stop reading and visualize. ▶	She snaps him up for dinner.

88   UNIT 3 | WHAT ...?

AFTER Reading

CHECKING FOR UNDERSTANDING

1. This poem comes in a unit called *What …?* With a partner, decide whether this poem fits in this unit. Give two reasons to support your answer. Share your answers with the class.

PURPOSE / AUDIENCE / FORM

2. As a class, decide on the **purpose** (see The Reference Shelf, page 263) that the poet might have had in mind when writing this poem. Give at least three reasons to support your answer. Record your answers in your notebook.

STYLE AND CONVENTIONS

3. Homophones are two (or more) words that sound the same but have different spellings and meanings (for example, there, their, they're; too, two, to; here, hear). Find the one set of homophones in this poem (hint: you have to look at **root words**). Describe the effect that homophones have on the reader.

CRITICAL THINKING

4. While you read this poem you were asked to visualize what was happening. Create a four-panel cartoon that shows the events of this poem. A logical place to divide the poem is at the end of every second line, where you were asked to stop reading. Remember to use the tips on how to read cartoons (see The Reference Shelf, page 282) to help you design your own cartoon. Post your cartoon in the classroom.

The Praying Mantis | POEM | 89

informational text

PURPOSE
- To separate interesting ideas from important ideas
- To **retell** this selection

Why Do People Yawn, and Why Are Yawns Contagious?

KATHY WOLLARD

BEFORE Reading

Create a chart like this one:

Interesting Ideas	Important Ideas

As you read, follow the instructions to stop and fill in your chart, using **jot notes**. Keep this chart for later.

AS YOU READ

(1) Yawns are more contagious than the common cold. Seeing someone else yawn, you'll almost certainly yawn, too. Just reading about yawning can set you off. Are you yawning yet?

Stop and fill in your chart. ▶

(2) If you are, you're in good company. Human beings yawn all day long. We yawn when we wake up in the morning. We yawn when we go to bed at night. We yawn a lot when we watch television, studies show. And we even yawn when we are jogging briskly through the park.

Stop and fill in your chart. ▶

(3) Human beings aren't the only creatures that yawn. Many other animals, from lions to fish, open their jaws wide in yawns, too.

Stop and fill in your chart. ▶

(4) When we see people yawn, we often think they are tired or bored. But when Siamese fighting fish yawn, watch out! Male fish begin to yawn when they see other males. More yawning follows—about one yawn every 10 minutes. Then fish attacks fish, and the battle explodes. Other animals, such as monkeys and lions, yawn when they are hungry.

Stop and fill in your chart. ▶

90   UNIT 3 | WHAT …?

(5) Why do people yawn? The common explanation is that we yawn to gulp in extra oxygen—for example, in a stuffy room. But Robert Provine, a psychologist who studies yawning, says that isn't true. People given pure oxygen yawn just as much as people breathing ordinary air.

(6) Provine said no one knows exactly why people yawn or why yawns are so contagious. But he is trying to find out.

(7) Over the years, Provine has run a number of yawning experiments at the University of Maryland. In one, he had volunteers sit alone in a quiet room and think about yawning. When they felt a yawn coming on, they pressed a button. When the yawn ended, they did the same.

(8) Provine found that the average yawn lasted about 6 seconds. One person who concentrated hard yawned 76 times in half an hour.

(9) Next, Provine videotaped himself yawning or smiling. When shown the tape, only about one of every five viewers smiled when they saw Provine smile. But more than half of the viewers yawned right along with the psychologist. The conclusion: Yawning appears to be much more contagious than friendliness.

> **The conclusion: Yawning appears to be much more contagious than friendliness.**

(10) When we yawn, the head tilts back, the jaw drops, the eyes squint, and the brow wrinkles. Provine pointed out that when we stretch, we usually yawn, too. Yawns, he said, may be a stretch for the head and neck. But yawning also briefly stops oxygen-carrying blood from leaving the brain. So yawning may simultaneously wake us up as well as calm us down.

(11) You can see for yourself that yawning isn't just about taking a deep breath by doing an experiment of your own, Provine said. Seal your lips at the beginning of a yawn and try to breathe through your nose. It's just about impossible. If a yawn were simply a deep breath, your nose would work as well as your mouth.

(12) Yawns are so contagious, Provine said, that our brains are probably "programmed" to respond to a yawning face. Since early humans lived in groups, yawning may have been a way to synchronize the group's behaviour. A yawn setting off another and another might mean it's bedtime—or hunting time.

AFTER Reading

CHECKING FOR UNDERSTANDING

1. Using the chart you created while reading, compare your interesting and important ideas. As a class, discuss the differences between interesting and important ideas and why we have to separate them from each other.

PURPOSE / AUDIENCE / FORM

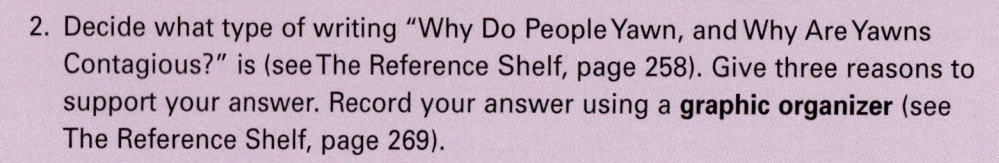

2. Decide what type of writing "Why Do People Yawn, and Why Are Yawns Contagious?" is (see The Reference Shelf, page 258). Give three reasons to support your answer. Record your answer using a **graphic organizer** (see The Reference Shelf, page 269).

STYLE AND CONVENTIONS

3. This author uses a **dash** (—) three times in this selection, in paragraphs 4, 5, and 12. As a class, locate the sentences that include a dash, and copy them on the board. Together, decide why the author has used a dash. Then, decide whether you think it is useful in helping you understand the writing. Give reasons to support your answer.

CRITICAL THINKING

4. a) As a class, make a list titled "Rules of Retelling" on the board. Copy the rules into your notebook.
   b) With a partner, retell (see The Reference Shelf, page 245) "Why Do People Yawn, and Why Are Yawns Contagious?" in your own words. Focus only on the reasons people yawn. Individually, record your work.
   c) Trade your work with another pair of students for peer editing. While you are editing, you should focus on the Rules of Retelling that the class decided on.
   d) Write a revised copy of your work, and post it in the classroom.

poem + magazine article

PURPOSE
- To compare two different types of writing

BONES

Bones

WALTER DE LA MARE

BEFORE Reading

Look at the titles of the poem and the article, and the graphics in each. **Predict** what each will be about.

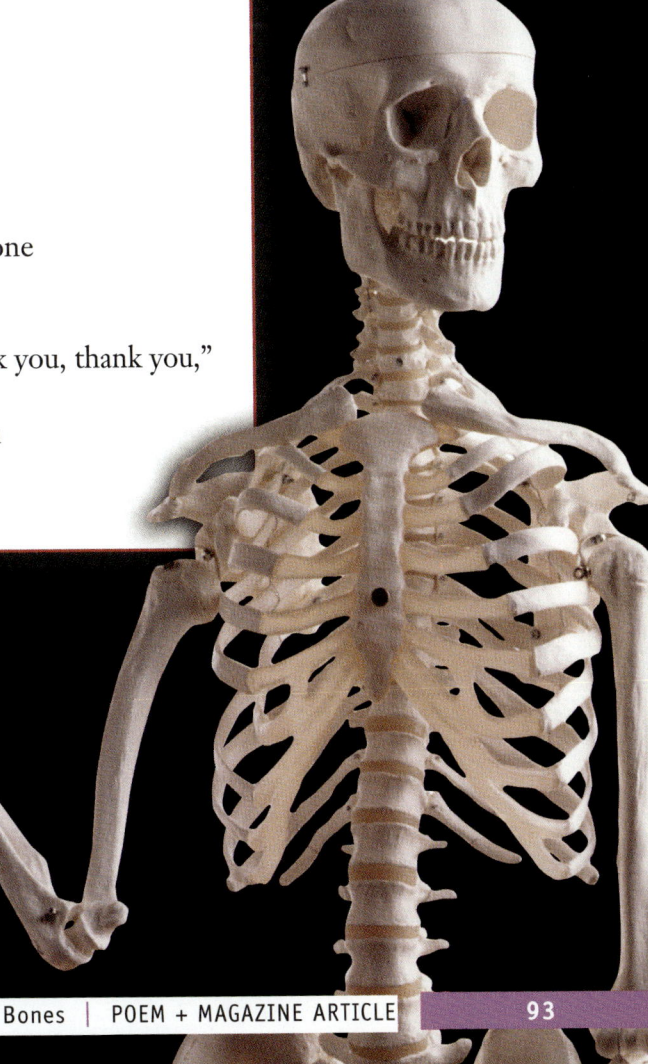

AS YOU READ

While you are reading, infer the meaning of each underlined word. Use the words surrounding the underlined word to help you figure out its meaning.

Said Mr. Smith, "I really cannot
   Tell you, Dr. Jones—
The most <u>peculiar</u> pain I'm in—
   I think it's in my bones."

5 Said Dr. Jones, "Oh, Mr. Smith,
   That's nothing. Without doubt
We have a simple cure for that;
   It is to take them out."

He laid <u>forthwith</u> poor Mr. Smith
10 <u>Close-clamped</u> upon the table,
And, cold as stone, took out his bone
   As fast as he was able.

And Smith said, "Thank you, thank you, thank you,"
   And wished him a good-day;
15 And with his parcel 'neath his arm
   He slowly moved away.

Bones | POEM + MAGAZINE ARTICLE   93

Gross Out?

BRITT NORLANDER

(1) Professional weight lifter Hossein Barkhah's performance took a serious turn for the worse at the 2003 World Weightlifting Championships. While trying to lift a 157.5 kilogram weight over his head, he wrenched his arm out of its socket. Ouch!

(2) What causes an elbow injury like Barkhah's? *Ligaments* (tough bands of tissue) normally hold together the bones in joints like your elbow. But an extreme *force* (push or pull) can cause the bones to *hyperextend* (increase the angle between the bones)—stretching or tearing the ligaments like a rubber band pulled too far. Dislocations like Barkhah's occur when the bones slide all the way out of position. "It takes a lot of force to dislocate a joint," says Dr. Tai David, physician for the San Diego Chargers. Barkhah was trying to lift more than twice his body weight! His bones moved so far out of place that his *humerus* (upper arm bone)—normally tucked safely in the joint—pressed right up against his skin.

(3) If no bones are broken, doctors can usually pop the elbow joint back into position by extending the patient's arm straight. But it's no treat. "We often have to sedate patients because the muscles are in spasm, and the patients are in a lot of pain," says David. It usually takes about six weeks for the joints to completely heal. But Barkhah also broke a bone in his elbow. So his doctors say it will take about three months for his elbow to heal.

Barkhah was trying to lift more than twice his body weight! His bones moved so far out of place that his humerus (upper arm bone)—normally tucked safely in the joint—pressed right up against his skin.

AFTER Reading

CHECKING FOR UNDERSTANDING

1. a) Fold a piece of paper in half lengthwise. In the left-hand column, make **jot notes** to record everything you can remember from reading the article "Gross Out?"
   b) **Reread** the article. In the right-hand column of your paper, record any new ideas you now remember after reading the article a second time.
   c) As a class, discuss the advantages and disadvantages of rereading.

PURPOSE / AUDIENCE / FORM

2. a) Find three ways "Bones" and "Gross Out?" are alike and three ways they are different (you can look at **audience**, **format**, **language**, punctuation, grammar, content, and so on). Use a **graphic organizer** to record your answers in your notebook (see The Reference Shelf, page 269).
   b) Return to the predictions you created in the Before Reading activity. Compare your first thoughts to your answers for question #2(a).
   c) **Brainstorm** why these selections would be placed together.

STYLE AND CONVENTIONS

3. The author of "Gross Out?" uses **italics** in paragraph 2. As a class find all the examples of italicized words, and record them on the board. Beside each italicized word, record what the author has included in brackets. Decide on the likely reason the author put some words in italics and some words in brackets. Discuss how this **text feature** helped or didn't help you understand the text.

CRITICAL THINKING

4. In a group of three, prepare a **reader's theatre** oral reading of "Bones." Decide who will be Mr. Smith, Dr. Jones, and the director. Decide what volume of voice you will use and what actions you will use. You might also like to put a **rhythm** to the poem. Practise your performance, and present it to the class.

5. With a partner, research either the proper way to lift weights or good warm-up exercises to do before weightlifting to prevent injury. Write out your recommendations in a procedure format (see The Reference Shelf, page 259). Present your procedure to the class.

Bones | POEM + MAGAZINE ARTICLE

newspaper article

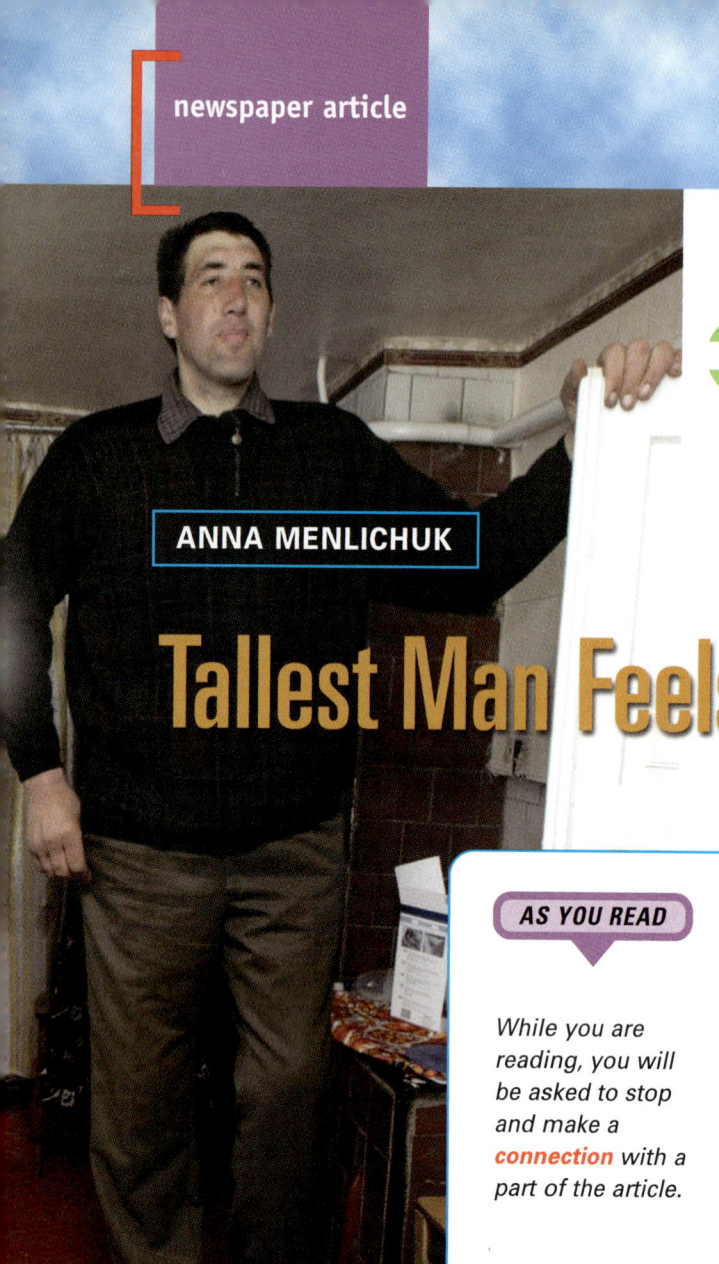

PURPOSE
- To write a **supported opinion** paragraph
- To detect **bias** in a piece of writing

Tallest Man Feels Lowly at the Top

ANNA MENLICHUK

BEFORE Reading

Your teacher will draw a line horizontally across the board with the words "Love It" at the left end, and "Hate It" at the right end. As a class, line up on this line based on how you feel about your height.

AS YOU READ

While you are reading, you will be asked to stop and make a **connection** with a part of the article.

(1) PODOLIANTSI, UKRAINE—At age 33, Leonid Stadnik wishes he would stop growing.

(2) He's already 8 feet, 4 inches (2.54 m) tall.

(3) Recent measurements show Stadnik is already 7 inches (18 cm) taller than Radhouane Charbib of Tunisia, listed by the *Guinness Book of World Records* as the tallest living man. He's also gaining on Robert Wadlow, who at 8 foot 11 (2.71 m) is the tallest man in history.

(4) Yet for Stadnik, the prospect of becoming a record-holder would be little comfort.

(5) "My 2-year-old suit's sleeves and pants are now 30 centimetres shorter than I need," he said.

(6) "My height is God's punishment. My life has no sense."

(7) Stadnik's height keeps him confined to this tiny village about 210 kilometres west of the capital, Kiev.

(8) "Taking a public bus for me is the same as getting into a car's trunk for a normal person," he said.

Stop reading and **visualize** what Leonid looks like.

(9) Stadnik's unusual growth began after a brain operation at age 14, which is believed to have stimulated his pituitary gland. Since then, life just keeps getting harder.

(10) Although he once was able to work as a veterinarian at a cattle farm, he had to quit three years ago after his 17-inch (43 cm) feet became frostbitten because he wasn't able to afford proper shoes. This month, he finally got a good pair, paid for by some businessmen. Their $200 (U.S.) cost was equivalent to about seven months' worth of the tiny pension that Stadnik receives in the economically struggling country.

(11) Stadnik sleeps on two beds joined lengthwise and moves in a crouch through the small one-storey house that he shares with his mother, Halyna.

(12) His weight of about 440 pounds (199.5 kg) aggravates a recently broken leg, and he suffers from constant knee pain.

◀ *Stop reading and decide how Leonid must feel abut his height.*

> **His weight of about 440 pounds (199.5 kg) aggravates a recently broken leg, and he suffers from constant knee pain.**

(13) Despite his aches, he tries to keep himself busy with the usual routine of country life. He works in the garden, tends the family's cows and pigs, and helps neighbours with their animals.

(14) To relax, he cultivates exotic plants and pampers his tiny blue and yellow pet parakeet with his huge hands.

(15) Bronyslav, a neighbour who wouldn't give his last name, described Stadnik as the "most unselfish, diligent man of a pure soul."

(16) His friends, in turn, treat him with the same sort of soft good humour. They're trying to organize a trip for him to the Carpathian Mountains to show him that "there's something in the world taller than you," Bronyslav said.

◀ *Stop reading and decide if you would like to be the same height as Leonid.*

AFTER Reading

CHECKING FOR UNDERSTANDING

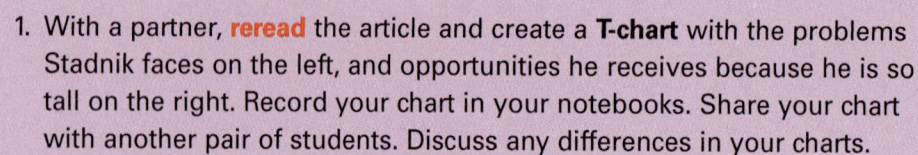

1. With a partner, **reread** the article and create a **T-chart** with the problems Stadnik faces on the left, and opportunities he receives because he is so tall on the right. Record your chart in your notebooks. Share your chart with another pair of students. Discuss any differences in your charts.

PURPOSE / AUDIENCE / FORM

2. Form a group of three students. Decide if the author is trying to make you feel sorry for or envious of Leonid Stadnik. Find three ideas from the text to support your **opinion**. Record your ideas in a **graphic organizer** (see The Reference Shelf, page 269).

STYLE AND CONVENTIONS

3. Return to the T-chart you created for question #1. As a class, decide how this article is biased. Discuss why the article shows a bias and the effects that the bias has on you as a reader.

CRITICAL THINKING

4. a) You will write a supported opinion paragraph on the statement "My height is perfect." As a class, review the rules for writing an opinion paragraph (see The Reference Shelf, page 259).
   b) Create a T-chart in your notebook to **brainstorm** your thoughts about your height, and to agree or disagree with the statement. Use this chart to plan your paragraph.
   c) Write the rough draft of your paragraph.
   d) In a group of three, pass your paragraph to the person on your left. Edit the paper you have in front of you. Look for proper **format**, clear meaning, supporting details, correct spelling, and proper sentence structure. Write your name at the top of the paper you have edited. Pass the paper you have to the person on your left, again. Edit the new paper you have. Put your name at the top when you have finished.
   e) Write a final draft of your paragraph. Be sure you can show all the process work leading up to this draft.

short story

Blue Eyes

MEGHAN WAFER

PURPOSE
- To understand how **suspense** is built in a story
- To create a **storyboard** for a film

BEFORE Reading

Read the title of this short story. Predict what the story will be about. Share your prediction with two other students.

While you are reading, you will be told to stop at certain places and connect with the text. To do this, finish each sentence starter you come to.

AS YOU READ

(1) Bizarre, weird, frightening. There was no word that could describe it. The dream had again happened.

◀ This reminds me of …

(2) A young man—well, the back of his head—was pulling me towards him. His dark hair was shining and his every move hypnotized me. I walked towards him, unable to turn away.

(3) I would always wake up as I approached him, his head slowly turning, my eyes popping open at the exact same time nightly.

(4) The strangest feeling came over me when I awoke, though. It was like I was trying to get away, trying to wake up, like this dream was against my will and unnatural.

> **On the front page was the heading:
> SCREAMING SLEEPERS DON'T AWAKE.**

(5) It was scary at times. I had a feeling like I might not be able to wake up and something bad would happen. I would see his face.

◀ I felt like this when …

(6) I had remembered reading the newspaper that day. Something I normally wouldn't do.

(7) It was just sitting there, so I decided to see what the headlines were.

Blue Eyes | SHORT STORY   99

AS YOU READ

(8) On the front page was the heading: SCREAMING SLEEPERS DON'T AWAKE. It sounded like something interesting, so I read it:

(9) "Ten people were found dead in their beds yesterday morning. All of them were of different residences, none knew each other. Spouses say that their loved ones were crying out in the night. 'Blue eyes,' they would scream continuously, unable to be awoken. They screamed for hours, and then in the morning, they were found dead. Cause of death is unknown."

(10) I could do nothing but stare, dumbfounded.

(11) Why were these people dying and why did no one know the reason for their deaths? Certainly they would find something in an autopsy. There had to be a reason.

(12) Deep down, I had the feeling that an explanation would not be found. Logic. Reality. All seemed to disappear from my mind. No solution could come to me.

> **Deep down, I had the feeling that an explanation would not be found. Logic. Reality. All seemed to disappear from my mind.**

(13) But why did I feel worried? Certainly this was some medical issue. I was healthy.

(14) At that moment, an image crossed my mind. An image of the man, walking slowly, in a way where I felt powerless. Did a silly dream scare me? Was this what worried me?

I can't sleep when …

(15) That night, I couldn't sleep. I would not let myself. I would just simply stay awake. I tried, I honestly did, but a power came over me, a power that I could not control.

(16) I began to close my eyes, prying them open once I realized what was happening. But my eyes closed. I slept.

(17) The man was there again. I was pulled towards him by the strange force.

(18) He turned, ever so silently. I slowly began to see the face of the person who had haunted my dreams. He had no face. Only blue eyes.

AFTER Reading

CHECKING FOR UNDERSTANDING

1. With two other students, discuss how accurate your predictions were. Discuss when in the story you realized your Before Reading predictions were accurate or inaccurate, and why. Next, discuss how predicting what a story will be about can help you understand it better.

PURPOSE / AUDIENCE / FORM

2. The author creates suspense by using the elements of a **narrative** (see The Reference Shelf, page 246). Complete the following chart. **Reread** the story to help you find examples. An example has been done for you.

Story Element	Quote or Example from Text	It creates suspense because …
Plot	"I would always wake up as I approached him, his head slowly turning, my eyes popping open at the exact same time nightly."	it shows repetition of the dream and that the dreamer does not really enjoy the dream.
Plot		
Atmosphere		
Language		
Character		
Character		
Setting		

STYLE AND CONVENTIONS

3. The author uses very short sentences. For example, the first sentence of the story is "Bizarre, weird, frightening." As a class, decide what effect(s) these short sentences have on the reader.

CRITICAL THINKING

4. a) As a class, divide this short story into scenes as if it were a film.
   b) Work with a partner to create the storyboard you would use to shoot one scene of this film. Remember to include camera angles, sound effects, and props needed. See The Reference Shelf, page 287 for help with features of a film.

Blue Eyes | SHORT STORY

drama/folktale

PURPOSE
- To identify a **simile** and explain how it helps create meaning
- To understand the **purpose** of a **folktale**

The Magic Sieve

BASED ON A JAPANESE FOLKTALE

IRENE N. WATTS

BEFORE Reading

Rank these items in order according to what you value most:
- friends
- family
- possessions
- school
- work
- relaxing

Record your list in a column in your notebook. Next, beside each word, write what you do that shows that you value this item. For example, if someone values family first, they might say, "I will say no to an activity with my friends if I have said I will do something with my family."

Read this play aloud. The roles needed are: narrator, wife, sister, brother, fisherwoman, goblin 1, goblin 2, goblin 3, goblin 4, goblin 5, neighbour 1, neighbour 2, neighbour 3, neighbour 4, neighbour 5, spirit of the sieve, sieve. You can combine the goblin roles or neighbour roles if you need to.

When the play opens, the two families are already on stage, side by side, separated by an imaginary thin wall between their houses. The characters are frozen, until each one begins to speak. The wealth of the sister may be suggested by her dress and jewels.

NARRATOR: Two relatives, whose fortunes had separated, prepared to welcome in the New Year.
BROTHER: The brother …
WIFE: His wife …
SISTER: And his sister …
NARRATOR: Lived next door to each other.
SISTER: The sister was very rich and had many things.

Sister puts on necklace and rings.

BROTHER: But her brother was poor; he did not even have enough coal left in his hibachi to heat his home.

The sister warms herself at her fire. The couple shivers.

WIFE: His wife longed to make rice cakes to celebrate the New Year, but alas, she had no rice. She asked her husband, "Please take this empty bowl and ask your sister, as a special favor, to lend us some rice."

Freeze.

BROTHER: So the brother went next door *(he bows)*. "We have no rice for New Year's breakfast. Will you lend us just a little? I will return it as soon as I can."

SISTER: I have none to spare *(turns him away)*.

He exits from the sister's house. Depending on staging, sister and wife should exit during next speech, removing any props with them.

BROTHER: The brother was ashamed to return home to his wife empty-handed. He decided to walk for a while. He took the path towards the sea. The day was as cold as his sister's words.

FISHERWOMAN: A fisherwoman was mending her nets. Her fingers were old and clumsy. She said, "Please, young man, help me turn my net."

BROTHER: Gladly.

FISHERWOMAN: Thank you, the net is heavy for my fingers. You are kind. Tell me, why do you look so sad? Don't you know that tomorrow is the New Year?

> **The world is a cold and selfish place.**

BROTHER: Yes, but my wife and I go hungry, while others celebrate. The world is a cold and selfish place.

FISHERWOMAN: Not all the world is bad. You helped me; now I will help you in return. Take this corncake and go back along the path until you reach the mountains. Wait quietly, and you will see the mountain men. They will beg you for that cake. You may give it to them *only* in exchange for their sieve. Don't forget.

She exits.

BROTHER: The young man bowed his thanks and began to walk towards the mountains.

Goblins appear.

NARRATOR: A noise like a swarm of bees around a hive filled the air.

The Magic Sieve | DRAMA/FOLKTALE

BROTHER: Those must be the mountain men the fisherwoman told me about. How noisy they are! I did not know they were goblins. They seem to be quarreling. I'll wait here and watch.

Goblins shout and push each other, trying to lift a log from a hole in the ground. They turn and see the brother and begin to drag him to the hole.

GOBLIN 1: A goblin was trapped there, and cried, "Help, murder, I'm caught under this log!"

BROTHER: The young man quickly freed him. "There you are," he said.

GOBLIN 1: The goblin did not bother to thank him. "I must have that corncake in your pocket; it smells better than all the things I have ever eaten."

BROTHER: The young man remembered what he had been told and said, "No, I cannot part with it."

NARRATOR: All the other goblins came 'round and offered him bribes for the cake.

GOBLIN 2: Give us the cake for our dinner and you shall have a bag of gold.

GOBLINS: Gold, gold, gold.

BROTHER: But the man would not change his mind. "I'll not exchange this cake for all the gold on the mountain."

NARRATOR: The goblins whispered together, greedily.

GOBLIN 3: "Not for all our mountain gold?" asked one.

GOBLIN 4: "That must be a very special cake," said another.

GOBLIN 5: "What *will* you take for it?" pleaded the last.

BROTHER: The man looked around, pretending to consider for a long time, then he spoke: "I'll give you this special corncake for …"

GOBLINS: Yes, yes, go on, for what?

BROTHER: In exchange for the sieve in which you shake the mountain earth.

NARRATOR: The goblins put their heads together and argued loudly, but at last they said:

GOBLINS: We are all agreed.

The brother holds out the cake temptingly, just out of the goblins' reach. One of them holds out the sieve.

GOBLIN 1: Here is our magic sieve. It cannot give you gold, but it will give you anything else that you really need. Treat it well.

GOBLIN 2: When you make a wish you must turn the sieve to the right …

GOBLIN 5: And when you have enough, then …

GOBLIN 3: Turn the sieve to the left.

GOBLIN 4: And don't forget to say, "Stop, sieve, stop."

GOBLIN 1: Here.

Grabs the cake and runs, with other goblins.

NARRATOR: And all the goblins ran with it into the mountain, and were never seen again.

BROTHER: Holding the precious sieve the brother went home.

WIFE: His wife had been waiting anxiously for his return, for it was getting dark and cold. "Where have you been for so long? It is almost New Year. I hope you have brought the rice."

BROTHER: I have brought you something much better than a bowl of rice. Here is a magic sieve that will give us whatever we really need. Let's try it right away.

NARRATOR: They spread a clean tatami mat and put the sieve on it.

WIFE: Sieve, sieve, please make us some rice.

> **Sieve, sieve, please make us some rice.**

BROTHER: And he turned it to the right.

WIFE: The wife was amazed to see so much rice appear, enough for many meals.

BROTHER: Then her husband turned the sieve to the left, and said, "Stop, sieve, stop."

WIFE: This is a wonderful magic sieve. Let's share our good fortune and make a New Year's feast for all our friends and neighbors. And of course, we'll invite your sister too."

NARRATOR: All their neighbors and friends came and enjoyed the feast.

NEIGHBOR 1: What excellent food, such tasty fish and chicken!

NEIGHBOR 2: How kind of you to share your good fortune!

NEIGHBOR 3: You must have worked hard to provide all this for us.

NEIGHBOR 4: A feast to remember.

NEIGHBOR 5: May fortune be with you all through the years.

WIFE: Indeed.

BROTHER: The brother said, "It is nothing at all. There is plenty more for all of you, as much as you can eat."

SISTER: The sister looked on and was so full of envy that she could not eat. How could her brother afford all this, and where did it come from? She asked her brother, "Did you have a big catch yesterday after all?"

BROTHER: An old fisherwoman showed me a lucky place. Thank you for honoring us with your presence.

The neighbors bow and leave, followed by the sister, looking doubtful.

SISTER: This time she had to turn away, but she was determined to discover her brother's secret. That night, when all was quiet, she waited outside in the darkness and looked and listened.

She holds an open fan—the "wall" at which she listens.

> **This time she had to turn away, but she was determined to discover her brother's secret.**

WIFE: The wife put the sieve in a safe place and said, "Thank you for your magic gifts." And then she went to sleep.

The couple exits or sleeps.

SISTER: The sister crept into the house and stole the sieve. She walked down to the sea and climbed into a boat that she kept there. She rowed out to sea so that she could not be seen or heard. "I'll wish for gold," she said, and started to shake the sieve as hard as she could. "Make gold for me, lots of gold …"

The spirit of the sieve appears upstage.

SPIRIT OF THE SIEVE: Those who wish gold from me will get white salt to fill the sea.

NARRATOR: Then the sieve started to make salt.

SISTER: Who spoke? I have been tricked. I want gold, not salt! Help me, the salt is too heavy for the boat. It will sink! Stop, help me!

SIEVE: But the sieve went on pouring salt, and soon the boat was covered in white salt. Slowly the boat and the selfish sister and the magic sieve sank to the bottom of the sea.

The spirit and the sister sink in slow motion to the ground, covered by a white cloth that the spirit places over them. Freeze.

NARRATOR: The sieve is still making salt, and that is why the sea will always taste salty.

AFTER Reading

CHECKING FOR UNDERSTANDING

1. In a group of three students, draw a placemat like this one. Your group will choose one role of either the brother, the wife, the sister, or the goblins. In the A sections, each person will write **jot notes** describing the **character traits** of the assigned character. Take turns talking about what each person wrote. Put check marks beside ideas in your list that have been said by others. In the centre, write a statement that explains what your character feels is important.

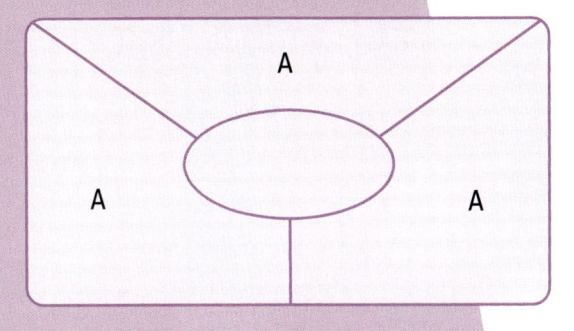

PURPOSE / AUDIENCE / FORM

2. Make a **T-chart** that shows the advantages and disadvantages of telling this story as a **drama** rather than as a story. Share your thoughts with the class.

STYLE AND CONVENTIONS

3. a) Find one example of a simile in this play and copy it into your notebook. As a class, discuss how the use of simile helps you understand the story better.
   b) With a partner, write a simile that describes the character trait(s) of the brother, wife, goblins, and sister.

CRITICAL THINKING

4. a) As a class, **brainstorm** a list of possible **subjects** for this play. Next, choose one or two subjects and write **theme** statements for them on the board. (See The Reference Shelf, page 251.)
   b) Use a **graphic organizer** like this one. Write your theme statement in the middle. Write each character's **opinion** on that theme statement.
   c) Compare your graphic organizer with two other students'.

Goblin | Brother
Theme Statement
Sister at End of Play | Sister at Beginning of Play

The Magic Sieve | DRAMA/FOLKTALE   107

short story

mirrors dot com

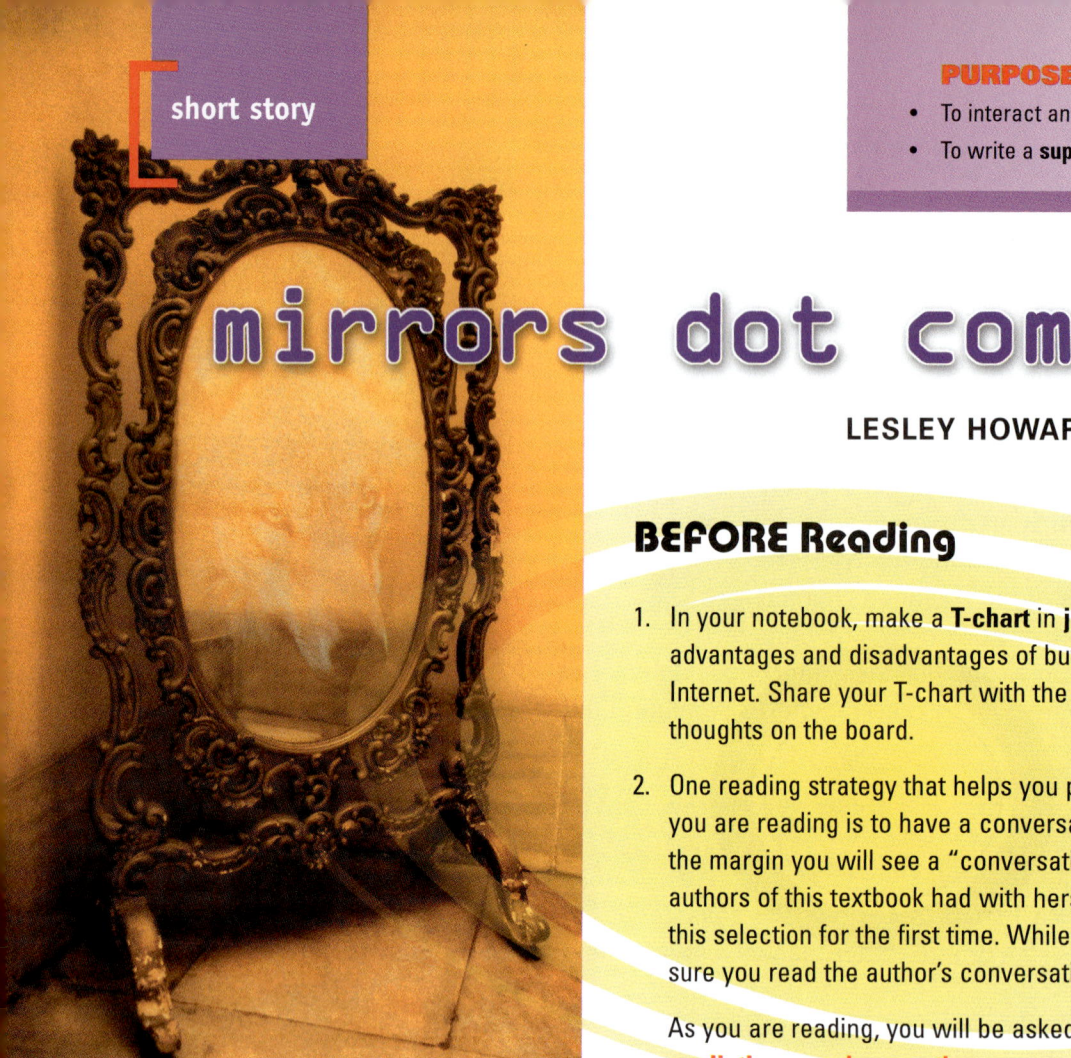

LESLEY HOWARTH

PURPOSE
- To interact and **connect** with a text
- To write a **supported opinion** paragraph

◀ "I've seen "dot com" before. It goes with Internet URLs, so I think some of this story will be about the Internet."

BEFORE Reading

1. In your notebook, make a **T-chart** in **jot-note** form that lists the advantages and disadvantages of buying products over the Internet. Share your T-chart with the class, and record your thoughts on the board.

2. One reading strategy that helps you pay attention to what you are reading is to have a conversation with the text. In the margin you will see a "conversation" that one of the authors of this textbook had with herself as she was reading this selection for the first time. While you are reading, make sure you read the author's conversation as well.

As you are reading, you will be asked to **comment**, make a **prediction**, or **ask a question**.

AS YOU READ

"I'm the year of the horse."

"I didn't know that. I wonder what my animal is."

"This is British slang, and I think it means to be stunned speechless. The story makes sense with this meaning, so I'll use it."

(1) It started four days before Samantha Lamb's birthday.
(2) You know there's a Year of the Rat, a Year of the Pig, the Dog, the Horse, in the Chinese calendar? They knew more than we did, the people who started that stuff.
(3) I know about that stuff now. Did you know there's an animal—a secret self—<u>hidden in your reflection</u>? Oh, yes. And the way to see it is—
(4) But I'd better start at the beginning.
(5) My friend Sam's birthday was coming up, so I searched the Internet for these mirrors. Sam likes stuff for her room, and I knew she'd just broken one. Finally I found a site selling mirrors. It took an age to download the graphics. But when they popped up, I was <u>gobsmacked</u>.
(6) They were pretty amazing mirrors. Twisted spirals of silver around shapes that looked like wolves' heads. Mirrors like the shields of knights in battle. Gilt 'chimney glasses' crested with eagles. Copies of Roman hand-mirrors shaped like the sun. Unbreakable mirrors of polished

108 UNIT 3 | WHAT …?

(7) metal. Used by explorers, the site said. And all at pub/mirror.com. I didn't know mirrors like that existed. I'd never seen anything like them.

(7) I actually never meant to order it.

(8) Those mirrors—especially the glaring wolf's head with the burning ruby eyes—seemed to jump out at me, to *make* me click on them and order them. I'll never know why I put the wolf-mirror into my 'shopping trolley'. Next thing, I'd OKd Mum's credit card number and the wolf man was on his way.

(9) He actually turned up in the cat flap next day. The postman pops parcels through the cat flap whenever there's no one at home. When I saw the package labelled PUB/MIRROR WORLDWIDE in the darkness of the garage, I felt very slightly sick. As though his burning ruby eyes could read my mind through the bubble-wrap already, and he knew that he wasn't wanted.

(10) 'And where are you going to put *that*?' Mum's reflection looked back at her disgustedly from the silvery depths of the wolf-mirror.

(11) 'I'm not. It's for Sam's birthday.'

(12) 'Good job. He gives me the creeps.'

(13) He gave me the creeps, too, actually.

(14) The wolf man curling around the mirror glared down at me before I went to school. His grinning face, resting on the top of the mirror and hanging down over the edge of it, glared down at me when I came home. His silver paws hugged the sides of it and glinted in the moonlight that leaked in at night around the sides of my blind, and felt like they'd like to hug me too, and not in a friendly way. I got up and put him outside.

(15) I forgot about him until I fell over him on my way to the bathroom next morning. He toppled over onto my feet and lay looking up at me, still creeping around his mirror like some twisted mythical beast.

(16) *I don't even like you. Get off me!*

(17) Three days until Sam's birthday.

(18) Why didn't I send him back?

(19) You know in fairy stories, there's always a forbidden thing, something the person in the story mustn't do, and then they always go and do it? DON'T forget to go home at midnight. DON'T go into the woods alone. DON'T forget to drop the enchanted nut into the sea for your magic griffin to rest on, all that stuff? I began to wonder about the

AS YOU READ

◀ Make a comment, make a prediction, or ask a question.

◀ "The author used *italics* on make. That usually means it's an important idea."

As though his burning ruby eyes could read my mind through the bubble-wrap already, and he knew that he wasn't wanted.

◀ Make a comment, make a prediction, or ask a question.

◀ "The author is talking about what happens in fairy stories. I think I'm getting a hint about something that is coming up."

mirrors dot com | SHORT STORY 109

AS YOU READ

Make a comment, make a prediction, or ask a question.

mirror man, the more his ruby eyes got to me. What did he do, to be stuck there like that, hugging his mirror and hoping someone might want him over the Net?

(20) 'Did you get me something?' Sam asked.

(21) 'Something?'

(22) 'A birthday present?'

(23) 'Oh, yeah,' I said. 'I got you a present. I got you a present, all right.'

(24) I tried to send him back that night, but Returns weren't optioned at all, and pub/mirror.com came up with some boring looking pub mirrors, as if that was what they were selling. 'What happened to the wolf-mirror?' I mailed them.

(25) 'Gothic Series Sold Out,' was the only reply. No Returns even mentioned, not even a PO Box to send them to.

(26) I was stuck with him, and I knew it. Two more days, then Sam would have to have him in *her* bedroom. Some birthday present. I knew, even then, I should bury him under the noodles and cans in the dustbin and buy Samantha Lamb something else.

(27) But by that time it was too late.

(28) It had come to me as I was lying in bed waiting to go to sleep. I'd just seen *ER* and my mind wouldn't stop. You know the feeling. Not good. The moonlight always came in around the side of my blind, and that night it silvered the claws of the wolf-mirror and made a pale glow in its depths.

I tried to send him back that night, but Returns weren't opened at all, and pub/mirror.com came up with some boring looking pub mirrors ...

(29) I got up and turned him to face the wall.

(30) Then I got back into bed.

(31) I could feel the power in his red-eyed glare, even with his back to the room. The moonlight flooded in anyway, and suddenly I knew what the forbidden thing was, as certainly as if it had been chalked on the back of the mirror, where his silver claws appeared around the backing.

Make a comment, make a prediction, or ask a question

(32) *Don't look into the mirror by moonlight, or you'll see what animal you are.*

(33) I sat up in bed. What *animal* you are?

(34) I got up and moved the mirror, very carefully, out of my room.

(35) 'What on earth are you doing?' Dad wondered, coming up the stairs to bed.

(36) 'I don't like him in my room at night,' I told him sheepishly.

(37) 'I'm not surprised, it's hideous. I thought it had four legs.'
(38) 'It has.' I checked him. 'There's one at the back.'
(39) 'Night, then,' Dad said.
(40) 'Night, night.'
(41) Sweet dreams, I almost added, except I didn't get any, myself. Instead, I had the moonlight leaking in around the blind and the feeling that grew and kept me awake until it was driving me mad.
(42) Two feelings, actually.
(43) One was the certainty that if I got up to go to the loo and had to walk past the wolf-man I wouldn't be able to stop myself *looking into the mirror by moonlight.*
(44) The other was the certainty that he'd had all four legs wrapped around the front of the mirror, and no leg down the back.
(45) In the end I had to get up.
(46) I made it past the mirror to the toilet, though his ruby eyes scorched my ankles. I made it back as far as the bedroom door before I let myself see, through half-closed eyes, the place where the wolf-man had been.
(47) His mirror glared down the stair-well, reflecting the outside light that leaked up the stairs in the darkness; a plain, silver-edged mirror, so ordinary you might even have ordered it from pub/mirror.com, or from any shop selling candles, or any department store.
(48) The wolf-man was gone, I didn't like to think where.
(48) I must have knocked him off his perch in passing; probably he'd rolled down the stairs. Probably if I looked I'd see him, forlorn and glinting, in the hall.
(50) But I didn't look.
(51) Instead I slept on the landing in the sleeping bag I found in the airing cupboard, too scared to go into my room.
(52) In the early hours, a flash of silver seemed to tumble into my dreams. The glare of ruby eyes reminded me, over and over again, of the *one thing I knew I mustn't do.*
(53) Dad fell over me at seven o'clock.
(54) 'Lisa! What on earth—?'
(55) I turned over. 'Dad.'
(56) A hammering headache filled the whole of my brain. Those burning eyes had drilled into the back of my head. They saw what I really was, reflected in their own fiery depths.

> Don't look into the mirror by moonlight, or you'll see what animal you are.

AS YOU READ

(57) 'Where's that—'

(58) 'Mirror?' Dad set it straight. 'Must have fallen over in the night.'

(59) There he was, but he didn't fool me.

(60) So the mirror-man was back on his mirror, with his wolf-legs folded around it as if he'd never been gone. Flashing around like a slip of silver all night. He'd changed his position, anyone could see. What did he think, we were stupid?

(61) 'Why aren't you in your bed?' Dad bleated.

(62) 'Doesn't matter, does it?' I said, turning over. 'Leave me alone,' I growled.

(63) The next night was Friday night, and we went to the cinema for Sam's birthday treat, as her party was going to be only *part* of her birthday, as Sam gets everything she wants. The film was OK, not great. We spilled a whole tub of popcorn over the floor, plus these stupid boys kept annoying us, but anyway, it was all right.

> Those burning eyes had drilled into the back of my head. They saw what I really was, reflected in their own fiery depths.

(64) When I got home I remembered him. The mirror-man upstairs. I delayed for as long as I could. But finally I had to go to bed.

(65) It was the worst night yet. I finally got off to sleep all right, which I don't usually after a Jumbo Cola and a giant pack of Pik 'n' Mix, which was pants, as they had the wrong prawns and massively big worms, so you have to pay five quid to get *one*.

(66) So at last I was just drifting off. I don't know, I may have been asleep—when I thought I saw him running round my room. Quick as quicksilver, the mirror-man, wolfing my slippers and flashing over my desk, his red eyes burning, his tongue slavering, his quick tail flicking and whipping.

(67) Who was he? The reflection of someone's secret self, the last person to look into that mirror in the moonlight, after they'd ordered it by mistake? That mirror, that mirror, that mirror. Had been the cause of it.

(68) I started up in fright and launched myself at that mirror.

(69) In the moment before I smashed it, I saw what animal I was. The wolf rolled off the top of it and raged and boiled on the carpet, *changing shape as I watched into the animal that was me*, until I put my pillow on top of it, and another pillow on top of that, and my dressing gown and a pile of books, and everything I could find to weigh it down and stop it, that reflection of my secret self …

"This sounds very British to me. I think the girl is saying she was disappointed with her "Pik 'n' Mix" treats because she paid a lot of money and didn't get the kind of treats she wanted."

▶ Make a comment, make a prediction, or ask a question.

(70)   'Happy birthday!' Sam wishes herself, her head around Lisa's bedroom door on Saturday morning. 'I let myself in, all right?'

(71)   Sam waits, but nothing happens; no move to get her her present. Instead, Lisa puzzles over the pieces of a mirror. Not a very nice mirror, either.

(72)   'What are you doing?'

(73)   'What does it look like? I just have to piece it together. Then I can send it back.'

(74)   Sam picks up a twist of silver. 'What's this?'

(75)   'What does it look like?'

(76)   'A dragon?'

(77)   'It *was* a wolf, but the wolf-man's gone.'

(78)   Sam looks at the dragon's curved limbs, at the shape it's designed to hold, its tail licking clean around an oval. 'What's this meant to be for?'

(79)   'He sits on top of the mirror,' Lisa supplies. 'When he's not—'

(80)   'What?'

(81)   'Broken.'

(82)   'You said, alive.'

(83)   Lisa's eyes flash. 'I said, broken.'

(84)   Sam looks at her friend. 'About my party tonight—'

(85)   'Mind if I take it back?' Lisa scratches Sam very slightly as she reached up to grab the figure. Blood wells up on Sam's hand, in a ruby-red spot on her thumb. Lisa watches her eyes, and Sam gets the strangest feeling she's looking into the mouth of a—

(86)   The dragon in Lisa's eyes smiles. 'Thanks.' Her fingernails close over the silver figure and place it over the top of the mirror-puzzle.

(87)   'It's my birthday.' Sam sucks the scratch on her hand. 'This isn't supposed to happen.'

(88)   But Lisa has eyes for no one but herself, mirrored in the scattered pieces of glass that make up a jigsaw on the floor. 'Ever look into a mirror at night? After I mend it, you can put this in your room and see what animal *you* are.'

(89)   <u>Sam Lamb knows already.</u> She leaves the bedroom, unnoticed, as downstairs Dad logs on to the computer and finds pub/mirrors.com offering 'Reduced Gothic Mirrors at a Fraction of their Former Price', over the search he makes for a book.

(90)   'Lisa! That dot com company's got those mirrors again!' Dad yells up the stairs as a range of extraordinary mirrors appear when he clicks on them without meaning to. 'Like that weird mirror you just got!'

In the moment before I smashed it, I saw what animal I was.

Make a comment, make a prediction, or ask a question.

(91)   His voice washes over Lisa, guarding her broken mirror upstairs, seeing her fragmented face in it.

(92)   *Me and not me. Who am I?*

(93)   *For a moment, I can see a reflection of myself as I might be. The girl in the mirror is me. Me, and not me, at the same time. I'm not sure I wanted to know, but I did what I knew I shouldn't …*

(94)   *I can hear Dad downstairs, ordering a mirror. I want to stop him, but I can't. He will release his inner self. What animal will he be? A pig, a rat, a rabbit?*

(95)   Dad's voice comes up the stairs. 'You know, these mirrors aren't bad—'Gothic Mirror in Gilt'—I think I might—oh, I *have* clicked on it, what a stupid donkey I am, I think I might have just ordered it …'

AFTER Reading

CHECKING FOR UNDERSTANDING

1. a) With a partner **retell** this story in jot-note form in your notebooks. Use 7 to 10 notes. You should **scan** the text if you need help remembering what happened.

   b) Join another pair of students. Orally retell your versions of the story to each other. Then, scan the text for any important details you left out, and add these to your list. If you've included any unnecessary points, cross them off your list.

PURPOSE / AUDIENCE / FORM

2. The author uses italics in paragraphs 92, 93, and 94 for a specific **purpose**. The author also uses italics in paragraph 95, but for a different purpose. As a class, discuss how italics are used for different purposes in these examples. Decide whether the use of italics helped you understand the story, or if it made the story more confusing for you. Give reasons to support your answer.

STYLE AND CONVENTIONS

3. a) Divide the class into four groups. Each group will be assigned a language **convention** to start with: **dash** (—), words all in CAPITAL LETTERS, single quotation marks ('/'), and italics. Copy the chart below onto a piece of paper (one chart per group). Write the language convention assigned to your group at the top of the left column. Find one example of the language convention and record it in your chart. Then determine the purpose of that language convention and record it in your chart.

   b) Pass your chart to another group, who will find a new example for the language convention written on the chart. Keep passing charts until you get the one you started with. Discuss what each language convention is used for, first as a small group and then as a class.

Language Convention	
An example from the story	The language convention is used to…

mirrors dot com | SHORT STORY | 115

CRITICAL THINKING

4. a) Create a word web about three different animals that you might be (see The Reference Shelf, page 270).

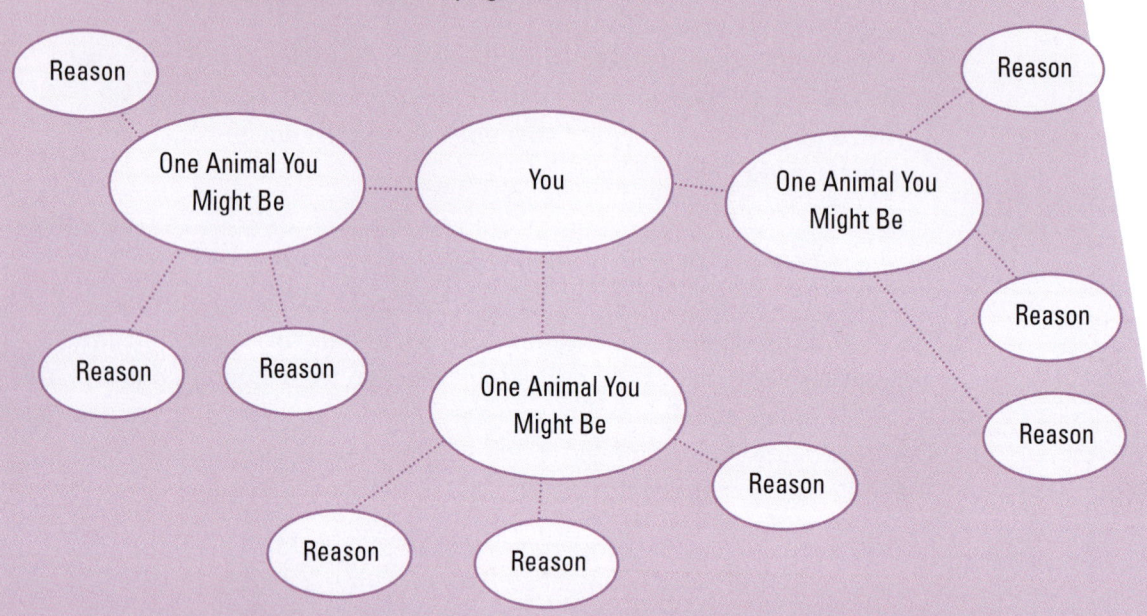

```
        Reason                                              Reason
             \                                              /
         One Animal You ····· You ····· One Animal You
          Might Be                        Might Be
         /      \          |              /       \
     Reason   Reason       |          Reason    Reason
                      One Animal You
                        Might Be
                      /     |     \
                Reason   Reason   Reason
```

b) Choose the one animal from your web that you think will be the most convincing for your **audience**. Write a supported opinion paragraph telling what kind of animal you would be (see The Reference Shelf, page 259).

c) In a group of three, pass your paragraph to the person on your left. Edit the paper you have. Then pass the paper you have to the person on your left, again. Edit the new paper you have. Refer to The Reference Shelf, page 273, to help you edit.

d) Revise your work using your editors' comments as a guide.

e) Create a final draft of your paragraph and post your finished product in the classroom.

Unit 3 Activity

For your project for this unit, you will be evaluated using a rubric your teacher will discuss with you before you start. You will be expected to keep any process work and submit it with your final product.

Choose <u>one</u> of the following activities to complete.

1. a) Consider the question, "What is normal?" Copy and complete the graphic organizer below. An example has been done for you.

Selection	List all the things in the text that are not normal.	Why are these things not normal?	Rank your opinion using a scale of 1 to 10 (1 is completely normal, and 10 is completely abnormal).	Explain your ranking.
"Tallest Man Feels Lowly at the Top" (page 97)	• Leonid Stadnik is 33 and still growing.	• Most males stop growing around age 18.	8	Stadnik is past the age where people stop growing.

Follow these steps:
1) Choose two selections.
2) Look for evidence of things that are not normal.
3) Narrow down your evidence to the two best examples.
4) Complete the chart.

b) Write a **supported opinion** paragraph to answer the question, "How does where we live and who we know help us define 'normal'?"

Follow these steps:
1) Choose one of these topics: music, teenagers, movies, tattoos, piercing, or fashion.
2) Make a **T-chart** with the left-hand side labelled "normal according to my community" and the right-hand side labelled "not normal according to my community." Brainstorm what is considered normal and not normal about your topic, according to the community you live in.
3) Think about this question: "Does my community have a fair definition of *normal* in relation to my topic?"
4) Highlight in your T-chart the three arguments you will use to support your opinion.
5) Write a supported opinion paragraph. Remember to give a topic sentence, supporting ideas, and a conclusion sentence. (See The Reference Shelf page 259.)
6) Edit your work using the guidelines in The Reference Shelf on page 273.
7) Create a polished copy of your supported opinion paragraph.

2. Think about the following questions from page 81.
   - How does the unexplained influence the way we define "normal"?
   - Why are people drawn to the unexplained?

   You will research one of these topics: crop circles, Easter Island, Big Foot, or ghosts.

   Follow these steps:
   1) Choose a topic and make up six questions you'd like to answer while researching.
   2) Research your questions, using the library to find books on this topic, or using the Internet. Take **jot notes** in your own words to record your findings.
   3) Group your research notes into subtopics such as: where, when, why, how, what, and who. Choose four subtopics you can write about.
   4) Choose at least three research facts to highlight per subtopic.
   5) Write a four-paragraph report (see The Reference Shelf, page 259) explaining your findings.
   6) Edit your work. (See The Reference Shelf, page 273.)
   7) Prepare a final copy of your report. Make sure you record where you found all your information and organize your process work.

3. Form a group of three students (you will be evaluated separately). You will write an extension of one of the selections from this unit. You can choose from: *The Magic Sieve*, "Blue Eyes," or "mirrors dot com."

   Follow these steps:
   1) Choose a story.
   2) **Brainstorm** ideas about what happens one month, one year, and five years in the future. What did the **characters** learn from their odd experiences? How have their personalities changed? Are they still affected by their unusual experiences? What has happened to them since their unusual experiences? Are they still having unusual experiences?
   3) Write a role-play **script** that extends the story one month, one year, or five years into the future. Each person must have a speaking role. You can use a **narrator** if you want to. Include any sound effects or props that you need. Your skit must be at least five minutes long.
   4) Practise your role play until it is polished and everyone knows their lines and actions.
   5) Perform your role play for the class.

> 1 > 2 > 3 > **UNIT 4** > 5 > 6

INVESTIGATIONS

You Have the Right to Remain … Informed PAGE 125

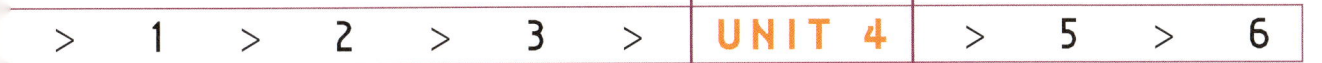

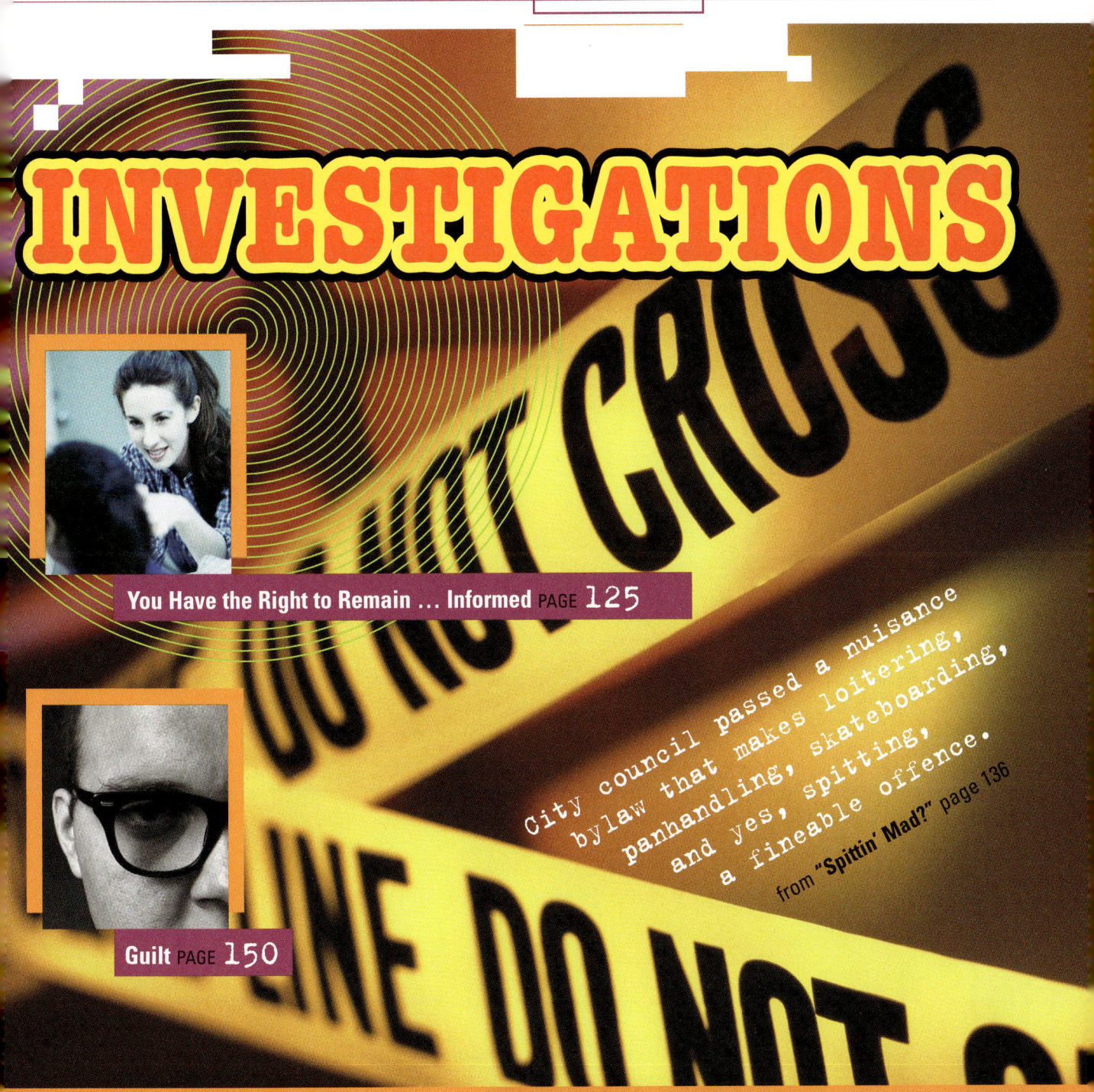

Guilt PAGE 150

City council passed a nuisance bylaw that makes loitering, panhandling, skateboarding, and yes, spitting, a fineable offence.

from **"Spittin' Mad?"** page 136

THINK ABOUT IT

- How does the media affect our understanding of crimes, investigations, and punishment?
- Why do people commit crimes?
- What is the impact on other people when someone commits a crime?

> > >

🍁 **Fingerprinting the Dead** by *David Owen* (informational text) ... **121**

🍁 **You Have the Right to Remain ... Informed**
by the *Department of Justice Canada* (informational text) ... **125**

🍁 **The Gift That Could Not Be Stolen** by *Burt Konzak* (short story) ... **132**

🍁 **Spittin' Mad? That'll Be $155** by *Robin MacLennan*
(newspaper article) ... **136**

Unbalanced by *William Sleator* (short story) ... **141**

Guilt by *Steve Barlow* and *Steve Skidmore* (drama) ... **150**

Unit 4 Activity ... **155**

UNIT 4

Investigations

Choose one selection from the list above. What do you think this selection will be about? How will it relate to the theme of "investigations"?

informational text

PURPOSE
- To practise specific reading strategies on your own
- To create a speech

Fingerprinting the Dead

DAVID OWEN

BEFORE Reading

Individually, make a list of things you do to help you understand what you are reading (reading strategies). As a class, compile a list of these reading strategies (see The Reference Shelf, page 239) and leave them on the board to use as a reference while you are reading.

AS YOU READ

For Paragraph 1: In the margin you will see a "conversation" one of the authors of this textbook had with herself as she was reading this selection for the first time. Someone in your class will read this paragraph aloud along with the author's conversation.

For Paragraph 2: Where you see words or sentences underlined, stop and have a conversation with yourself. Create a chart like the one below to record your conversation using words or pictures.

The book says …	I wonder …, I am reminded of …, I think …
rigor mortis	
decomposed	
Mummified bodies may need to have the fingertips softened by soaking them in a mixture of glycol, lactic acid, and distilled water, sometimes for several weeks, before prints can be taken.	

For Paragraph 3: You will need to form groups of three. Number yourselves one, two, and three. Each person, starting with number one, will take a turn reading one sentence from paragraph 3 aloud to the others. At the end of the sentence that you read, you will say something about what you have read, and your group members will respond to what you have said. Look back at your reading strategies to help you. If you cannot think of anything to say, **reread** the sentence and think again.

> I know what evidence is, but I don't really know what trace is. I know how to trace something, but that meaning doesn't make sense here.

> I watch those crime shows, so I know an autopsy is what they do to tell how a person died. They look inside the person and do a lot of tests.

> What is "standard part"? Standard: I think of standards like industry standards. I guess that means "normal" or the least I can expect. So "standard part" must be normal part.

> I know what construct means—to make—and "re" means again. So they must be making the fingerprints again. Why are there quotation marks?

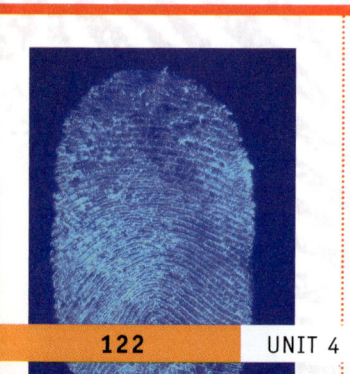

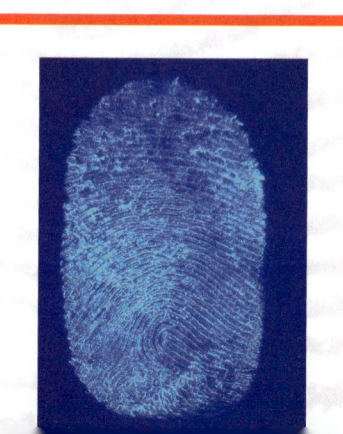

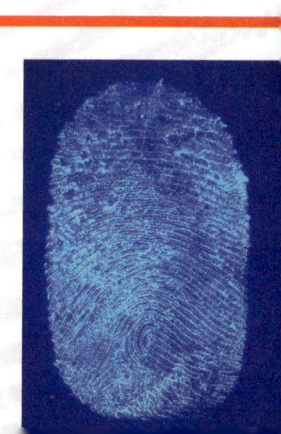

AS YOU READ

I say ... ▶

I say ... ▶

I say ... ▶

(1) Fingerprinting has now become a <u>standard part</u> of <u>autopsy</u> procedure, conducted after all other possible <u>trace evidence</u> has been removed from the fingertips and fingernails. If time has passed since the victim's death, examiners may undertake "<u>reconstructive</u>" procedures to obtain a clear set of prints.

(2) Fingerprints are usually taken from dead bodies when <u>*rigor mortis*</u> has passed off and after the body has been kept in cold storage. Sometimes, when bodies are badly <u>decomposed</u>, the hands, or occasionally individual fingers, must be removed in order to take the prints. <u>Mummified bodies may need to have the fingertips softened by soaking them in a mixture of glycol, lactic acid, and distilled water, sometimes for several weeks, before prints can be taken.</u>

(3) The most difficult subjects are those in which the skin has been softened by dampness or immersion in water. In some cases, glycerine or liquid wax has to be injected into the fingertip from below the joint. If the damage to the tissues is more extensive, the skin can be stripped away from the hand, then mounted on a surgical glove in order to obtain prints.

122 UNIT 4 | INVESTIGATIONS

AFTER Reading

CHECKING FOR UNDERSTANDING

1. **Reread** paragraphs 2 and 3. Make a list of the strategies you and your group members used to help you understand these two paragraphs. Beside each strategy, explain how it made the content clearer.

PURPOSE / AUDIENCE / FORM

2. a) Make **jot notes** to describe three different ways people might react to this selection.
   b) Divide the class into number ones and number twos. The number ones will argue that this selection should be included in a Grade 9 textbook and the number twos will argue that it should not be included.
   c) Create a **graphic organizer** (see The Reference Shelf, page 269) to gather ideas that support your argument.
   d) Share your ideas with a partner and add new ideas to your graphic organizer.
   e) Present your ideas to the class.

STYLE AND CONVENTIONS

3. In jot-note form, using headings for each note, describe the vocabulary, the length of the sentences, and the difficulty of the content. In one opinion paragraph, state whether or not the author intended this article for Grade 9 students. Use your jot notes to support your opinion.

CRITICAL THINKING

4. Write a speech agreeing or disagreeing with this statement: "Should everyone's fingerprints be kept on file?"
   a) Choose three points from the selection to support your opinion and make an organizer like the one on page 124.

Fingerprinting the Dead | INFORMATIONAL TEXT

| Opening line |
| Point 1 |
| Explanation of Point 1 |
| Point 2 |
| Explanation of Point 2 |
| Point 3 |
| Explanation of Point 3 |
| Conclusion |

b) Write your speech.
c) In a group of four, take turns reading your speech. Each listener should ask one of these questions:
- How does your opening line grab the listener's attention?
- What are your major points?
- How have you explained each of your points?

The writer must answer each of the questions aloud to the rest of the group, referring to his or her speech. If the writer cannot answer the questions, he or she should make a note to revise his or her writing.

d) Revise your speech. Create cue cards for your speech and be prepared to present it to the class.

informational text

PURPOSE
- To understand specialized vocabulary
- To work as a pair to create an interview

You Have the Right to Remain ... Informed

DEPARTMENT OF JUSTICE CANADA

BEFORE Reading

Discuss with a partner what you know about the justice system from watching TV or reading newspapers and magazines.

QUIZ Time!

AS YOU READ

Answer the questions in your notebook.

1. **True or False:** A youth record is automatically erased when a person turns 18 years of age.

2. A cop stops a person for questioning about his or her possible involvement in a minor crime. The person says, "But I didn't do anything." Is that an official statement and can it be used against the person?

3. Under the YCJA, young people who receive a six-month custody sentence will most likely:
   a) Spend three months in a facility and three months being supervised in the community
   b) Spend four months in a facility and two months being supervised in the community
   c) Spend weekdays in a facility and weekends at their parents' cabin on Lake Ontario
   d) Spend the entire time in a facility

4. What's incorrect about this statement? *"I was on trial for armed robbery, and by entering a guilty plea, duty counsel got me a lighter sentence that included custody and community supervision."*

5. Which of these youth crimes may result in an adult sentence?
   a) manslaughter
   b) an indecent wardrobe malfunction at a major sporting event
   c) pouring intoxicants into soda cans
   d) aggravated sexual assault

6. Lorraine, 16, has been found guilty of committing a serious crime. The judge is sentencing her as an adult. This means:
   a) Her name can be released to the media
   b) Her criminal record becomes permanent, unless she is pardoned
   c) She could face the maximum sentence an adult can get
   d) All of the above

7. **True or False:** Under the YCJA, if a youth has committed a crime against someone, the victim is not allowed to be provided with any information on the case.

8. **Fill in the blank:** *A judge's sentence must include measures that focus on the youth's _____ into the community.*
   a) rest and relaxation
   b) rehabilitation and reintegration
   c) regurgitation and rejuvenation
   d) repositioning and disintegration

9. Jaret was 15 when he was found guilty of a minor crime. He finished his sentence at age 16. At age 18, he is found guilty of another minor crime. What happens to his youth record?
   a) It is completely erased
   b) Ryan Seacrest plays it on *American Top 40*
   c) It becomes a permanent adult record
   d) It becomes a major plot line on *Moose Jaw Law & Order*

10. **True or False:** Even after a person's youth record is closed in Canada, he or she can still have a criminal file in the U.S.

(1) No one means to break the law. Or, more accurately, no one means to get caught breaking the law. But it happens. And if it ever happens to a person, would he or she know what his or her rights are or the consequences he or she faces?

(2) The answers to these questions and more are in this guide to the *Youth Criminal Justice Act*. The YCJA is designed to make the youth justice system more fair and effective. Its main goals are to provide meaningful consequences that help offenders understand the impact of their actions, to help rehabilitate those who offend, and to provide support and supervision for those young people so they can fit back into society.

(3) So think of this YCJA primer sort of like life insurance, a kidney donor, or even a barf bag on an airplane—it's something people hope they never need, but if they do, they'll be eternally grateful that it was there.

There's No Such Thing as a Victimless Crime

(4) This is one of the main ideas behind <u>Community Justice Forums</u>, a form of <u>restorative justice</u> that brings together the victim, the offender, and community members to decide how to repair the harm done to the victim and the community or if any other <u>reparation</u> is desired.

(5) For the 12- to 17-year-old who has committed a crime like theft, assault, or property damage, being seated face to face with the victim can be a powerful experience.

> **For the 12- to 17-year-old who has committed a crime like theft, assault, or property damage, being seated face to face with the victim can be a powerful experience.**

The purpose is to help the youth to realize what he or she has done, how the offence affected others, and how the youth can take action to make amends. It also gives the victim a forum to voice how he or she felt about the crime.

(6) Richard Kennett, a trained facilitator and forum coordinator in Winnipeg, says that assisting the young person who has committed the offence to repair the harm with those who have been affected by his or her actions goes a long way to ensure the youth does not re-offend.

(7) "It doesn't make sense for a kid who has smashed the window of a store to be sentenced to 72 hours of cleaning up cat poop at an animal shelter," he says. "It's an <u>unrelated consequence</u> that doesn't fit the crime, doesn't benefit the store owner, and it may lead to the youth feeling more anger and resentment towards the community."

(8) Kennett says that with Community Justice Forums, a more meaningful act of reparation that might be suggested is for the young person who has offended to work in the owner's store after school for two weeks. "That way the owner can <u>recoup</u> their losses and the youth can come to realize that the owner is a real person. Their relationship will be transformed. The young person is more likely to feel good about what they're giving back to the person that has been harmed—as well as the community."

(9) Under the Youth Criminal Justice Act, Community Justice Forums are now more available to those affected by crime.

(10) Before the YCJA became law, it was estimated that one in six youths found guilty of a crime received a <u>secure custody</u> sentence and only one in 35 participated in any kind of process involving the community and victim. The YCJA was implemented to help the Canadian criminal justice system move towards more meaningful consequences in order to promote rehabilitation—protecting the community from further victimization and the young person from further offending.

> ... within two years of introducing the conference concept, the rate of young re-offenders dropped from 40 percent to less than four percent.

(11) To date, there have been no official Canadian statistics released on the effectiveness of the YCJA or related programs like Community Justice Forums. However, Kennett points to one 1996 case study from Sparwood, BC (population 5,000), reporting that within two years of introducing the conference concept, the rate of young re-offenders dropped from 40 percent to less than four percent.

(12) In the long run, it is hoped that the "new attitude" of the Youth Criminal Justice Act will decrease the quantity of youth in jail for minor and non-violent crimes and increase the quality of life in safer, more secure communities.

Arrested Developments

These four teens have all had run-ins with the law, but others can learn from their mistakes.

DAN, 15

Dan stole a purse from an elderly woman. During the theft, the woman's arm was broken. At the request of the judge, an <u>advisory group</u> was set up to make recommendations on Dan's sentence. The advisory group recommended that Dan perform volunteer work for groups specializing in elder care.

JOE, 16

Joe was stopped by the police after stealing a CD from a record store. Because he had no prior convictions, the police officer used his <u>discretionary powers</u> to release him after serving him with a <u>warning</u>.

CHARLIE, 16

Charlie was <u>arrested</u> for vandalizing a bus shelter. The officers read him his rights and took him to the police station. He made use of his right to call a lawyer. After a short investigation, all parties agreed to forgo formal legal proceedings. Charlie accepted responsibility for the offence and agreed to an <u>extrajudicial sanction</u>. He became enrolled in a program on the costs of crime and also had to repair the damage he caused.

JILL, 15

Jill was caught shoplifting a sweater. A month earlier, she'd been issued a warning for having stolen a ring. This time, the police and Jill's parents were called. Jill and her dad went to the police station, where she received an official <u>caution</u>.

Glossary

Advisory Group (or "Conference"): A conference is an advisory group put together by a police officer, a prosecutor, a judge or other key decision-makers in the youth justice system. Depending on the type of conference, the victim, the offender, their families, others affected by the crime, along with people from different sectors involved with the youth, could meet to discuss the offence.

You Have the Right to Remain ... Informed | INFORMATIONAL TEXT

Arrest: When a person in authority (i.e., a police officer) restrains someone believed to have committed a crime so that it is clear that the person is not free to leave.

Caution: An extrajudicial measure (i.e., an action that does not use the formal justice system) that police or the Crown can utilize to deal with a youth who commits a less serious offence. The youth would receive a written caution and his or her parents would be involved.

Discretionary Powers: In the youth justice system, police and other professionals have some freedom to make certain decisions based on their own judgement.

Extrajudicial Sanction: The most formal type of extrajudicial measure. A youth must accept responsibility and agree to participate. Examples could be restitutional community service and apologies to victims.

Record: If a young person is found guilty of an offence, the record is automatically provided to the RCMP. As long as the youth doesn't re-offend, the record will be destroyed after a certain period. If convicted of a summary offence (less serious), the offence usually stays on the record for three years after the sentence is completed. For an indictable offence (more serious), the period is about five years after the sentence is completed. And for a violent indictable offence, the record will exist for at least 10 years after the sentence has been completed.

Warning: An extrajudicial measure that police can use for less serious offences to alert a youth that his/her behaviour is considered an offence.

AFTER Reading

CHECKING FOR UNDERSTANDING

1. Look back at your answers to the quiz at the beginning of the selection (page 125). Your teacher will assign one question to you and a partner to work on. **Skim** the article to find the answer to your question and revise your answers based on the information in the text.

PURPOSE / AUDIENCE / FORM

2. The information contained in this text is very serious and could discourage young people from reading it. Name at least four different ways the author and editor have made the information easier and more interesting for teenagers to read.

STYLE AND CONVENTIONS

3. As a class, create a glossary for these terms from the selection:
   - community justice (paragraphs 4, 8, 9, and 11)
   - restorative justice (paragraph 4)
   - reparation (paragraphs 4 and 8)
   - unrelated consequence (paragraph 7)
   - recoup (paragraph 8)
   - secure custody (paragraph 10)

For each term, write a sentence that will help you remember its meaning.

CRITICAL THINKING

4. a) With a partner, choose one of the young people you read about on page 129.
   b) Gather your facts in a chart like the one below:

Name	Crime	Consequence	Meaning of Consequence

   c) Create four questions a crime reporter might ask this person. Make sure the questions are ones that your audience would be interested in knowing about.
   d) Write answers from the young person's point of view.
   e) Perform your interview for the class.

short story

BURT KONZAK

THE Gift THAT Could Not BE STOLEN

PURPOSE
- To think about the form and **style** of the selection
- To create a television **news report**

BEFORE Reading

When readers connect to what they are reading, the reading becomes more personal and easier to remember (see The Reference Shelf, page 244). As you are reading, you will see some sentence starters that will help you make a connection to what you are reading. Write out the sentence starter in your notebook and complete it in your own words. Share your sentences with a partner. If you could not think of anything, talk it over with your partner, and try again to complete the sentences after your discussion.

AS YOU READ

This character makes me think of …

(1) Shichiri Kojun was seated in evening meditation at his small house on the outskirts of town. The house was dark, for Shichiri had no need of light during meditation, or for the martial arts practice he had just finished. For over fifty years, he had practiced the martial arts diligently. Even now, no longer in the prime of his life, he never missed a day of training.

(2) Seeing no light and hearing no noise from within, a passing robber thought that the house was an ideal place to finish his lucrative evening's work. He unsheathed his long sword and crept into the house.

(3) "You are making too much noise," a voice called out. "My money is in a silk purse under the tatami mat."

(4) Through the darkness, the thief saw a man seated motionless on a cushion in the adjacent room. He found the purse, and in it was a small pile of money. "Don't take it all. I have to pay my bills tomorrow," the seated man called out. "And ask politely when you want something."

(5) "May I have some money?" the thief asked, surprising himself.

◀ I've never …

(6) "Yes," Shichiri replied.

(7) The thief took half the coins and put the rest back. "Thank a person when he gives you a gift," the voice called out again. Without understanding why he was doing so, the thief obeyed the man and thanked him, then bowed, and quickly ran out of the house and down the street leading to the woods outside of town.

(8) Later that night, the thief was caught. The authorities made every attempt to return stolen items to their owners and to collect statements concerning the guilt of their prisoner. Shichiri was the last to be consulted, since all that was stolen from him was money, and it was difficult to tell from whom it had been taken. A neighbor said he had seen a man running from Shichiri's house that evening. The authorities knocked at the samurai's door, explaining that they had his stolen money.

> "As far as I am concerned, this man is no thief. He came into my house and politely asked for money. I gave it to him. He thanked me for it. If he were indeed a thief, he would have taken the rest of my money."

(9) Shichiri responded. "As far as I am concerned, this man is no thief. He came into my house and politely asked for money. I gave it to him. He thanked me for it. If he were indeed a thief, he would have taken the rest of my money." Shichiri drew the string on the silk purse and showed the coins still in it. "He is an unfortunate man, poorer than I. I wish I could have given him something more. I wish I could have taught him how to appreciate the beauty of the moon." Shichiri motioned toward the sky where the full moon was glowing.

◀ The difference between the police and Shichiri is …

(10) Several years later, when the thief had finished his prison term, he sought out Shichiri. "I see you want to learn how to appreciate the

The Gift That Could Not Be Stolen | SHORT STORY

> **AS YOU READ**
>
> This reminds me of …

beauty of the moon," the old man said when he saw the former thief. He looked not the least bit surprised or disturbed—no more than he had that first night when the man broke into his house.

(11) The man who had been a burglar studied devotedly with Shichiri until the day that the master died.

(12) The money Shichiri gave the burglar could not be stolen, because it was a gift. The samurai was so generous that he wanted to give the thief an even greater gift, the ability to appreciate the beauty of the moon, the wonder of the things we see around us every day that have a value beyond money.

Ideals in an Imperfect World

(13) Musashi Miyamoto became wise, turning his back on the shallow ambition of defeating others and concentrating on improving himself. But he knew that the world was a dangerous place, full of wars and famine, and that even in peacetime rogues exist. Peace and relative prosperity had arrived in Japan many years before, but it was still necessary to train just as hard as in war, in order to live in peace.

(14) Musashi hoped that his own life would inspire others to train hard and pursue the arts in order to develop themselves and create a better world. He knew a better world comes not just from high ideals, but also the personal power to pursue these ideals.

AFTER Reading

CHECKING FOR UNDERSTANDING

1. a) Complete the following sentence: "Trying to make some connections with this text was … because …"
   b) Create three questions you have as a result of reading this story. In a group of three, read all of your questions aloud and try to answer them.

PURPOSE / AUDIENCE / FORM

2. a) What is the **purpose** of this story?
   b) This story sounds like a **folktale**. As a class, discuss why the folktale form suits the purpose of this story.

STYLE AND CONVENTIONS

3. This story is told simply, but the style is quite formal. Refer to The Reference Shelf (page 262) and make **jot notes** on formal style. **Scan** the story again and find three examples of formal style. Copy the examples into your notebook, and explain why each example is formal.

CRITICAL THINKING

4. a) As a class, **brainstorm** things you should consider when creating a news report for television. Record these ideas in your notebook.
   b) Number off one to four. Number ones will be the police officer. Number twos will be the thief. Number threes will be Shichiri. Number fours will be a newspaper reporter.
   c) If you are a number one, two, or three, think about what happened in this story from your character's point of view. Gather your ideas in a **graphic organizer** (see The Reference Shelf, page 269). If you are a number four, create some questions you could ask the three other people in order to get your story.
   d) In groups of four, making sure your group has all four characters, prepare a television news report that includes interviews with the police officer, the thief, and Shichiri.
   e) Present your report to the class.

The Gift That Could Not Be Stolen | SHORT STORY

newspaper article

PURPOSE
- To explore **bias** in a **news report**
- To examine **organization** and **conventions** of a news report, and apply that learning to your own writing

Spittin' Mad? That'll Be $155

ROBIN MacLENNAN

BEFORE Reading

1. Read paragraph 3 of this article. According to this paragraph, what four offences could you be charged for?

2. Read the headline for this article. As a class, discuss why the reporter and headline writer would choose to focus on spitting rather than on any of the other offences mentioned in paragraph 3 of the article.

3. In your notebook, create a chart like the one below. As you are reading the article, record the arguments for and against the law and the person who made the statement. An example has been done for you.

Person	Argument For Law	Person	Argument Against Law
Tom Moore	Spitting is repugnant.		

This article was written on May 12, 2004.

(1) BARRIE, ONTARIO—In downtown Barrie, they'll no longer be able to spit in your eye. Or anywhere else for that matter.

(2) The city north of Toronto has big revitalization plans that call for a drastic makeover of its downtown landscape.

(3) And to make its core feel safer, city council passed a nuisance bylaw that makes loitering, panhandling, skateboarding, and yes, spitting, a fineable offence.

(4) It's not new. But it is rare. Moose Jaw, Sask., passed a spitting law 18 years ago, but has never issued a fine.

(5) And 100 years ago, Toronto and Hamilton approved bylaws to "prohibit expectoration." Toronto's law was approved after fines were cut from $50 to $1, and the jail terms from 6 months to 3 days. It was still in place in pre-merger Toronto.

(6) The bylaws are hardly ever enforced, and today Toronto only charges a $15 fine for spitting.

(7) But Barrie's new bylaw will be enforced by city police and bylaw enforcement officers.

(8) And it could cost you $155.

(9) The fine has already drawn comparisons to fine-happy Singapore.

(10) The tiny Asian island with the aim of having one of the most prosperous, cleanest communities in the world offers fines for eating on the subway, jaywalking, not flushing a public toilet, and, of course, spitting.

(11) "I understand if you are caught putting graffiti on a building in Singapore you can be caned," said councillor Tom Moore.

(12) "Our fines, by comparison, are very modest."

(13) He said the issue of spitting was raised more than once during his election campaign last fall.

> **"We don't go around with a team of spitting police that would be looking for offenders, but if somebody complains, we would investigate,"**
> —*Saskatoon city solicitor Steven Schiefner*

(14) "It's repugnant … We don't expect that people would be spitting on the sidewalk, just like we don't expect they would be spitting in a public building or in a restaurant."

(15) And it could be hard to make a charge of spitting stick, so to speak.

(16) "We don't go around with a team of spitting police that would be looking for offenders, but if somebody complains, we would investigate," said Saskatoon city solicitor Steven Schiefner.

(17) For starters, it would have to be proved that the spit actually belonged to the offender, he added.

(18) Downtown Barrie hairstylist Doug Samson is thrilled that spitting is officially illegal.

(19) "It's nasty, it's disgusting, and I am glad they can't spit anymore," he said.

(20)   "We saw it all the time, especially when there was a tattoo parlour right across the street. There would be a group of guys, and the girls were right there with them, standing there talking and spitting all over the sidewalk.

(21)   "We were all grossed out by it, and that's part of the perception people have of the downtown," he added. "It's important to make the area more friendly, more comfortable, more safe, so that people want to come here."

(22)   Saliva aside, critics say the real aim of the bylaw is to push its homeless out of town.

(23)   "I really believe our people are not wanted downtown, and if this bylaw is enforced, it will make it almost impossible for them to be there," said Ann Burke, coordinator at the David Busby Street Centre.

(24)   Burke points to the removal of benches last year from Memorial Square, a downtown park, as a signal of the concerted effort to push the homeless out.

(25)   And last summer, with threats of $20,000 fines, the city shut down a homeless tent city that had been erected at a private lot.

> **"I was offended by the language that was expressed to describe some of the homeless …"**

(26)   "They are not always the prettiest, or they don't smell the nicest or look the nicest, but this is about human rights," said Burke.

(27)   She heads a shelter visited by as many as 160 homeless people each day and was a member of the committee that drew up the new rules.

(28)   Burke said her opinions were often shot down.

(29)   "I was offended by the language that was expressed to describe some of the homeless," she said.

(30)   Kimberly Dawson, coordinator of the Simcoe County Alliance to End Homelessness, criticized council for being "narrow" and "railroading the changes through."

(31)   "It seems to me that there were a number of people who helped get the mayor elected, and maybe that's who they are listening to."

(32)   But councillor Barry Ward, a downtown business owner, disagrees.

(33)   "That's a red herring. If it targets anyone, it's the people leaving the bars at three in the morning," said Ward, who said the aim is to generally keep loiterers away.

(34)   "People said when they came downtown they had to fight their way

(35) down the sidewalk. We are trying to get the sidewalks clear of people doing anything but walking."

Newspaper boxes have been removed from corners, park benches have been relocated away from the sidewalk, and planters will be equipped with sharp edges to deter people from sitting.

(36) Moore said they're simply raising the bar and making expectations clear.

(37) "In over two decades of experience as a secondary school principal, I learned that people will generally rise to the level of expectations you have of them," he said. "In doing so, we are not targeting any group, but are identifying behaviours that are not acceptable."

(38) He said the issue is respect.

(39) "You don't have the right to ride your bicycle on the sidewalk," he said. "And we are saying, 'Don't skateboard on the sidewalk where you will be running over pedestrians. Take your skateboard around the corner to the park we built for you, and enjoy yourself there.'"

(40) Councillor Dave Aspden was alone in his opposition to the new bylaw, which he said would be too tough to enforce.

(41) "I do agree that improvements are needed," he said.

(42) Ward said the bylaw will be enforced by city police and bylaw enforcement officers who witness the behaviour, or act on complaints from citizens.

(43) Three new bylaw officers were hired last year to work night shifts, primarily for parking infractions.

(44) "But there's no reason they can't be downtown, as well," Ward said.

AFTER Reading

CHECKING FOR UNDERSTANDING

1. a) With a partner, compare your lists of arguments for and against the law. **Scan** the article again and add any missed information to each of your charts.
   b) Look back over your list and decide if this article presents
   - a biased view <u>against</u> the law
   - a biased view <u>for</u> the law
   - a balanced view of both sides

   Be prepared to give two good reasons that support your choice.

PURPOSE / AUDIENCE / FORM

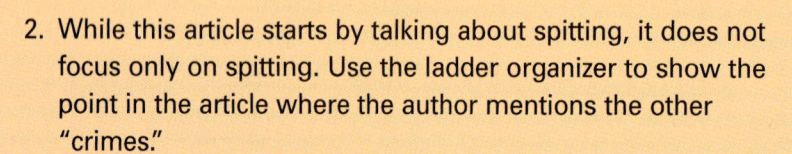

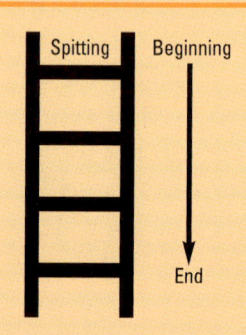

2. While this article starts by talking about spitting, it does not focus only on spitting. Use the ladder organizer to show the point in the article where the author mentions the other "crimes."

STYLE AND CONVENTIONS

3. Make a list of "rules" you can **infer** from the article about how a newspaper article should be written. You should be able to infer at least seven rules. (Hint: some things to think about include **text features, organization, style,** and **tone**.)

CRITICAL THINKING

4. a) Research in your school library, public library, or city or town hall some of the bylaws for the area where you live. Record the bylaws and the fines for breaking them. Choose one bylaw and write a newspaper report for television news about it.
   b) Record who the bylaw is aimed at controlling. Decide whether or not it is a good bylaw, and make notes on why or why not. Ask others in your class or in your school their **opinions** on the bylaw, and copy their words exactly so that you can use them in your report.
   c) Create a ladder organizer for your report.
   d) Create your report.
   e) Work with a partner. Read each other's writing aloud and restate each other's paragraphs in your own words. Talk about how well the ideas flow and about any parts that don't make sense.
   f) Revise your writing and perform your broadcast for the class.

short story

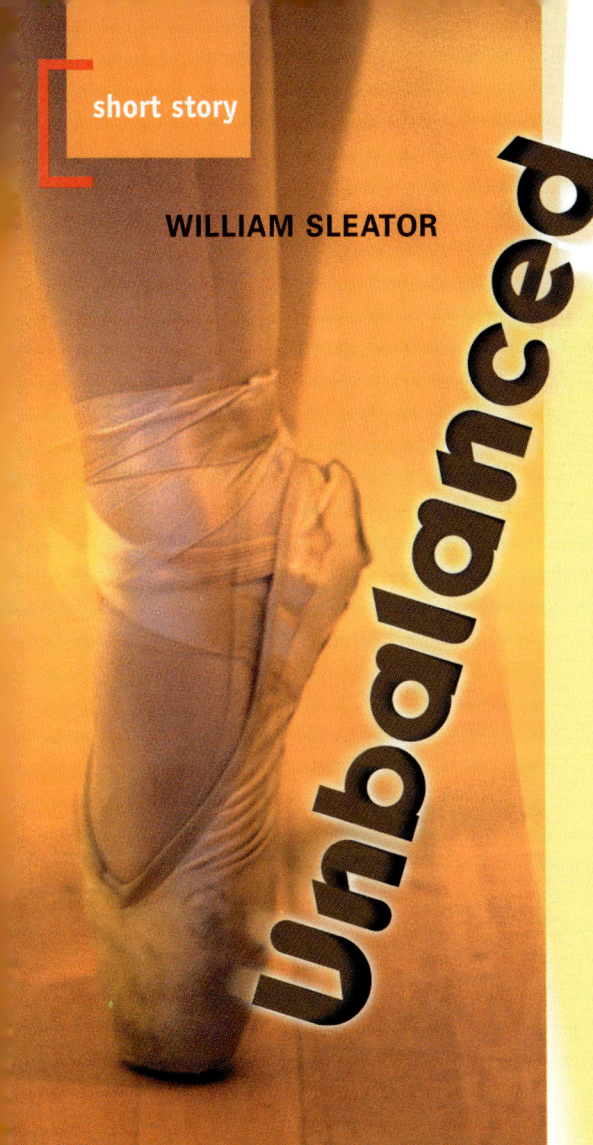

Unbalanced

WILLIAM SLEATOR

PURPOSE
- To examine the elements of a **narrative**
- To adapt a piece of literature into different forms

BEFORE Reading

Create a word web (see The Reference Shelf, page 270) like the one below for these five elements of a narrative:

- plot
- language
- atmosphere
- characters
- setting

(See The Reference Shelf, page 246.) Read only the title and paragraph 1 of "Unbalanced," and then write down one **fact** linked to each element.

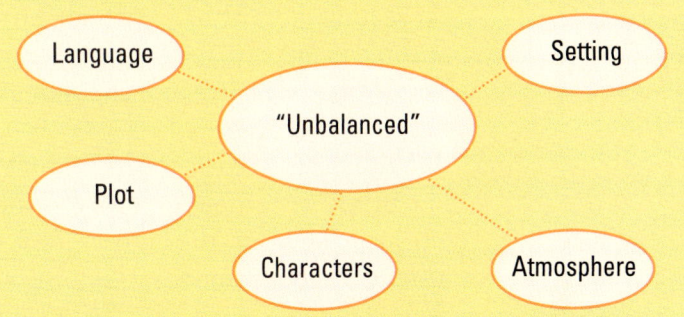

```
        Language              Setting
                 "Unbalanced"
        Plot
              Characters    Atmosphere
```

Each time you see an asterisk (*) in the margin, add to your web by writing down one observation for at least two of the narrative elements on it. Try to choose different elements of your web each time.

---

(1) "Oh, that was close!" she gasped, just offstage, bent over with her hands on her knees, gulping air. "If you weren't so quick, it would have been a fracture for sure."

(2) He rested his hand lightly, comfortingly on her shoulder. "I'm there for you," he said, breathing as hard as she was. "I just want to know who made that place slippery."

(3) Linda felt the panic, which had just been subsiding, start to rise again. "You think somebody put Vaseline there on purpose?"

(4) "How else did it get there?" Jimmy said.

(5) They ran out to take their bows.

(6) It was a bad, tricky step. She had to run toward the specific place upstage left, marked with a piece of tape, which would be right under

Unbalanced | SHORT STORY | 141

AS YOU READ

the follow spotlight, and then suddenly stop, on pointe, in arabesque, one leg out behind her. It was hard, but she had finally got it in rehearsal. Tonight, in performance, she had reached the place and gone up on pointe. But this time there was no friction to stop her—her foot was sliding horribly out from under her, her arms flailing. She was going over backward, her spine heading for the stage.

(7) Jimmy rushed out of the choreography, lifted her before she fell, and carried her offstage for their exit.

(8) Back in the wing, their bows over, she asked, "But why would somebody do that to me?" Her breath was coming easier now, but the sweat on her body chilled her. "What did I ever do to anybody?" Her voice sounded like a little girl's.

(9) Which she nearly was. To be a soloist at seventeen was unusual. All those long years at ballet school, and then acceptance by the company at fifteen, and two years later—last week, in fact—promotion to soloist. Maybe she was naive, but she thought promotion meant people were on her side.

(10) "You haven't learned yet?" Jimmy said. "You don't know what they're like here?" He stood up now, tall and beautiful. He was twenty-five and a principal dancer, the highest level. "There are other people who wanted to get promoted to soloist, who've been in the company longer than you. Older than you. They could do anything. You've got to know that. You've got to … watch out for it."

(11) She tightened. It had been magical being promoted so soon, a dream. Now suddenly what it meant was fear.

(12) "Linda, what happened?" It was Carla, her best friend in the company.

(13) "Somebody put Vaseline on the stage," Jimmy said, looking hard at Carla, his voice dead calm. "And I'm going to find out who, and I'm going to kill her. See you in class tomorrow." He strode away.

(14) They were in different dressing rooms now—Carla had not been promoted from the corps. But they lived close enough to each other to walk partway home together. Carla was twenty-two, and she had taken Linda under her wing. "Jimmy really thinks somebody's out to get you?" Carla asked her, walking through the leaves on the sidewalk.

(15) "He says it's because I got promoted and other people who've been in the company longer didn't." She shook her head. "But it's not my

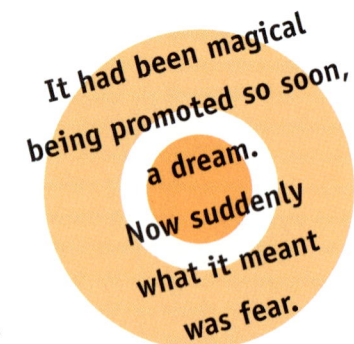

It had been magical being promoted so soon, a dream. Now suddenly what it meant was fear.

142 UNIT 4 | INVESTIGATIONS

fault. I can't help it if Maggie promoted me. I didn't walk over anybody to make it happen."

(16) "They don't care," Carla said, her face hard. Linda knew how unhappy Carla had been when she found out she hadn't been promoted, but it didn't seem to change her feelings for Linda. She squeezed Linda's shoulder. "Jimmy's watching out for you, and I am too," she said warmly. "We'll find out who it is and stop her. I don't want you worrying about it. You've got to concentrate on dancing now, more than ever."

(17) Linda didn't sleep well. It would be very easy for someone to put Vaseline on the stage. All the girls had Vaseline. They wore it on their lips, inside and out, during performance, so that when their mouth got dry, their lips wouldn't stick to their teeth, giving their stage smile a snaggle-toothed look. Before the show the stage was always swarming with dancers, warming up and practicing steps. Whoever had done it would most likely not have been noticed.

(18) In class the next morning, at the barre, she looked around at the thirty-six dancers in the company, twenty-four of them female. Everyone was rumpled, sloppy in baggy, unraveling leg warmers and old, falling-apart slippers. Which one was it?

(19) She could rule out the four principal girls—they were above her and had no reason to feel competitive or envious. The same was true of the four other soloists, who routinely had better parts than she did. She could rule out Carla, her best friend. That left the fourteen other girls in the corps. Which ones had been hoping to get promoted? Which one was desperate and cruel enough to try to injure her so she could take her place?

Which one was desperate and cruel enough to try to injure her so she could take her place?

(20) Dora and Eloise were reputed to be almost thirty. They were too old to have any hope of getting out of the corps now. A lot of the others were so young and fresh that they were still thrilled to be in the company at all—they had time and didn't need to do anything drastic to get ahead. So that left …

(21) Her eyes fixed on Helen, then quickly slipped away before Helen noticed, looking straight ahead now as she sank down into a *grande plié*. Helen was twenty-three. Helen was a good dancer. Helen didn't have a lot of friends. She was cool and inward. She lived with her boyfriend, a law student, and kept away from company parties. Was it her?

Unbalanced | SHORT STORY

AS YOU READ

(22) Before the performance that night, onstage behind the closed curtain, Linda and Jimmy went through some of their lifts and catches. Jimmy was a wonderful partner, attuned to her body, right on the music, always gentle, never rough like some of the less experienced boys. It was so reassuring to have a partner like Jimmy, since she was so small and your partner was in complete control when you were dancing.

(23) The applause for the conductor rose up, the signal to get off the stage just before curtain. In the wing she whispered to him, "Do you think it could be Helen?"

(24) He looked down at her—he was almost six feet, and she was five two—and furrowed his brow. "She *is* getting old to be in the corps, if she wants to have a real career," he murmured. "And she's good. If you weren't around, they probably would have promoted her. I'll ask Al if he noticed her doing anything unusual before the performance last night." He stepped away, muscles moving under his tight unitard.

(25) Al was the dancer-friendly stagehand, the one who seemed to regard all of them as his children. Linda waited nervously, pacing. She always had a certain amount of stage fright, but that was normal; it gave you the adrenaline to do your best. But now she had an extra and very real worry: What was going to happen tonight when she ran for that spot?

(26) Was there time to check it out? Why hadn't she thought of this before? They weren't supposed to be onstage now; in an instant the conductor would raise his baton and the curtain would go up. But she had a few seconds. She dashed onto the stage and over to the tape. She bent over and felt the stage with her hand. It was tacky, from all the rosin on the dancers' shoes. No Vaseline tonight, within a foot of the spot. And too late for anybody to put it there. She heard the deep *swoosh* of the curtain opening and rushed back into the wings just in time.

* ▶

(27) Jimmy was waiting for her as the music began. "It's clean," she said. "What did Al say?"

(28) Jimmy looked grim. "He saw Helen backstage with a jar of Vaseline last night, but he sees that all the time. He didn't notice her doing anything unusual onstage before the show. No help."

(29) They stepped aside as a line of corps girls ran out on stage, led by Helen.

(30) "Did you tell him what happened so he can watch out for it?" Linda whispered.

> She always had a certain amount of stage fright, but that was normal; it gave you the adrenaline to do your best.

(31) "No. I don't want to say anything until I'm sure. But I did ask him to keep his eye out for anybody bringing Vaseline onstage. He knew enough not to ask why." He touched her elbow comfortingly. "So you checked the spot? That was smart of you. I did too, before you came up. Don't worry, Lindy. I hate to see you look worried. Everything's going to be okay. We'll stop this. I'm here for you." He paused. "Maggie say anything to you about last night?"

(32) Maggie was Margaret Stephens, the artistic director, the boss. All the dancers called her Maggie behind her back. "No. She didn't. But she must have noticed and thought it was my fault. And just promoted me! I've got to make up for it tonight."

(33) The beginning of their dance went better tonight than last night—the nerves might be good for both of them. The hardest part—except for Linda's run to arabesque—was the lift in the slow section. Jimmy held her above him upside down, and then she had to slowly slide down his body to the floor. He lifted one arm and used the other hand to guide and support her from behind, unseen by the audience. She had to keep both hands up in the air, against the natural instinct to hold them down and in front of her to protect her in case she slipped—that was the beauty of the step, her hands in the air as she slithered down him headfirst toward the floor. Tonight it went so smoothly, no jerks, no fumbling, his invisible hand keeping her safe and steady. They had never done it that well before, even in rehearsal. No other partner she had ever danced with could have guided and protected her so well.

(34) Her torso made gentle contact with the floor, her hands still lifted. Then he pulled her up and she ran upstage right to start her hops on pointe.

(35) Thirty-two hops on one toe, moving diagonally across the stage, the other leg held in the air in front of her. The audience always went nuts over this step, but she had practiced it so many times that it didn't unnerve her anymore.

(36) And then the ribbons fell off—the ribbons that attached the shoe she was hopping on to her foot.

(37) Toe shoes came without ribbons. Dancers spent a lot of time sewing ribbons to the shoes. The shoe had to be part of the foot in order to

support you in the highly unnatural and difficult position of being on pointe. The ribbons were what made the shoe part of the foot, sewn to the shoe and then carefully and tightly tied around the ankle.

(38) And now the ribbons had come off. The shoe she was hopping in was not part of her foot, it was a floppy appendage, giving her no support. She tried to keep on hopping, but she could feel that in a matter of seconds her wobbling ankle would give way, it could fracture, she would fall—unless she just stopped in the middle of the step.

(39) But that was impossible. She couldn't do that, what would Maggie say—two mistakes onstage on two consecutive nights, just after being promoted. She couldn't stop the hops.

(40) But if she kept them up, she would be injured. Her heart was thudding, she was trembling, her ankle was screaming in pain, the shoe felt like it was about to fall off.

(41) And then Jimmy was beside her, lifting her gently, setting her down on both flat feet, nudging her into an easy *balancee* waltz step. The audience wouldn't know anything was wrong. Maggie would, but at least she hadn't been injured. And—thank God!—the run into arabesque, the one that was safe to do tonight, was on the foot with the good shoe. She did it perfectly.

(42) Jimmy had saved her again.

(43) Backstage after the bows she pulled off the shoe. "I *know* I sewed these on as good as ever!" she said. And the neat, tiny stitches were all there. She and Jimmy and Carla examined the ribbon just above the stitches, where it had broken.

(44) "Smooth," Carla murmured. "Smooth almost all the way across, and then ragged. She cut your ribbons, Lindy. Not enough so you would notice, but enough so they'd break when there was a lot of pressure on them."

(45) Now it was a struggle for Linda to hold back her tears. "What am I going to do? Something different every night! How do I know what to look for next, what to be afraid of?"

(46) For a long moment Jimmy's and Carla's eyes met. It was as though they were making a silent pact to protect her. "It won't happen again," Jimmy said. "We'll take care of that."

(47) They were older, they had been dancing longer, and they were going to protect her. At least she had that going for her.

(48) Maggie spoke to her after class the next morning, when the other dancers were leaving the studio. "Twice in two nights you almost fell onstage, Linda," Maggie said, shaking her head. "You're lucky Jimmy was fast enough to save you both times—if it weren't for him, you would have made a fool of yourself, and me. If anything else happens, you're never doing that part again. I hope it wasn't a mistake to promote you."

(49) "But … but it wasn't my fault," Linda couldn't keep from saying, though it sounded so babyish.

(50) "Whose fault could it have been then, may I ask?" Maggie said coldly. She was fat—though she was always telling the dancers *they* were too fat—and she wore a smocklike dress that barely reached her knees, to show off what she thought were her good legs.

(51) "I don't know who," Linda said. "But somebody put Vaseline on the stage the first night, and last night my ribbons were cut."

(52) Maggie lifted her chin angrily. "Things like that don't happen in my company," she said. "Don't blame your own mistakes on childish imaginary enemies. You do a perfect performance tonight, or else. Understood?" She turned and walked away.

(53) "We're going to confront Helen tonight, after the show," Carla told her backstage before the performance. She had just told Jimmy and Carla what Maggie had said—and how Maggie had noticed that Jimmy had saved her both times.

(54) "You probably shouldn't have said anything to her about the Vaseline and the ribbons before you had proof of who did it," Jimmy said kindly. "Maggie doesn't like to think about things like that."

(55) "But tonight we'll get Helen to admit," Carla reassured her again. "And then …" She ran her finger across her throat.

(56) She was more nervous about performing now than she had ever been in her life. She had checked her shoes, she had checked the spot for Vaseline, and both were fine. But something else could still happen, something she wasn't expecting, like both times before.

(57) She was trembling as they danced, but she was also determined. It wasn't as perfect as it had been at the beginning last night, but it went well enough. She began to hope that this time nothing would happen—maybe Helen had run out of tricks. And afterward they would confront her, and that would be the end of it.

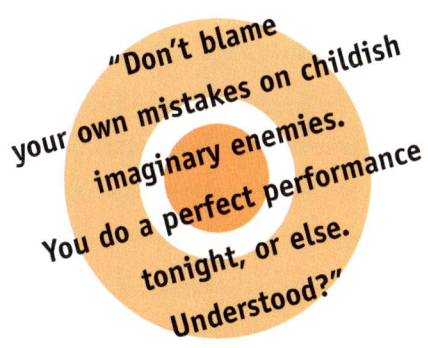

> "Don't blame your own mistakes on childish imaginary enemies. You do a perfect performance tonight, or else. Understood?"

AS YOU READ

(58) Jimmy lifted her. He positioned her tiny body upside down in front of his tall torso. He held his left hand in the air and with his right began easing her slowly down his body. She kept her hands lifted.

*▶ (59) And then he let go of her.

(60) Her head hit the floor, hard. She felt something snap at the top of her neck. And then she didn't feel anything else at all.

(61) The music stopped. Murmurs and cries of alarm reached her from the audience. Jimmy knew enough not to move her. The curtain came down. And she was thinking, *Nobody will ever believe he did this. He saved me two times before.*

(62) Dancers hovered around her until the stretcher came. Helen was especially kind and concerned, bringing a wet towel for her face, comforting her.

(63) As they bore her away in the stretcher, her head lying limply to one side, she saw Jimmy and Carla walk away together.

*▶ (64) Holding hands.

AFTER Reading

CHECKING FOR UNDERSTANDING

1. a) Number off the class from one to five. Each numbered group will be assigned one element.
   - One: plot
   - Two: language
   - Three: atmosphere
   - Four: characters
   - Five: setting

   b) Move into your numbered groups. In your group, define the element of the story you have been assigned (see The Reference Shelf, page 246). Find a partner within your group and compare the comments you have made about your element throughout the story

   c) In your group, explain how and why your element changes or stays the same from the start to the finish of the story. Be ready to represent your group's ideas.

PURPOSE / AUDIENCE / FORM

2. a) Imagine you are making this story into an after-school television show. Your **audience** will be mainly young people between the ages of nine and twelve. You want to give your audience a clue that Carla is involved. Choose one part of the story where you could use camera shots, angles, or movements to suggest Carla's involvement. Create a shooting **script** for that scene. You can use words or **thumbnail sketches** (see The Reference Shelf, page 285). One example has been done for you.

Character's Actions and Words	Camera Shot	Camera Angle	Camera Movement
"Somebody put Vaseline on the stage." Carla could look at Jimmy out of the corner of her eye and give a little smirk.	Carla is in the background. The shot is taken over Linda's shoulder from Jimmy's point of view.	Slightly worm's eye.	Zoom in slowly toward Carla.

b) Share your ideas with one other person.

STYLE AND CONVENTIONS

3. Short stories can be written from **first-person** or from **third-person** point of view. Using a Venn diagram like this one, show the similarities and differences between the two points of view.

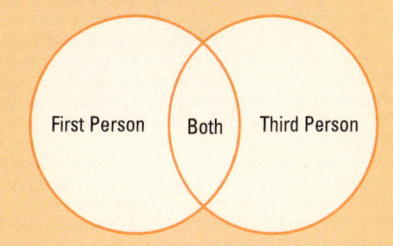

CRITICAL THINKING

4. a) Using events from the story, write the confession that either Carla or Jimmy makes to the police after they investigate Linda's accident.
   b) Trade your confession with a partner and ask questions (see The Reference Shelf, page 273) that will help your partner improve the confession.
   c) Revise your confession and perform it for the class.

drama

PURPOSE
- To explore the differences between **scripts** and **narratives**
- To defend a position with proofs

Guilt

STEVE BARLOW AND STEVE SKIDMORE

BEFORE Reading

1. As a class, create a word web (see The Reference Shelf, page 270) that lists everything you know about cloning and clones.

2. Create a chart like the one below in your notebook. You will use this chart while you are reading.

Judge Adam's Character Trait	What I Think of Him

Each time you see an asterisk (*), record one character trait the judge is showing and what you think of him at that point in the story.

Guilt: Characters
David, Jonathan, Judge Adam, Doctor Connor

A medical room. There are two chairs. David sits in one, Jonathan in the other. There is a machine beside them. Judge Adam comes in, followed by Doctor Connor.

JUDGE ADAM: So, these are the clones. Which is which?
DAVID: I am David.
JONATHAN: Are you? I thought I was David.
DAVID: Perhaps you are. Perhaps I'm Jonathan. I forget.
JUDGE ADAM: Doctor Connor?

(Doctor Connor holds up David's arm. There is a number "1" tattooed on the inside of his wrist.)

150 UNIT 4 | INVESTIGATIONS

DR CONNOR: This is David. He was the first.
JUDGE ADAM: It is foolish of you to waste time. You know why I'm here?
DAVID: To ask questions.
JONATHAN: To find the truth.
DAVID: If you can.
JUDGE ADAM: Oh, I shall, have no fear. Do you know who I am?
DAVID: You are Judge Adam.
JUDGE ADAM: Yes. And I am here to find out who murdered Chief Scientist Faber.

(The clones say nothing.)

JUDGE ADAM: The Chief Scientist was the man who created both of you. He was beaten to death in this laboratory. We know that one of you is guilty. Your fingerprints were found at the scene.
DAVID: *(To Jonathan)* It's an open and shut case.
JONATHAN: *(To David)* He's got us bang to rights.
DAVID: *(To Jonathan)* There's just one problem.

We're clones. Our fingerprints are identical.

JONATHAN: *(To David)* We're clones. Our fingerprints are identical.
DAVID & JONATHAN: *(Together)* So, which of us did it?

(They both turn to face Judge Adam.)

JUDGE ADAM: I'm not here to play games.
DAVID: That's a pity.
JONATHAN: We like games.
JUDGE ADAM: Do you think this is funny?
JONATHAN: Oh, no.
JUDGE ADAM: We're wasting time. *(To Doctor Connor)* Test them.
DR CONNOR: *(To both clones)* Roll up your sleeves.
DAVID: What for?
JUDGE ADAM: A DNA test. There was a struggle. We found traces of the murderer's DNA at the scene. Hair. Flesh beneath the victim's finger nails.

(David and Jonathan look at each other, then shrug and roll up their sleeves. Doctor Connor takes a sample of blood from David and tests it on the machine.)

JUDGE ADAM: Do I have to remind you what happens to a clone that malfunctions?
DAVID: We know.
JONATHAN: You made the law on clones.
DAVID: A clone is not a human being.
JONATHAN: A clone is made, not born.

AS YOU READ

DAVID: A clone has no rights.
JONATHAN: A clone that malfunctions …
DAVID: … is terminated.
DR CONNOR: This sample matches the DNA found at the scene of the crime.

(Dr Connor repeats the test with Jonathan.)

JUDGE ADAM: Very well. One of you killed Chief Scientist Faber. That is a malfunction.
DAVID: But that means only one of us has malfunctioned.
* ▶ **JUDGE ADAM:** No. Because the other is telling lies to protect the murderer. Lying is also a malfunction. I could have you both terminated.
JONATHAN: But then, you'd never know the truth.
DAVID: We've heard that the truth is important to you.
DR CONNOR: This sample also matches the DNA found at the scene.
JONATHAN: What does that prove?
JUDGE ADAM: It is further proof that one of you was the murderer. Or perhaps both of you.
DAVID: Why should we trust that machine?
JONATHAN: It could be wrong. Maybe it would say that *any* blood sample matched the one from the murder.
JUDGE ADAM: The machine does not make mistakes.
DAVID: Prove it. Test a sample of *your* DNA in the machine.
* ▶ **JUDGE ADAM:** *(Sighs)* Very well, if it will speed up the process.

(Doctor Connor takes a sample of blood from Judge Adam and tests it in the machine.)

JUDGE ADAM: Now, you have wasted enough of my time. This is my last case. I am due to retire tomorrow.
DAVID: You have never lost a case.
JONATHAN: You have always found out the truth. Everyone says so.
JUDGE ADAM: And I shall find out the truth here. For the last time, which of you killed Chief Scientist Faber?
DR CONNOR: Ah … sir …
JUDGE ADAM: What is it?
DR CONNOR: Your DNA sample, sir. It *does* match the one from the murder scene.
* ▶ **JUDGE ADAM:** What? That's impossible! The machine must be wrong.
DR CONNOR: The machine cannot be wrong, sir.
JUDGE ADAM: But I didn't kill Faber!
DAVID: Can you prove that?
JUDGE ADAM: This is insane! There's no way my DNA could match that from the murder scene. Unless …

DAVID: Unless your DNA is identical to ours.
JONATHAN: Unless we were cloned from you.
JUDGE ADAM: No! Impossible!
JONATHAN: You had to provide a DNA sample when you became a judge.
DAVID: Every government official does.
JONATHAN: Did you ever wonder what happened to it?
DAVID: It came to the lab, here. And Chief Scientist Faber must have thought, why not make clones of the famous Judge Adam?
JONATHAN: The great Judge Adam.
DAVID: The noble Judge Adam, who believes that clones are not human beings.
JONATHAN: That clones should have no rights.
JUDGE ADAM: This can't be true! You're lying.
JONATHAN: Don't act so surprised. You knew, didn't you?
JUDGE ADAM: No!
DAVID: You hate clones. And when you found out that Chief Scientist Faber had created clones from your own DNA …
JONATHAN: You were so angry, that you came here in secret and beat him to death.
JUDGE ADAM: This is madness!

Will you destroy your own flesh and blood?

DAVID: We asked for you to try this case.
JONATHAN: So judge this. Will you destroy your own flesh and blood?
DAVID: After all, we are your flesh and blood.
JONATHAN: We truly are. More than your sons could ever be.
DAVID: So who is guilty, father? Where does that guilt begin? With the man who created us?
JONATHAN: Or with the man whose DNA made us what we are?
DAVID: Which of us will you terminate?
JONATHAN: Or will you terminate both of us?
JUDGE ADAM: Stop this!
DAVID: But we forgot—you're a suspect now, too, aren't you, father?
JONATHAN: There is no way of telling which of the three of us killed Chief Scientist Faber.
DAVID: So who is guilty, father?
JONATHAN: Is it me?
DAVID: Is it me?
DAVID & JONATHAN: *(Together)* Is it you?

AFTER Reading

CHECKING FOR UNDERSTANDING

1. a) Look back at the chart you completed while you were reading. How did it make you pay attention to what you were reading?
   b) Talk about the following questions with your classmates: How did your **opinion** of the judge change over the course of the story? Do you think the writers wanted your opinion to change? Why or why not?

PURPOSE / AUDIENCE / FORM

2. a) Make a Venn diagram (see The Reference Shelf, page 270) that shows the differences and similarities between a **drama** and a short story (**narrative**). (See The Reference Shelf, page 246 and page 251.)
   b) With a partner, rewrite the beginning of this drama into the beginning of a short story. Write no more than four paragraphs. Include information and events up to the end of Jonathan's first speech.

STYLE AND CONVENTIONS

3. **Scan** the play to make up **script**-writing rules for the following:
   - showing when one character is talking
   - showing when a new character starts talking
   - giving **stage directions**

CRITICAL THINKING

4. a) Make a list of points that suggest the clones killed Chief Scientist Faber. Beside your list, make another list of points that suggest Judge Adam did it. Think about the motive that each side had to kill the scientist. Think about the evidence that has been gathered.
   b) Form four groups to represent the following:
   Group 1: lawyers who defend the clones
   Group 2: lawyers who defend Judge Adam
   Group 3: the clones
   Group 4: Judge Adam
   Create a fifth group who will act as members of the public who have learned about the case from the media. Your class will become the court. Group 4 and then group 3 will be questioned by groups 1, 2, and 5. Group 5 will decide who will be found innocent.

Unit 4 Activity

For your project for this unit, you will be evaluated using a rubric your teacher will discuss with you before you start. You will be expected to keep any process work and submit it with your final product.

Choose <u>one</u> of the following activities to complete. For each of the activities you will think about at least one of these questions.

> Question #1: What is the impact on other people when someone commits a crime?
> Question #2: How does the media affect our understanding of the law, crime, and investigations?
> Question #3: Why do people commit crime?

1. In a group of four, present a panel discussion on one aspect of crime and investigations. You will become one of the fictional characters or real people you have read about in this unit.

   Follow these steps:
   1) As a group, choose the question you want to answer.
   2) Individually, choose the person or character you would like to portray.
   3) Individually, gather six to eight pieces of information on your character or person's opinions in a chart like this one:

Character's Name:		
Selection title:		
Question:		
Character's opinion about the question	Proof from the selection	How does this proof help answer the question from the character's point of view?

   4) From your chart, choose three to five points you think your character would make in response to the question.
   5) Prepare the speech your character will make during the panel discussion.
   6) As a group, perform your panel discussion.

2. In a group of four, role-play a roving reporter who asks people on the street to answer two questions. The others in the group will portray characters or people from the selections you have read in this unit.

   Follow these steps:
   1) Decide who in the group will role-play the reporter and who will role-play characters from the selections. Decide which three characters will be portrayed.
   2) As a group, choose the two questions the reporter will ask.

   If you are a character from a selection
   3) Gather six to eight points in chart like the one from Activity 1, step 3.
   4) From your chart, choose three to five points you think your character would make in response to the question.

   If you are the reporter
   3) Find out which characters the other group members are portraying.
   4) Make a "know/want to know" chart to gather the information you will need to conduct your interviews.

Character's name	What I know about the character	What I want to know about the character

   5) As a group, write the script for the interviews.
   6) Present the role play to the class.

3. Individually, create a news broadcast. The broadcast will feature at least two news reports, each about one of the characters or people from the selections you have read in this unit. Each report will focus on a different question.

   Follow these steps:
   1) Choose the characters each report will focus on.
   2) Choose the questions each report will ask.
   3) Fill out a chart like this one:

Character's Name	
Selection Title	
How would the character respond to the question?	

   4) Use the information you have gathered in your chart to prepare your broadcast.
   5) Rehearse your broadcast.
   6) Perform the broadcast.

> 1 > 2 > 3 > 4 > **Unit 5** > 6

EMPOWERMENT

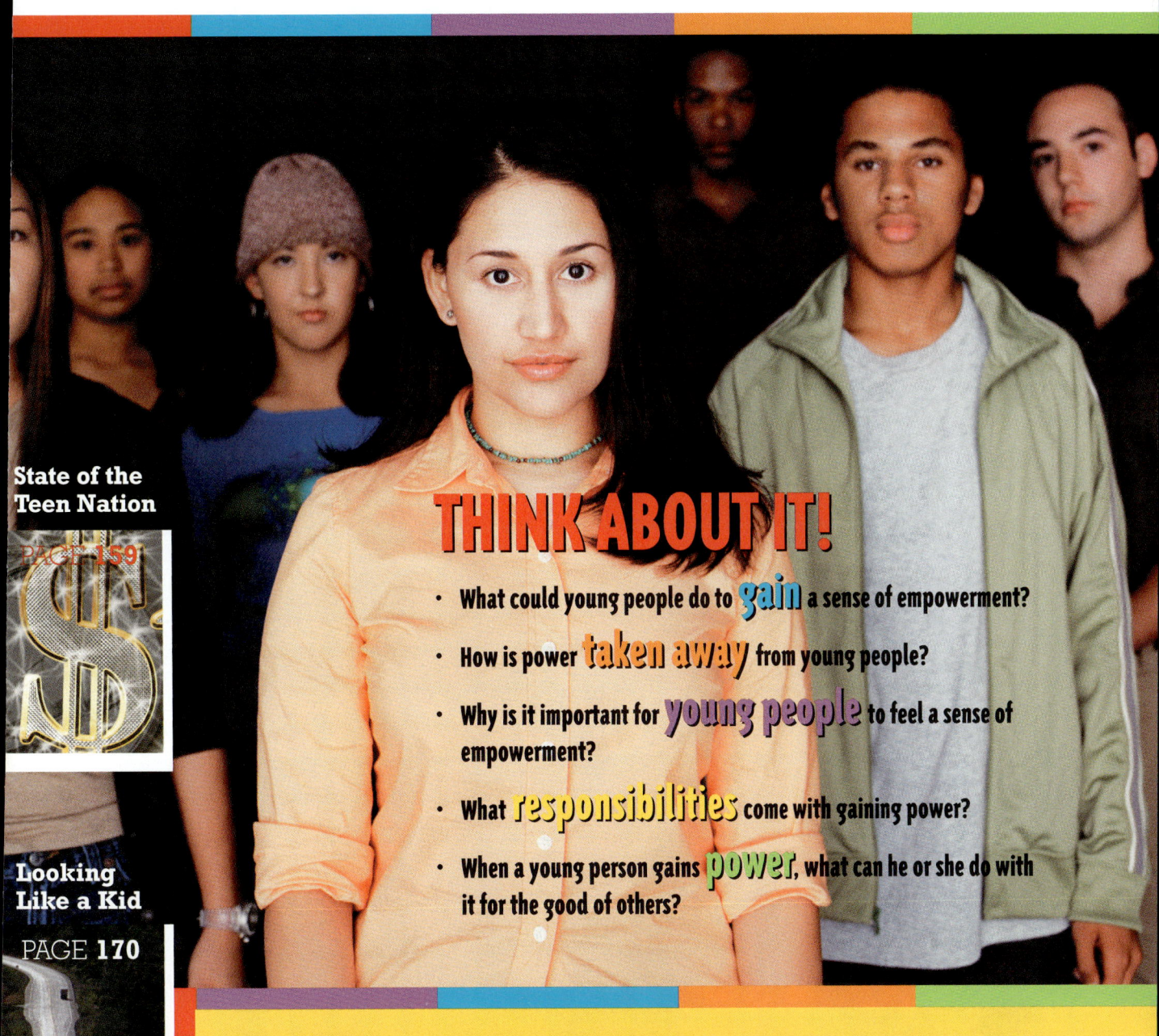

State of the Teen Nation
PAGE 159

Looking Like a Kid
PAGE 170

THINK ABOUT IT!

- What could young people do to **gain** a sense of empowerment?
- How is power **taken away** from young people?
- Why is it important for **young people** to feel a sense of empowerment?
- What **responsibilities** come with gaining power?
- When a young person gains **power**, what can he or she do with it for the good of others?

Vinny thought he heard a voice, small and distant. Yes. Something inside him, a tiny voice pleading, *Don't do it. Walk away. Just turn and go and walk back down.* "... I can't," Vinny whispered.

from "**The Ravine**," page 190

- **State of the Teen Nation** by *Youth Culture Research: Trendscan* (magazine article) ... 159

- **Helping Kids Make Sense of the Media** by *Terry Price* (newspaper article) ... 163

- **What Dreams May Come** by *Jody Roach* (poem) ... 168

- **Looking Like a Kid** by *André Mayer* with *Scott Colbourne* (magazine article) ... 170

- **What Are You Waiting For?** by *Jaclyn Law* (quiz) ... 175

Two Selections on Our Roots
- **slang tongue twist** by *Vera Wabegijig* (poem) ... 179
- **Mother Tongue** by *Susan Lee* (poem) ... 180

The Ravine by *Graham Salisbury* (short story) ... 182

Unit 5 Activity ... 193

UNIT 5

Empowerment

Look at the titles above. What do you think each title is about? How are the titles related to the theme of "empowerment"?

magazine article

PURPOSE
- To read and interpret a bar graph
- To compare yourself to teens in the survey

$tate of the Teen Nation

Youth Culture Research: Trendscan
FUEL MAGAZINE

BEFORE Reading

1. a) Survey your classmates to find answers to the following questions:
   - How much money do you have to spend each week?
   - Do you have a job?
   - Do you get an allowance?
   - How many days in a week do you buy your lunch?
   - How many days in a week do you bring your lunch from home, or go home for lunch?
   - Do you pay for your own entertainment?
   - Who pays for your clothes: your parents or you?

   b) Record your answers on the board.

(1) For the past five years, Youth Culture Group (the company that publishes *Fuel Magazine*), hits the phones to get the lowdown from 1,800 young Canadians between the ages of 12 to 24. We do our best to learn more about what makes your generation tick. You tell us everything from your opinion on the government programs to what your fave deodorant is. You even give us the inside scoop on what you like about reading magazines! Then, every spring, we feature some of our key findings from the survey. We've gotten such positive reader feedback that we've decided to feature Trendscan in every issue! Keep your peepers peeled for future highlights, so you can get connected to what other Canadian teens are thinking, feeling, and doing across our diverse country.

State of the Teen Nation | MAGAZINE ARTICLE   159

You're Large, Rich and in Demand, Baby!

(2) As you've probably figured out, teens are an increasingly hot commodity to marketers. Regular teens, like yourself, both drive and adopt fashion, music, and sports trends. You have your own TV channels, clothing brands, stores, magazines, websites, games, movies—the list is endless! There are teen-friendly hotels being built and even automobile companies are designing cars with the young consumer in mind. Many consumer products, especially technology, are being developed specifically for the teen market. But, why? What makes you so special? "The teen market has been growing in value," says Hollis Hopkins, director of research at Youth Culture, "not only because of the sheer number of teens with a considerable amount of disposable income, but because many of today's teens are the trendsetters and 'Early Style Adopters' of technology, fashion, music … they are not afraid to try new products and are incredibly brand-conscious and savvy."

(3) Yup, you read right, there are a whole lot of you. You are part of the second-largest generation of teens in Canada's history, behind your Baby Boomer parents. Youth (12- to 19-year-olds) represent a population of approximately 3.2 million in Canada.

You're Showing Us the Money!

(4) You guys are raking it in. At the time of our Trendscan survey in the fall of 2002, teens were bringing in an average of $156 per week per teen. That translates to approximately $25.5 billion dollars in personal income from the teen market.

(5) And your income levels have been increasing steadily over the last few years. Between the first Trendscan survey we conducted in 2000 and the last one in 2002, the average teen income has increased by 46 percent! Even your parents don't get raises like that!!! And speaking of parents, this is not money you're getting from Mom and Dad—about 80 percent of that money is earned on the job.

(6) "When people hear that teens are getting on average as much as $156 per week, they think, no way! It seems like an incredible amount of money and nothing like the $5 per week allowance many of us got for taking out the garbage or cleaning our room when we were younger," says Hopkins. But, the fact is, most kids simply don't get an allowance anymore. They ask their parents for $20 to go to a movie or $10 to get bus tickets or pocket money. "Then, busy Boomer parents give $5 to $10 for lunch every day—because, who has time to make and pack lunches every morning? Parents are essentially walking wallets for their kids," Hopkins adds.

You Know How to Work It!

(7) Teens are entering the workforce early in life, with 35 percent of you guys holding down some kind of employment. Thirty-three percent of teens have a part-time job, but there are some of you (eight percent) who are actually working full-time. (Not surprisingly, most full-time teen workers are 18 to 19 years old.) Younger teens (33 percent of 12- to 13-year-olds) are the most likely to be doing some kind of occasional job, such as babysitting.

(8) Now, these figures mean that more of you are trying to balance school and some kind of job. No wonder you're stressed! The summer is a different story, but it's your parents that are taking the vacation. They're giving two percent less to you in the summertime than they do during the school year. Guess they figure you're outta school and can get a job!

JENN AND LEE
"We both need a job desperately. We're **stressing about money** and our futures."

MAYA
"I'm **very** influential on my parents. My Mom asked me if she should buy the car she bought."

You've got THE POWER!

(9) But, it isn't enough that you are a large group and have a lot of disposable income. Oh no, you also wield the mighty sword of influence. You're a powerful group because of your size and wealth … and … insert drum roll here … you also have an incredible amount of influence over you parents!

JENNIFER, J.R. AND LILY

"I have a lot of influence over my parents. They **always** listen to me."

"We're **worried** about our careers."

"My parents **will be** paying for my post-secondary education, but I have no influence on them whatsoever."

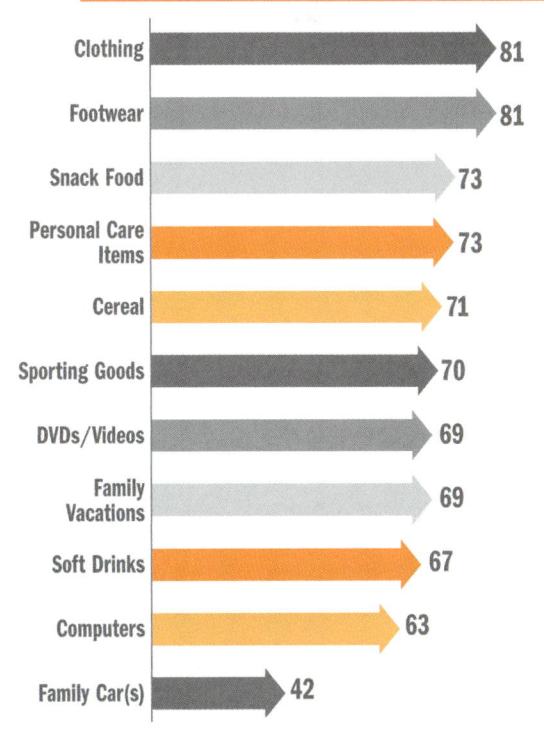

TEEN INFLUENCE ON PARENT PURCHASES:
(% HAVING A LOT/SOME INFLUENCE ON THE PURCHASE OF:)

Category	%
Clothing	81
Footwear	81
Snack Food	73
Personal Care Items	73
Cereal	71
Sporting Goods	70
DVDs/Videos	69
Family Vacations	69
Soft Drinks	67
Computers	63
Family Car(s)	42

SOURCE: Trendscan Wave III, Sample Size = 1806

State of the Teen Nation | MAGAZINE ARTICLE

AFTER Reading

CHECKING FOR UNDERSTANDING

1. a) **Reread** the article and make **jot notes** to answer the following questions:
   - What is the average amount of money a teen has per week?
   - Do most kids get an allowance?
   - Who pays for lunches every day?
   - What percentage of teens work?

   b) As a class, discuss your answers to part (a). Record the answers on the board. Using your survey results from the Before Reading activity and your answers to part (a), compare your class to the teens surveyed in the article. Discuss reasons why your class is similar to, or different from, those teens.

PURPOSE / AUDIENCE / FORM

2. a) This article contains a graph that shows the percentage of teens that can influence their parents' purchases. Make a list of the features of this graph that help you read and understand it.
   b) As a class, **brainstorm** other visual ways you could show this data. Form groups and have each group recreate the data in a new **format**.
   c) Post your visuals around the class.
   d) As a class, discuss which new visuals are easiest to read and understand. Decide which visual features work best to display the information.

STYLE AND CONVENTIONS

3. a) With a partner, **scan** a section of the article looking for words or phrases that appeal to teens. Record these words or phrases in your notebook.
   b) Discuss with another group why these words or phrases appeal to teens.

CRITICAL THINKING

4. a) As a class, review the features of a **summary** (see The Reference Shelf, page 260). Record the features on the board.
   b) Reread the article and make a jot-note list of the important **facts**.
   c) Individually, write a summary of this article. Refer to the list you made to help you determine the information that is important.
   d) Trade your summary with two other students and edit each other's work.
   e) Write a final draft of your summary. Be prepared to hand in your summary as well as your process work.

newspaper article

PURPOSE
- To understand that the media affect teens
- To find **facts** and form an **opinion**

Helping Kids Make Sense of the Media

BEFORE Reading

Draw a continuum line across the board that says "Never" on the left-hand side, "Sometimes" in the middle, and "Usually" on the right-hand side. Place yourself on the continuum in response to each of the statements below. One person should tally the results in terms of where the majority of students are standing.

- The violence in movies or television affects me in a negative way.
- I play video games that have a violent rating.
- I buy the kind of clothes I see people wearing in magazines, on television, or in the movies.
- I use the Internet unsupervised at home.
- My parents/guardians talk to me about what I see on television and in movies.

TERRY PRICE

AS YOU READ

Think about whether the article supports the question, "Should teens aged 13 to 16 be allowed unrestricted and unsupervised access to various media?"

(1) "What did you learn in school today?"

(2) It's a frequent parental question and, depending on the age and mood of your child, the response it elicits may range from a dismissive shrug to a torrent of enthusiasm.

(3) But these days, there may be a much more important question to ask: "What did you learn from *the media* today?"

(4) We've known for years that kids spend as much or more time interacting with television, video games and computers than they do in school. The lessons that teachers deliver are constantly scrutinized and tested for their relevance and effectiveness at building informed and responsible future citizens. The same can't be said, however, for the lessons learned from after school sitcoms, Internet immersion and weekend gaming.

(5)　　Yet the impact of this "alternative curriculum" is being felt in Canadian classrooms every day. Students who watch the news at home regularly show up at school with questions and concerns about everything from birth control to international terrorism. And educators frequently report witnessing kids imitating dangerous stunts and violent behaviour that they've seen on TV.

(6)　　So the Canadian Teachers' Federation decided to ask the second question itself. We commissioned Erin Research Inc. to conduct a national survey of more than 5,700 students across the country in Grades 3 to 10 to find out what media products they watch and play, and what they think about their experiences.

(7)　　The results, published in a report released today and titled *Kids' Take On Media*, are illuminating.

(8)　　**Choices**: Despite the amount of time students spend watching TV, surfing the Internet or playing video games, both boys and girls rate hanging out with their friends as their preferred activity—and it becomes more popular the older they get.

(9)　　Conversely, reading for pleasure decreases as students age.

(10)　　In a finding that should be of interest to TV producers and programmers, "exciting" and "funny" topped the list of attributes of the students' favourite TV programs, the majority of which don't contain violence. Excitement and competition were also key aspects of what attracted both girls and boys to video and computer games.

(11)　　**Violence**: However, the survey responses did reflect some stereotypical trends, with girls expressing a decided preference for non-violent TV shows, and being much less interested in games. In fact, violence in video and computer games seems to be one of the attractions for male students and by Grade 10, boys are choosing electronic entertainment as a preferred weekend activity at twice the rate of girls.

(12)　　One of the favorite games for boys across all grades surveyed is *Grand Theft Auto*, a game designed for mature audiences. The extreme violence in this game—it involves murder, bludgeoning and prostitution—raises questions about the definition of "mature," but more disturbing is the fact that the game is very popular among boys even in Grade 3.

(13)　　Hundreds of previous studies have documented the impact of media violence on

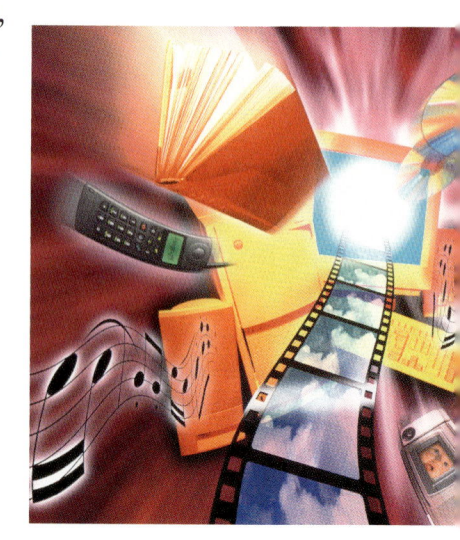

(14) society. We know that repeated exposure to violent depictions, whether real or fictionalized, increases people's fears, desensitizes them to the suffering of others, and encourages aggressive behaviour. And in the real world of schools, that sometimes translates into the kind of bullying and violence that can have a profound effect on students.

(14) In fact, in this survey, 51 per cent of Grade 7 to 10 kids said that they had personally witnessed the real life imitation of some "violent act" from a movie or TV show. What can we do about this?

(15) **Supervision**: The results from *Kids' Take On Media* suggest many children receive little or no parental restriction when it comes to their media consumption. Forty-eight per cent have their own TV, and 26 per cent have their own computer and Internet access.

> **51 per cent of Grade 7 to 10 kids said that they had personally witnessed the real life imitation of some "violent act" from a movie or TV show.**

(16) Nearly half of those surveyed say there are no household rules regarding which TV shows they can watch, and two-thirds report that no one dictates which video or computer games they can play, or for how long. Perhaps not surprisingly, kids who experience little supervision of their media use are more likely to regard media violence as benign.

(17) At the same time, many of the students recognized the value of adult restrictions. They identified TV programs such as *The Simpsons* and *South Park* that they felt should be off limits to younger children and believed that there should be tighter age restrictions on mature-rated computer and video games than on R-rated movies.

(18) **Opportunities:** The survey also found that children who do watch TV with their parents and are encouraged to talk about what they see are more aware of the potential impact of media violence, and more likely to have discussed the issues of racism and sexism. They also tend to spend more time doing homework, reading and participating in extra-curricular sports, clubs and hobbies.

(19) *Kids' Take On Media* demonstrates some of the ways children benefit from adult perspectives on the media's alternative lessons.

(20) It also shows that the older kids get, the more they themselves see the value of studying media in school.

(21)   Clearly, parents and teachers have a crucial role to play in helping young people to sort through the wealth of media that's available to them—much of it intended for older eyes and ears. We can and should provide context for the "lessons" being taught by the news, entertainment and advertising media.

(22)   This is why media literacy should not be considered a frill but a life skill we should be teaching our young people. In addition to the traditional literacies of reading and numeracy, students need to learn to understand and analyze some of the messages they see and hear in the media.

AFTER Reading

CHECKING FOR UNDERSTANDING

1. a) Copy the chart below into your notebook. With a partner, **reread** the article and find evidence that supports and opposes the question, "Should teens aged 13 to 16 be allowed unrestricted and unsupervised access to various media?"

Question: Should teens aged 13 to 16 be allowed unrestricted and unsupervised access to various media?	
Evidence That Supports:	Evidence That Opposes:
Your Opinion:	Reasons:

b) Share and discuss your chart with the class.

PURPOSE / AUDIENCE / FORM

2. As a class, decide on the **purpose** of the bolded words in the article. Next, decide how this feature helps you better understand what you are reading. Record your ideas on the board.

STYLE AND CONVENTIONS

3. a) Reread paragraphs 1 to 4 to find each of these words. Decide if each word is formal or informal and fill in a chart like the one below.

Word	Is it informal or formal language?
elicits (paragraph 2)	
dismissive (paragraph 2)	
torrent (paragraph 2)	
interacting (paragraph 4)	
scrutinized (paragraph 4)	
relevance (paragraph 4)	
immersion (paragraph 4)	

b) As a class, decide who the intended **audience** is for this article. Think about your answers to question #2 and #3(a). Give reasons to support your answers.

CRITICAL THINKING

4. a) In a group of four, you will be assigned one of these statements:
    - 13- to 16-year-olds should have supervised and restricted access to media.
    - 13- to 16-year-olds should have access to media that is within their target age group (for example, not rated 18A).
   b) Number off from one to four. Numbers one and two will agree with your group's statement. Numbers three and four will disagree with the statement.
   c) Number one will state one point to support the statement. Number three will add a point against the statement. Number two will add a point to support the statement. Number four will add a point against the statement. Number one will add a point to support the statement.
   d) Continue until all points have been said.
   e) Discuss how the focused discussion process worked with your group.

poem

What Dreams May Come

JODY ROACH, AGE 18
INUK

PURPOSE
- To see how something written in another language may not translate directly to English
- To compare your dreams for the future with the poet's experience of dreaming of her future

BEFORE Reading

1. Think about the dreams you have for your future in terms of
   - a job/career
   - family
   - relationships
   - money
   - where you'd like to live

   Record your dreams in **jot-note** form in your notebook.

2. When you are reading, how do you know if you must stop and look a word up in the dictionary, or if you can skip it and keep reading?

AS YOU READ
Stop when you are asked to, and answer the question.

What does "RCMP" stand for?

Where is Nunavut? Do you need to know?

People's dream for me
is for me to become a successful RCMP officer.
If this dream would come true,
then I would be one of the very first women in Nunavut
5   to be a female RCMP officer.

My father's dream for me
is just to follow my own dreams.
He wants me to enjoy life as much as possible
and to travel the world.

What is a midwife? Use the clues in the next lines to figure it out.

10   But I do have my own dreams.
I want to become a midwife here in Nunavut.
That is my dream.
I would be so proud to be able to deliver
a new and beautiful child into this world.

15   Dreams come in many different sizes.
It's totally up to you to make that dream come true.

168   UNIT 5 | EMPOWERMENT

AFTER Reading

CHECKING FOR UNDERSTANDING

1. In your own words, **retell** this poem to a partner. Help each other answer the questions in the margins. Check each other's answers for accuracy and make sure important points are not left out.

PURPOSE / AUDIENCE / FORM

2. This poem was written first in Inuktitut, the native language of the poet. As a class, decide how the title in Inuktitut looks different from the title in English. Suggest reasons why the titles appear different.

STYLE AND CONVENTIONS

3. The translation of the first sentence of this poem sounds a bit awkward in English. Decide if the grammar in the first sentence affects your understanding of what the poet means. Discuss with the class why you are still able to understand the poet, or why this grammar creates a problem for you.

CRITICAL THINKING

4. In this poem, the poet talks about how three different people or groups of people are influencing her future career choice. In your notebook, create a **graphic organizer** (see The Reference Shelf, page 269) that shows the various future career choices you have in mind, the people who have influenced you, why you want to seek those careers, and any obstacles that might be in the way of those careers. Post your graphic organizers around the room.

What Dreams May Come | POEM

magazine article

Looking Like a Kid

ANDRÉ MAYER WITH SCOTT COLBOURNE

PURPOSE
- To see that teens can reach their goals through hard work
- To research a topic and give an oral presentation

BEFORE Reading

The following things have been invented in the last century: fax machines, cell phones, the microwave, the television, automated teller machines (ATMs), the credit card, and pop in a can. On your own, rank the inventions in order of importance, from most important to least important. As a class, discuss your rankings. Remember to have reasons supporting your ranking choices.

AS YOU READ

Monitor if or when you stop understanding what you read. If you stop understanding the text, use a reading strategy you've learned to help. Record the strategy you used in your notebook.

(1) It's late March in Prince George, B.C., at the Central Interior Science Exhibition. Held on the picturesque campus of the University of Northern British Columbia, this is one of the biggest events of the year in the city of 72,000, luring the brightest kids from Grades 4 to 12 to enlighten judges with such projects as "Let-tuce Eat Healthy" and "Heavyweight Championships of Velcro." Science is cool these days, like the internet was in the late 1990s.

(2) Sixteen-year-old Gina Gallant's entry in the fair is called "PAR III: Paving Our Future." It chronicles her trials with a new kind of asphalt, PolyAggreRoad (PAR), which contains recycled plastic.

(3) A teenage boy swaggers over to Gina's table, friends in tow. "You're the one who made crackers that don't get soggy." Indeed, in Grade 5, Gina had invented crackers that remain crisp in soup (By adding a secret compound she self-referentially calls "substance G"). The invention had made all the local papers.

(4) "So where are they?" quips the lad.

(5) "You're so stupid," groans one of his pals. Gina indulges the boy's insolence, graciously explaining that the project he's looking at concerns asphalt.

UNIT 5 | EMPOWERMENT

(6) He points at her display and blurts, "Did you make that that?"

(7) "What?" she asks.

(8) "The laptop!"

(9) Everyone bursts out in laughter, though in Prince George, the consensus does seem to be that Gina Gallant can do anything.

(10) Her business card reads "Inventor," and for more than a decade, Gina has demonstrated a head for all sorts of clever ideas. Her dictum: "I like to fix problems." In Grade 1, she made paper by crushing broccoli, blending it with ripped-up used brown and white paper and water, and then flattening it into sheets with an iron. In 1999, her younger brother, Jordan, was hit by a car while riding his bike. According to the police, a helmet saved his life. This inspired Gina to devise headgear with light-emitting diodes that make cyclists more visible to drivers.

(11) All of which has made Gina a veritable celebrity. She has the ear of Mayor Colin Kinsley. Strangers stop the freckled teen for autographs when she's out and about (one guy even joked about selling it on eBay). Word around Kelly Road Secondary School is that Gina Gallant employs paid bodyguards. She says the rumour is bunk, but students give her a wide berth in the halls.

> **Her business card reads "Inventor," and for more than a decade, Gina has demonstrated a head for all sorts of clever ideas. Her dictum: "I like to fix problems."**

(12) Her work with asphalt was instigated by her dad, Ken Gallant, head lab technician at the nearby Husky Oil refinery. Through him, Gina began doing some unpaid work with asphalt for the company. Having learned that one-third of most landfills contain plastics, Gina pondered a way to reuse discarded bottles. She came up with a hypothesis: "Plastic is based on hydrocarbons and asphalt is based on hydrocarbons, therefore they'd have a natural bond."

(13) Months of experimentation at Husky followed, and Gina discovered that the ideal mix for PAR was 3% plastic (the kind used for laundry detergent bottles), 6% asphalt, and 91% aggregate (crushed stone and gravel). She pitched the idea of testing PAR to Mayor Kinsley, a family friend. He loved the plan, and designated a little strip of Cranbrook Hill Road, a rutted, winding thoroughfare north of downtown "PG," as

(14)   a test site. The project went ahead on Oct. 24, 2002. Husky Oil donated the asphalt, Calgary-based Ingenia Polymers the plastic. Columbia Bitulithic did the paving, and AMEC Earth and Environmental took core samples to test PAR's efficacy.

(14)   "The fact that this project in particular has been supported by a number of businesses in Prince George—that's a fair testament to what she's done," says Roy Warnock, vice-president of upgrading and refining at Husky Oil.

(15)   Gina expounded on her new paving material at a recent annual general meeting of the B.C. Roadbuilders & Heavy Construction Association. She remembers it as "harsh"—a high-pressure presentation for a teenager.

(16)   Ken Gallant isn't an outwardly emotional type, but you can tell that his daughter's anxieties weigh on him. Being the parent of an inventor-enfantrepreneur requires delicacy: Do you bridle the kid, in a well-intentioned effort to keep them grounded, or do you resign yourself to the role of anxious observer, hopeful that the pressure doesn't cause your child to flame out?

> "For me, I have to write my feelings down," she (Gina) says, alluding to a notebook of poetry. "Like, if I don't, then I end up freaking at somebody for no reason."

(17)   "As a parent, you worry," says Ken. "When you see it's getting heavy, you have to take them bowling."

(18)   Gina is acutely aware of the need for relief. "For me, I have to write my feelings down," she says, alluding to a notebook of poetry. "Like, if I don't, then I end up freaking at somebody for no reason." She also skateboards, and follows Eminem, Vin Diesel, Avril Lavigne, and the local minor-league hockey team, the Prince George Cougars. Gina's mom, Crystal, swears that when she listens to Cougars game on the radio, she can actually make out her daughter's hoots and cheers.

(19)   It's Crystal who drives us in the family minivan to see Gina's handiwork on Cranbrook Hill Road. The PAR was laid in an L-shaped patch, like a lopsided Band-Aid.

(20)   "I can't believe it," Crystal swoons. "The cracks are gone." When the PAR was laid, it incurred a few fissures, known in engineering jargon as "laying fatalities," the result of underlying layers of paving. Now, six

months after the PAR was laid, something subtle but miraculous has occurred: Some of the cracks have healed themselves.

(21) "I had a theory that it might happen," Gina later observes. "Like, if the plastic melts, it would weave in and out of the lane, causing better expansion and contraction through the four seasons. But that was still yet to be proven. And right now it's proving itself."

(22) This revelation is the crux of Gina's science-fair project. If PAR continues to exhibit its restorative qualities, it might become marketable. And Gina predicts PAR will exceed the typical 20-year lifespan of regular paving material—perhaps even double it. As yet, however, none of her innovations has earned her any money. She still relies on baby-sitting for her disposable income.

(23) "I never started [inventing] thinking that I was going to get rich," says Gina. "I went in it because it's fun. It's like opening a present, or a door when you don't know what's behind it. It's a mystery. It's the excitement of doing competitions and things. If I get awards and money and stuff like that, it's a bonus."

(24) To no one's surprise, "PAR III: Paving Our Future" cleans up at the 2003 Central Interior Science Exhibition. Not only does Gina take a gold medal, but she wins three sponsored awards, including one from the Society for Canadian Women in Science and Technology, which comes with a $100 prize.

(25) The next morning, as she orders her customary French vanilla cappuccino at Tim Horton's, the girl behind the counter congratulates her. Same thing happens with the girl buttering Gina's bagel. She gets recognized at Tim Horton's a lot. A while back, an elderly lady, a complete stranger, asked for an autograph.

(26) "That was when I still had my old signature," she says. She scribbles her name on a scrap of paper. "Now I have a pro signature." For the new look, first and last names, with the G doing double-duty. Instead of dotting the "i," Gina substitutes a tiny heart shape. It all looks grown-up but not too grown-up.

AFTER Reading

CHECKING FOR UNDERSTANDING:

1. a) Create a **graphic organizer** (see The Reference Shelf, page 269) that explains the following aspects of Gina's life: inventions, school, and friends/social activity
   b) Compare yourself to Gina in terms of school and friends/social activity. Decide how you are alike or different.

PURPOSE / AUDIENCE / FORM

2. **Scan** the text again to determine what type of writing this piece is (see The Reference Shelf, page 258). Record your answer in your notebook, and give at least two reasons to support your answer. Share your answer with the class.

STYLE AND CONVENTIONS

3. The titles of some of the Science Exhibition displays are: "Let-tuce Eat Healthy," "Heavyweight Championships of Velcro," and "PAR III: Paving Our Future." Each of these titles is a **pun**, which means it has a double meaning by making a "play" on words. For each title, describe the double meaning.

CRITICAL THINKING

4. a) Return to the inventions that you ranked in the Before Reading activity.
   b) With a partner, choose one of the inventions to research. Make up eight questions you would like to answer in your research.
   c) Conduct your research using print, human, and/or electronic resources. Make **jot notes** of the information. Remember to put your notes in your own words and write down the source(s) of your information.
   d) With your partner, combine and organize your research notes into at least three different categories. Give each category a **subtitle**. Write out each subtitle on a cue card, and record your information in sentence **format** under each subtitle.
   e) Prepare a three- to five-minute oral presentation that tells about what you've learned. Divide up the speaking parts so that each partner speaks for the same amount of time.
   f) Organize your research notes so that your teacher or another student looking at your project can understand your process.

quiz

PURPOSE
- To see that procrastination habits may keep students from reaching their full potential
- To review good work habits

What Are You Waiting For?

BEFORE Reading

As a class, define the word *procrastination*. Next, write a **brainstorm** list on the board of all the things you do to procrastinate. If possible, organize your list into categories.

When you've got a task to complete, do you take the long and leisurely route or do you cram everything into a couple of hours? Take our quiz and find out if your planning style is holding you back.

AS YOU READ

Keep track of your answer to each question in your notebook.

Quiz

1. **You must complete 40 hours of volunteer service before you can graduate from high school. How do you plan to finish your volunteering?**
   a) Wait until your senior year—40 hours isn't that long.
   b) Start scouting for volunteer opportunities now—who needs the stress of cramming all 40 hours into the last months of school?
   c) Volunteer every year during summer and Christmas holidays until you've done 40 hours.

2. **Your sister's birthday is coming up in a month and, for a gift, she's asked for a DVD that's difficult to find. What do you do?**
   a) Go to the video store as soon as possible and, if they don't have it in stock, ask them to order it for you.
   b) Wait until a few days before her birthday, try one or two stores, give up, and buy her something else.
   c) Give your sister the cash and tell her to buy it herself.

3. **You have a book report due in one week. How do you plan your time?**
   a) Start reading the book NOW! Then, spend a couple of days thinking about it before you start writing.
   b) Read a little bit every day and write the paper the night before the due date.
   c) Rent the movie that's based on the book the night before the deadline and use the flick as the basis for your assignment.

4. **When faced with an important decision, do you usually:**
   a) Put off making a choice for as long as you possibly can.
   b) Make a decision as fast as possible.
   c) Talk to your friends, ask for opinions, think it over, and then decide.

5. **Your parents are taking you on a trip to Europe in one month, and it's your responsibility to get your own passport. What do you do?**
   a) Pick up an application, fill it out, have photos taken, and drop it all off at the passport office immediately after they tell you about the trip.
   b) Spend a couple of weeks preparing the application before you take it to the passport office.
   c) Get so excited about the trip that you forget about the passport until a few days before the trip, then race to the passport office and pay a hefty extra fee for rush service.

6. **Have friends or family ever gotten upset with you because you show up late when you're meeting them?**
   a) All the time—oops, I'm supposed to be meeting someone right now!
   b) Sometimes, but I usually have a good reason.
   c) Never—you could set your watch by me!

7. **Your school is holding a formal dance in two months and you need a new outfit. What do you do?**
   a) Go shopping regularly with friends until you find the right outfit.
   b) Wait until the last minute and buy whatever is left or on sale.
   c) Visit a seamstress or tailor immediately and have something custom-made, leaving lots of time for alterations.

Tally up your scores here:

1. a) 0   b) 2   c) 1
2. a) 2   b) 1   c) 0
3. a) 2   b) 1   c) 0
4. a) 0   b) 0   c) 2

5. a) 2   b) 1   c) 0
6. a) 0   b) 1   c) 2
7. a) 1   b) 0   c) 2

TOTAL: _____ points

How Did You Do?

0–5 POINTS:
We all procrastinate now and then, but you've made it a way of life and you're probably stressed out! Don't put off tasks because you don't enjoy doing them—they'll be twice as unpleasant when you have to do them with deadlines looming, and who needs the added pressure? Overhaul your habits. Start by using a school planner to keep track of deadlines and appointments and work back from those dates (for example, if you have a big project due in two months, schedule time to work on it every week until then). Bonus: you'll find that your grades improve when your assignments aren't thrown together the night before they're due. If you think you need a little help to change your last-minute ways, talk to your guidance counsellor.

6–10 POINTS:
You've learned to prioritize and, as a result, you're usually on top of all the deadlines in your life. Now take it one step further: make a log of how you spend your days for one week and see if you can shave more time off your routine. Think about how you can make your study habits more efficient (so you can free up more time to do fun stuff!). Apply your good planning skills to all aspects of your life (family, friends, jobs), not just school, and you're well on your way to being a master planner.

11–14 POINTS:
You're a planning superstar! Everyone knows they can count on you to get the job done, on time. You know that a little bit of forethought goes a long way in reducing stress and helping you do your best work. Just remember that being too rushed to get things done can be a bad thing—make sure you take the time to find out all your options, ask the right questions, and give yourself time to think things over before making important decisions. Now, take a break from your busy schedule and do something fun—you've earned it!

AFTER Reading

CHECKING FOR UNDERSTANDING:

1. With a partner, discuss whether you agree or disagree with your quiz score rating, and give reasons to support your answer.

PURPOSE / AUDIENCE / FORM

2. As a class, discuss who you think the intended **audience** for this quiz is. Give reasons to support your answer.

STYLE AND CONVENTIONS

3. There are only three possible answers to each quiz question. As a class, discuss the positive and negative aspects of only having three options for an answer.

CRITICAL THINKING

4. a) As a class, make a list on the board of strategies anyone could use to stop (or do less) procrastinating and develop better work habits. You can use ideas you've heard before, check your student agenda book (if you have one), or refer back to the quiz.
   b) You are going to create a poster that will explain to others how to use a strategy to stop procrastinating. Your information on the poster needs to be written using procedure **format** (see The Reference Shelf, page 259). Choose a strategy from the board that you would like to explain.
   c) Make a rough outline of your poster. Remember to use clear **language** and procedure format.
   d) Trade your rough outline with two other students and edit for the following:
      - use of clear language
      - proper use of procedure format
      - visual appeal (use of colour, lettering, and layout)
   e) Consider the suggestions made by your peer editors. Create a final copy of your poster, and display it in your classroom.
   f) Read the posters in the classroom, and decide on one strategy that you will use to help you improve your work habits.

Our Roots

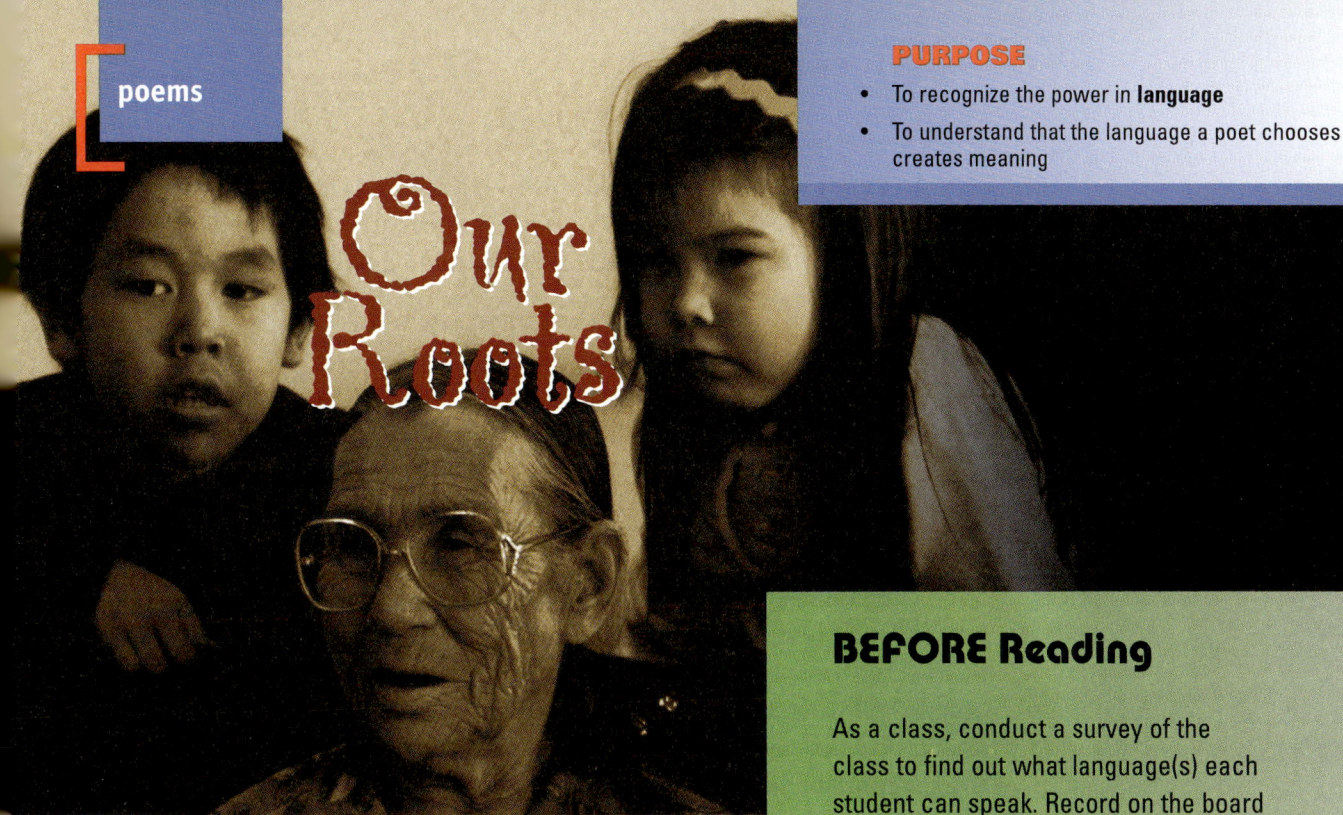

PURPOSE
- To recognize the power in **language**
- To understand that the language a poet chooses creates meaning

BEFORE Reading

As a class, conduct a survey of the class to find out what language(s) each student can speak. Record on the board languages spoken and/or understood. Together, discuss the advantages and disadvantages of knowing a language other than English.

slang tongue twist
VERA WABEGIJIG

brand extension on the rez:
hilfiger, adidas, nike, klein
hang loose on brown bodies,
from hats to pants even cool undies.

5   walking billboards is the latest trend
on our littered pow-wow grounds,
there's not enough long braids that dangle
or mother tongue words that tangle

skins dance,
10   but not to the pow-wow drum
it's a hip-hop beat from the ghetto streets.
here they break dance, a funky horse prance,
flip high fives and slam each other's mothers
and lay the beats to their blood brothers

15   brand extension reaches
bush rez and rezurbia,
a disillusion of community
where skin is against skin
in a neo-warrior gang clash

AS YOU READ

If you find a word you do not know, try to *infer* the meaning from the text. If the word is still a problem, ask another student for help or look up the word in the dictionary.

Mother Tongue
SUSAN LEE

My tongue was given to me by my mother
in the land of the Other
with this tongue
sounds, words, and meanings
5   were given and exchanged
My tongue,
freely floated, darted and
created
centred in my mouth
10   it created an ability
to be heard

When I came to this land
I was fed another tongue
and, bit by bit,
15   it filled my mouth
until I could not speak
I was forced to swallow
My mother tongue
to form new words
20   in order to be heard

My mother's tongue
swallowed, digested and
expelled
almost forgotten except
25   for the taste which lingers in my mouth

AFTER Reading

CHECKING FOR UNDERSTANDING

1. a) Write a **summary** in your own words of each poem.
   b) Form a group of three. Trade and read each other's summaries. Discuss the similarities and differences of your summaries. Edit your own summary by adding or taking away information.

PURPOSE / AUDIENCE / FORM

2. The **audience** for each poem is different, even though the **subjects** of the poems are similar. (See The Reference Shelf, page 251.) Work with a partner to complete this chart.

Audience Feature	"slang tongue twist"	Support	"Mother Tongue"	Support
Age				
Gender				
Music Style				
Clothing Style				
Level of Education				
Cultural Background				

STYLE AND CONVENTIONS

3. As a class, discuss whether the lack of periods in "Mother Tongue" and the lack of capital letters in "slang tongue twist" make the meaning of the poems confusing.

CRITICAL THINKING

4. a) **Theme** is the "big idea" of a story (see The Reference Shelf, page 251). As a class, **brainstorm** a list of subjects that each poem is about. Record the list on the board.
   b) With a partner, choose a subject from the board that you can write a theme statement on. Start by saying, "In the poem … the poet is saying…." Record your theme statement in your notebooks.
   c) Trade your theme statement with two other pairs of students and edit each other's work
   d) Discuss which poem you think does a better job of communicating the theme.

Our Roots | POEMS

short story

PURPOSE
- To see how peers can influence a decision
- To see that making a decision is not always easy

The Ravine

GRAHAM SALISBURY

BEFORE Reading

In your notebook, make a **jot-note** list of all the decisions (hard and easy ones) teenagers often have to make. Next, make a jot-note list of the people, things, or ideas that influence teens' decisions.

AS YOU READ

You will be asked several times to stop reading and ask a question or make a comment.

(1) When Vinny and three others dropped down into the ravine, they entered a jungle thick with tangled trees and rumors of what might have happened to the dead boy's body.

(2) The muddy trail was slick and, in places where it had fallen away, flat-out dangerous. The cool breeze that swept the Hawaiian hillside pastures above died early in the descent.

(3) There were four of them—Vinny; his best friend, Joe-Boy; Mo, who was afraid of nothing; and Joe-Boy's *haole* girlfriend, Starlene—all fifteen. It was a Tuesday in July, two weeks and a day after the boy had drowned. If, in fact, that's what had happened to him.

(4) Vinny slipped, and dropped his towel in the mud. He picked it up and tried to brush it off, but instead smeared the mud spot around until the towel resembled something someone's dog had slept on. "Tst," he said.

(5) Joe-Boy, hiking down just behind him, laughed. "Hey, Vinny, just think, that kid walked where you walking."

(6) "Shuddup," Vinny said.

(7) "You prob'ly stepping right where his foot was."

(8) Vinny moved to the edge of the trail, where the ravine fell through a twisted jungle of gnarly trees and underbrush to the stream far below.

(9) Joy-Boy laughed again. "You such a queen, Vinny. You know that?"

◀ Make a comment.

(10) Vinny could see Starlene and Mo farther ahead, their heads bobbing as they walked, both almost down to the pond where the boy had died.

(11) "Hey," Joe-Boy went on, "maybe you going be the one to find his body."

(12) "You don't cut it out, Joe-Boy, I going … I going …"

(13) "What, cry?"

(14) Vinny scowled. Sometimes Joe-Boy was a big fat babooze.

(15) They slid down the trail. Mud oozed between Vinny's toes. He grabbed at roots and branches to keep from falling. Mo and Starlene were out of sight now, the trail ahead having cut back.

(16) Joe-Boy said, "You going jump in the water and go down and your hand going touch his face, stuck under the rocks. *Ha ha ha … a ha ha ha!*"

◀ Make a comment. Joe-Boy reminds me of …

(17) Vinny winced. He didn't want to be here. It was too soon, way too soon. Two weeks and one day.

(18) He saw a footprint in the mud and stepped around it.

(19) The dead boy had jumped and had never come back up. Four search and rescue divers hunted for two days straight and never found him. Not a trace. Gave Vinny the creeps. It didn't make sense. The pond wasn't that big.

(20) He wondered why it didn't seem to bother anyone else. Maybe it did and they just didn't want to say.

(21) Butchie was the kid's name. Only fourteen.

(22) Fourteen.

(23) Two weeks and one day ago he was walking down this trail. Now nobody could find him.

(24) The jungle crushed in, reaching over the trail, and Vinny brushed leafy branches aside. The roar of the waterfall got louder, louder.

(25) Starlene said it was the goddess that took him, the one that lives in the stone down by the road. She did that every now and then, Starlene said, took somebody when she got lonely. Took him and kept him. Vinny had heard that legend before, but he'd never believed in it.

(26) Now he didn't know what he believed.

(27) The body had to be stuck down there. But still, four divers and they couldn't find it?

(28) Vinny decided he'd better believe in the legend. If he didn't, the goddess might get mad and send him bad luck. Or maybe take *him*, too.

◀ Make a comment. Vinny feels …

(29) *Stopstopstop! Don't think like that.*

The Ravine | SHORT STORY 183

AS YOU READ

(30)　"Come on," Joe-Boy said, nudging Vinny from behind. "Hurry it up."

(31)　Just then Starlene whooped, her voice bouncing around the walls of the ravine.

(32)　"Let's *go*," Joe-Boy said. "They there already."

(33)　Moments later, Vinny jumped up onto a large boulder at the edge of the pond. Starlene was swimming out in the brown water. It wasn't murky brown, but clean and clear to a depth of maybe three or four feet (about 1 m). Because of the waterfall you had to yell if you wanted to say something. The whole place smelled of mud and ginger and iron.

(34)　Starlene swam across to the waterfall on the far side of the pond and ducked under it, then climbed out and edged along the rock wall behind it, moving slowly, like a spider. Above, sun-sparkling stream water spilled over the lip of a one-hundred-foot (33-metre) drop.

(35)　Mo and Joe-Boy threw their towels onto the rocks and dove into the pond. Vinny watched, his muddy towel hooked around his neck. Reluctantly, he let it fall, then dove in after them.

Ask a question.

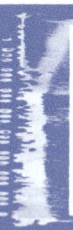

> **The cold mountain water tasted tangy. Was it because the boy's body was down there decomposing? He spit it out.**

(36)　The cold mountain water tasted tangy. Was it because the boy's body was down there decomposing? He spit it out.

(37)　He followed Joe-Boy and Mo to the waterfall and ducked under it. They climbed up onto the rock ledge, just as Starlene had done, then spidered their way over to where you could climb to a small ledge about fifteen feet (5 metres) up. They took their time because the hand and footholds were slimy with moss.

(38)　Starlene jumped first. Her shriek echoed off the rocky cliff, then died in the dense green jungle.

(39)　Mo jumped, then Joe-Boy, then Vinny.

(40)　The fifteen-foot (5-metre) ledge was not the problem.

(41)　It was the one above it, the one you had to work up to, the big one, where you had to take a deadly zigzag trail that climbed up and away from the waterfall, then cut back and forth to a foot-wide (30-cm wide) ledge something more like fifty feet (16.5 metres) up.

(42)　That was the problem.

(43)　That was where the boy had jumped from.

(44) Joe-Boy and Starlene swam out to the middle of the pond. Mo swam back under the waterfall and climbed once again to the fifteen-foot (5-metre) ledge.

(45) Vinny started to swim out toward Joe-Boy but stopped when he saw Starlene put her arms around him. She kissed him. They sank under for a long time, then came back up, still kissing.

(46) Joe-Boy saw Vinny looking and winked. "You like that, Vinny? Watch, I show you how." He kissed Starlene again.

(47) Vinny turned away and swam back over to the other side of the pond, where he'd first gotten in. His mother would kill him if she ever heard about where he'd come. After the boy drowned, or was taken by the goddess, or whatever happened to him, she said never to come to this pond again. Ever. It was off-limits. Permanently.

(48) But not his dad. He said, "You fall off a horse, you get back on, right? Or else you going be scared of it all your life."

(49) His mother scoffed and waved him off. "Don't listen to him, Vinny, listen to me. Don't go there. That pond is haunted." Which had made his dad laugh.

(50) But Vinny promised he'd stay away.

(51) But then Starlene and Joe-Boy said, "Come with us anyway. You let your mommy run your life, or what?" And Vinny said, "But what if I get caught?" And Joe-Boy said, "So?"

(52) Vinny mashed his lips. He was so weak. Couldn't even say no. But if he'd said, "I can't go, my mother won't like it," they would have laughed him right off the island. No, he had to go. No choice.

(53) So he'd come along, and so far it was fine. He'd even gone in the water. Everyone was happy. All he had to do now was wait it out and go home and hope his mother never heard about it.

(54) When he looked up, Starlene was gone.

(55) He glanced around the pond until he spotted her starting up the zigzag trail to the fifty-foot (16.5 metre) ledge. She was moving slowly, hanging on to roots and branches on the upside of the cliff. He couldn't believe she was going there. He wanted to yell, *Hey, Starlene, that's where he* died!

(56) But she already knew that.

(57) Mo jumped from the lower ledge, yelling, "Banzaiiii!" An explosion of coffee-colored water erupted when he hit.

(58) Joe-Boy swam over to where Starlene had gotten out. He waved to Vinny, grinning like a fool, then followed Starlene up the zigzag trail.

(59) Now Starlene was twenty-five, thirty feet (10 metres) up. Vinny watched her for a while, then lost sight of her when she slipped behind

AS YOU READ

◀ Make a comment. If I were Vinny, I would have ...

AS YOU READ

a wall of jungle that blocked his view. A few minutes later she popped back out, now almost at the top, where the trail ended, where there was nothing but mud and a few plants to grab on to if you slipped, plants that would rip right out of the ground, plants that wouldn't stop you if you fell, nothing but your screams between you and the rocks below.

(60) Vinny's stomach tingled just watching her. He couldn't imagine what it must feel like to be up there, especially if you were afraid of heights, like he was. *She has no fear,* Vinny thought, *no fear at all. Pleasepleaseplease, Starlene. I don't want to see you die.*

> **Vinny's stomach tingled just watching her. He couldn't imagine what it must feel like to be up there, especially if you were afraid of heights, like he was.**

(61) Starlene crept forward, making her way to the end of the trail, where the small ledge was.

(62) Joe-Boy popped out of the jungle behind her. He stopped, waiting for her to jump before going on.

(63) Vinny held his breath.

(64) Starlene, in her cutoff jeans and soaked T-shirt, stood perfectly still, her arms at her sides. Vinny suddenly felt like hugging her. Why, he couldn't tell. *Starlene, please.*

Ask a question. Why do you think Vinny wants to hug Starlene?

(65) She reached behind her and took a wide leaf from a plant, then eased down and scooped up a finger of mud. She made a brown cross on her forehead, then wiped her muddy fingers on her jeans.

(66) She waited.

(67) Was she thinking about the dead boy?

(68) She stuck the stem end of the leaf in her mouth, leaving the rest of it to hang out. When she jumped, the leaf would flap up and cover her nose and keep water from rushing into it. An old island trick.

(69) She jumped.

(70) Down, down.

(71) Almost in slow motion, it seemed at first, then faster and faster. She fell feetfirst, arms flapping to keep balance so she wouldn't land on her back, or stomach, which would probably almost kill her.

(72) Just before she hit, she crossed her arms over her chest and vanished within a small explosion of rusty water.

(73) Vinny stood, not breathing at all, praying.

(74) Ten seconds. Twenty, thirty …

(75) She came back up, laughing.

(76) *She shouldn't make fun that way*, Vinny thought. It was dangerous, disrespectful. It was asking for it.

(77) Vinny looked up when he heard Joe-Boy shout, "Hey, Vinny, watch how a man does it! Look!"

(78) Joe-Boy scooped up some mud and drew a stroke of lightning across his chest. When he jumped, he threw himself out, face and body parallel to the pond, his arms and legs spread out. *He's crazy*, Vinny thought, *absolutely insane*. At the last second, Joe-Boy folded into a ball and hit. *Ca-roomp!* He came up whooping and yelling, "*Wooo! So good!* Come on, Vinny, it's hot!"

(79) Vinny faked a laugh. He waved, shouting, "Naah, the water's too cold!"

> **Vinny knew then that he would have to jump. Jump, or never live it down.**

(80) Now Mo was heading up the zigzag trail—Mo, who hardly ever said a word and would do anything anyone ever challenged him to do. *Come on, Mo, not you, too.*

(81) Vinny knew then that he would have to jump.

(82) Jump, or never live it down.

(83) Mo jumped in the same way Joe-Boy had, man-style, splayed out in a suicide fall. He came up grinning.

(84) Starlene and Joe-Boy turned toward Vinny.

(85) Vinny got up and hiked around the edge of the pond, walking in the muddy shallows, looking at the school of small brown-backed fish near a ginger patch.

(86) Maybe they'd forget about him.

(87) Starlene torpedoed over, swimming underwater. Her body glittered in the small amount of sunlight that penetrated the trees around the rim of the ravine. When she came up, she broke the surface smoothly, gracefully, like a swan. Her blond hair sleeked back like river grass.

(88) She smiled a sweet smile. "Joe-Boy says you're afraid to jump. I didn't believe him. He's wrong, right?"

(89) Vinny said quickly, "Of course he's wrong. I just don't want to, that's all. The water's cold."

(90) "Naah, it's nice."

AS YOU READ

(91)   Vinny looked away. On the other side of the pond Joe-Boy and Mo were on the cliff behind the waterfall.

(92)   "Joe-Boy says your mom told you not to come here. Is that true?"

(93)   Vinny nodded. "Yeah. Stupid, but she thinks it's haunted."

(94)   "She's right."

(95)   "What?"

(96)   "That boy didn't die, Vinny. The stone goddess took him. He's in a good place right now. He's her prince."

(97)   Vinny scowled. He couldn't tell if Starlene was teasing him or if she really believed that. He said, "Yeah, prob'ly."

Make a comment. This reminds me of …

(98)   "Are you going to jump, or is Joe-Boy right?"

(99)   "Joe-Boy's an idiot. Sure I'm going to jump."

(100)   Starlene grinned, staring at Vinny a little too long. "He is an idiot, isn't he? But I love him."

(101)   "Yeah, well …"

(102)   "Go to it, big boy. I'll be watching."

(103)   Starlene sank down and swam out into the pond.

(104)   *Ca-ripes.*

(105)   Vinny ripped a hank of white ginger from the ginger patch and smelled it, and prayed he'd still be alive after the sun went down.

(106)   He took his time climbing the zigzag trail. When he got to the part where the jungle hid him from view, he stopped and smelled the ginger again. So sweet and alive it made Vinny wish for all he was worth that he was climbing out of the ravine right now, heading home.

(107)   But of course, there was no way he could do that.

(108)   Not before jumping.

(109)   He tossed the ginger onto the muddy trail and continued on. He slipped once or twice, maybe three times. He didn't keep track. He was too numb now, too caught up in the insane thing he was about to do. He'd never been this far up the trail before. Once he'd tried to go all the way, but couldn't. It made him dizzy.

(110)   When he stepped out and the jungle opened into a huge bowl where he could look down, way down, he could see their three heads in the water, heads with arms moving slowly to keep them

188 | UNIT 5 | EMPOWERMENT

afloat, and a few bright rays of sunlight pouring down onto them, and when he saw this, his stomach fluttered and rose. Something sour came up and he spit it out.

(111) It made him wobble to look down. He closed his eyes. His whole body trembled. The trail was no wider than the length of his foot. And it was wet and muddy from little rivulets of water that bled from the side of the cliff.

(112) The next few steps were the hardest he'd ever taken in his life. He tried not to look down, but he couldn't help it. His gaze was drawn there. He struggled to push back an urge to fly, just jump off and fly. He could almost see himself spiraling down like a glider, or a bird, or a leaf.

> **The next few steps were the hardest he'd ever taken in his life. He tried not to look down, but he couldn't help it. His gaze was drawn there.**

(113) His hands shook as if he were freezing. He wondered, *Had the dead boy felt this way?* Or had he felt brave, like Starlene or Joe-Boy, or Mo, who seemed to feel nothing.

(114) Somebody from below shouted, but Vinny couldn't make it out over the waterfall, roaring down just feet beyond the ledge where he would soon be standing, cascading past so close its mist dampened the air he breathed.

(115) *The dead boy had just come to the ravine to have fun*, Vinny thought. Just a regular kid like himself, come to swim and be with his friends, then go home and eat macaroni and cheese and watch TV, maybe play with his dog or wander around after dark.

(116) But he'd done none of that.

(117) Where was he?

(118) Inch by inch Vinny made it to the ledge. He stood, swaying slightly, the tips of his toes one small movement from the precipice.

(119) Far below, Joe-Boy waved his arm back and forth. It was dreamy to see—back and forth, back and forth. He looked so small down there.

(120) For a moment Vinny's mind went blank, as if he were in some trance, some dream where he could so easily lean out and fall, and think or feel nothing.

AS YOU READ

Ask a question. Who or what is the voice in Vinny's head?

(121) A breeze picked up and moved the trees on the ridgeline, but not a breath of it reached the fifty-foot (16.5-metre) ledge.

(122) Vinny thought he heard a voice, small and distant. Yes. Something inside him, a tiny voice pleading, *Don't do it. Walk away. Just turn and go and walk back down.*

(123) "... I can't," Vinny whispered.

(124) *You can, you can, you can. Walk back down.*

(125) Vinny waited.

(126) And waited.

(127) Joe-Boy yelled, then Starlene, both of them waving.

(128) Then something very strange happened.

(129) Vinny felt at peace. Completely and totally calm and at peace. He had not made up his mind about jumping. But something else inside him had.

(130) Thoughts and feeling swarmed, stinging him: *Jump! Jump! Jump! Jump!*

(131) But deep inside, where the peace was, where his mind wasn't, he would not jump. He would walk back down.

(132) *No! No, no, no!*

(133) Vinny eased down and fingered up some mud and made a cross on his chest, big and bold. He grabbed a leaf, stuck it in his mouth. *Be calm, be calm. Don't look down.*

(134) After a long pause he spit the leaf out and rubbed the cross to a blur.

(135) They walked out of the ravine in silence, Starlene, Joe-Boy, and Mo far ahead of him. They hadn't said a word since he'd come down off the trail. He knew what they were thinking. He knew, he knew, he knew.

(136) At the same time the peace was still there. He had no idea what it was. But he prayed it wouldn't leave him now, prayed it wouldn't go away, would never go away, because in there, in that place where the peace was, it didn't matter what they thought.

(137) Vinny emerged from the ravine into a brilliance that surprised him. Joe-Boy, Starlene, and Mo were now almost down to the road.

(138) Vinny breathed deeply, and looked up and out over the island. He saw, from there, a land that rolled away like honey, easing down a descent of rich Kikuyu grass pastureland, flowing from there over vast highlands of brown and green, then, finally, falling massively to the coast and flat blue sea.

(139) He'd never seen anything like it.

(140) Had it always been here? This view of the island?

(141) He stared and stared, then sat, taking it in.

(142) He'd never seen anything to beautiful in all his life.

AFTER Reading

CHECKING FOR UNDERSTANDING

1. Vinny has to make several decisions in this story. He must decide whether to
   - believe if the dead boy drowned or was taken by the goddess
   - swim in the pond when they arrive
   - go with his friends, since his mother told him to stay away from the pond
   - climb the ledge to jump
   - jump

   a) Complete the graphic organizer below in your notebook for each decision.
   b) As a class, discuss whether Vinny made the right decisions.

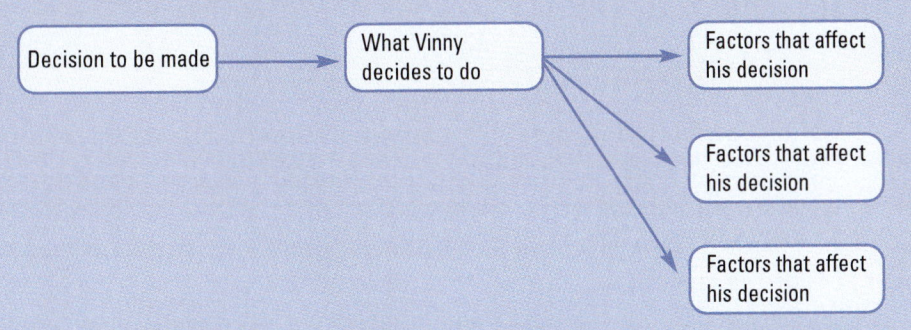

   Decision to be made → What Vinny decides to do → Factors that affect his decision / Factors that affect his decision / Factors that affect his decision

PURPOSE / AUDIENCE / FORM

2. a) The events of this story are not told in **chronological order**, which is the order in which events occur in real time. Copy the chart below into your notebook. **Reread** or **scan** the story to refresh your memory.

List of Events	Number the Events in Chronological Order	Number the Events in Story Order
Vinny, Joe-Boy, Mo, and Starlene walk to the pond.		
Vinny doesn't jump.		
Butchie drowns.		
Vinny's mom says don't go to the pond.		
Vinny returns home.		

b) As a class, discuss your answers and decide why an author might tell a story using chronological order, and not using chronological order.

The Ravine | SHORT STORY | 191

STYLE AND CONVENTIONS

3. The author of this story uses **italics** to show what is going on in Vinny's head. Sometimes, the author puts these thinking words together without spaces or punctuation between them. Examples are in paragraph 29 (*"Stopstopstop!"*) and paragraph 60 (*"Pleasepleaseplease."*). As a class, discuss the meaning and feelings that the author is trying to create by putting the thinking words together in this way. Rank the effect of writing in this way as follows:
   - helpful to my understanding of the story
   - a little distracting, but I understand
   - confusing

CRITICAL THINKING

4. Write a **supported opinion** piece based on Vinny's final decision. Your topic is: "Did Vinny do the right thing by not jumping?"
   a) Make a **T-chart** in your notebook that has "Yes" on the left and "No" on the right. Fill in as many ideas as you can about why you think Vinny did or didn't do the right thing.
   b) Decide on your **opinion**. Remember, you must choose "yes" or "no"; you can't choose "maybe" or "sort of."
   c) Write a rough draft of your supported opinion piece (see The Reference Shelf, page 259).
   d) As a class, **brainstorm** specific things you should look for while editing this supported opinion piece. Edit your own work, then trade your writing with two other students. Edit each other's work.
   e) Create a final copy of your supported opinion piece. Remember to keep all your process work.
   f) Divide the class into two groups based on whether they agreed or disagreed with Vinny's decision. Each person will choose their best argument and read the paragraph out loud to the class.

UNIT 5 Activity

For your project for this unit, you will be evaluated using a rubric your teacher will discuss with you before you start. You will be expected to keep any process work and submit it with your final product.

Choose one of the following activities to complete.

1. One of the focus questions for this unit is "What could young people do to gain a sense of empowerment?"
    a) Choose three selections from this unit. For each, develop a **theme** statement that explains what the author is saying about how young people can gain a sense of empowerment. (See The Reference Shelf, page 251.) Record your theme statements in your notebook.
    b) From each selection, find at least three examples, quotes, or ideas that support your theme statement for that selection. Record these supports in your notebook.
    c) Using the theme statements and supports, create a visual display that shows your ideas. You could design a poster, a brochure, or a web page. If you have another suggestion on how you could visually represent your ideas, check with your teacher before your start. Remember to use easy-to-read print and a clear and eye-catching layout.
    d) Hand in your visual display and your process work.

2. Some of the selections in this unit focus on the idea that with power comes responsibility. Form a group of three students. You will create a play that shows this idea. Your writing must be original, and you cannot borrow ideas from the stories you read. You will be evaluated separately for this assignment.
    a) **Brainstorm** and record ideas about ways that young people can gain power. Choose one idea as the topic for your play.
    b) Brainstorm all the jobs (besides the **script**) that will need to be done to create your play (for example, props, costumes, writing and revision, and sound effects). Divide up the jobs evenly and put each person's name beside their job. Keep this list to hand in later.
    c) Write a rough draft of your play, and edit your work. Each person in the group should be responsible for writing the words of at least one character in the play.
    d) Now, write a polished version of your play. Practise your play until it is smooth and polished. Perform your play for an **audience**. Remember that you are being evaluated separately.
    e) Hand in the polished copy of your play, all your process work, and the list of the jobs you brainstormed for part (b).

3. Choose three selections from this unit that you feel you can relate to. Write a minimum of three paragraphs in reflection **format** (see The Reference Shelf, page 261) that explain how or why you relate to each piece. You should include references to power or loss of power. You can also talk about how you have had experiences similar to those of the characters, and you can talk about how your own **outcomes** of the experiences were similar to or different from those of the characters. Edit your own work for clarity, spelling, grammar, and sentence structure. Create a polished draft to hand in, along with all your process work.

4. Choose four selections from this unit that you think focus on how gaining power can help an individual or a group of people. Copy and complete the chart below. You can complete the chart in **jot-note** form.

Title of Piece from This Unit	What power is gained?	How is the person helped by the power?	How could this power help a group of people?	How could this power hurt others?	What needs to happen to prevent this power from hurting others?

Hand in your finished chart.

> 1 > 2 > 3 > 4 > 5 > **Unit 6**

TECH TALK

If u were messaging on your cell would u key in words properly or use the shortcuts like most ppl do? Abbreviated sentences have become the standard lingo for communication through electronic means.

from "Tech Talk," page 207

PAGE 197
Future World

PAGE 201
Bubble Chamber

Think About It

- How does technology affect the way we live?
- How has technology affected the way we communicate with each other?

Future World by Michael N. Smith (magazine article) ... 197

🍁 **Bubble Chamber** by Tania Nepveu (short story) ... 201

🍁 **New Science of Body Measurement** (graphic text) ... 205

Two Selections on Text Messaging

🍁 **Tech Talk** by Ted Kritsonis (magazine article) ... 207

Zits by Jerry Scott and Jim Borgman (cartoon) ... 209

🍁 **Best Advice: Handle with Care** (graphic text) ... 211

The Toynbee Convector by Ray Bradbury (adapted by Ray Zone and Chuck Roblin) (graphic fiction) ... 214

Unit 6 Activity ... 229

UNIT 6
Tech Talk

> The online boom of the last 10 years has created an entirely different way for people to express themselves, though the real key to it all is the speed that goes with it.
> *from "Tech Talk," page 208*

[magazine article]

PURPOSE
- Create your own view of the future

FUTURE WORLD

MICHAEL N. SMITH

BEFORE Reading

1. a) Choose one of the following people to role-play: teenager, senior citizen, farmer, business person, environmentalist, homeless person, a person who believes the world should slow down, inventor, scientist.

   b) As a class, name five pieces of technology invented recently that we use regularly.

   c) Think to yourself about how the person you have chosen to role-play would feel about these pieces of technology. When you have had time to think about the technology from that person's point of view, find one other person in the class who is role-playing the same person and talk about your reactions to technology.

   d) As a class, discuss why different people have different feelings about technology.

AS YOU READ

As you read this article make a list of three pieces of technology that the person you chose to be would love or hate. Beside each item explain why.

(1) It's Friday morning in the year 2025, and you're running late. You got distracted watching the **music video** that was playing in the corner of your bathroom mirror while you were brushing your teeth. How will you get to your office at Mega Giga Industries on time?

(2) A quick check of your **Internet-connected refrigerator magnet** tells you your train—which travels at speeds up to 250 miles an hour as it **electromagnetically hovers** above its guide track—is a bit behind schedule, too. So you decide to drive your environmentally friendly **hydrogen fuel cell car** instead—or rather, let your car drive you. It's programmed to know the way, and it will get you there without speeding, getting lost, or crashing.

Future World | MAGAZINE ARTICLE   197

(3) Settling into your office chair, which **changes colour** to match what you're wearing, you pick up yesterday morning's newspaper. Printed on **reusable electronic paper,** it instantly rewrites itself with today's headlines. Now it's time for your big meeting. Uh-oh! You've left your handwritten notes at home. No problem. The **digital ink pen** you used has stored an electronic copy of what you wrote.

(4) Your **wristwatch videophone** suddenly rings. Your best friend's face pops up on the organic light-emitting diode screen asking what you're doing this weekend. Will you slap on your **3-D contact lenses** and play virtual soccer with the U.S. Olympic team? No, no, your friend says, you *so* have to take the **new nanotube elevator** (made of microscopic fibers many times stronger than steel) 60,000 miles into space.

(5) Could this scene really take place in just a couple of decades? The researchers who are currently developing all this stuff think so. Read further to check out more cool gadgets that may be as common in 20 years as cell phones and DVD players are today.

MUST-HAVE TV
GADGET: Roll-up television
WHY IT'S COOL: Built from a glowing plastic compound, these flexible, thin-as-paper TVs roll up like window shades.
BONUS: Heavy, bulky, big-screen TVs? They're so 2004. These lightweight, retractable monitors free up valuable space and allow you to carry your TV and watch it just about anywhere.
THE NEXT STEP: Roll-up maps for soldiers that display satellite footage of enemy troop movements

SAY, THAT SHIRT SMELLS GOOD ON YOU.
GADGET: Aroma clothes
WHY IT'S COOL: Electronic sensors woven into the fabric of these garments react to changes in your body and deliver scents from a perfume reservoir hidden in the lining.
BONUS: Feeling stressed? An aroma shirt will release the calming fragrance of vanilla from its collar to ease your mind. Dragging a bit later in the day? These clothes know—and emit the energy-enhancing aroma of geraniums to jump-start your brain.
THE NEXT STEP: Pajamas that "scent" you to sleep and hospital gowns that monitor your vital signs

LIVE, IN CONCERT, 'BOT-182!

GADGET: Entertainment robot

WHY IT'S COOL: It's a talking, singing, dancing mechanical party animal.

BONUS: This awesome automaton can recognize your friends, carry on a conversation, sing a heartfelt love song, and with its 38 flexible joints, tirelessly dance till dawn—all the while checking out audience reaction and adjusting its "act" to please the crowd.

THE NEXT STEP: Robots that serve as personal assistants, coordinating all your electronic gizmos to make sure your food, clothing, home, and car are kept just the way you like them

> **THE NEXT STEP:** Robots that serve as personal assistants, coordinating all your electronic gizmos to make sure your food, clothing, home, and car are kept just the way you like them

HEY, THAT PICTURE OF UNCLE ED JUST BURPED.

GADGET: Talking portraits

WHY IT'S COOL: You can get your pictures to spring to life with full motion and sound.

BONUS: Point a camera that's implanted with an imaging chip at the specially framed family portrait on your mantel. See each person in the picture wave hello or spin his or her life story—just like those wizardly portraits in the Harry Potter books.

THE NEXT STEP: Business cards that play a video about your company and billboards that show movie trailers as you drive by

DON'T PLAY IT BY EAR, PLAY IT BY FOOT.

GADGET: Cyber dance shoes

WHY IT'S COOL: This fancy footwear lets the dancer control the music instead of the other way around.

BONUS: Sensors in the insole and on the sides of these hip-hopping high-tops "feel" your movements, then "describe" them to an interactive sound system. The system cues the style, tempo, and volume of the music as you dance.

THE NEXT STEP: A cyber jogging sneaker that creates and plays music according to the pace and intensity of your running

AFTER Reading

CHECKING FOR UNDERSTANDING

1. a) Pair up with the person who shared your role in the Before Reading activity. With that person, compare the lists and explanations you made as you were reading.
   b) Choose one of the gadgets you agreed your character would hate and, in role as that character, have a discussion about why you dislike the technology. Be prepared to repeat your discussion for the class.

PURPOSE / AUDIENCE / FORM

2. Based on the way the writer describes the technology of the future, is he **biased** for or against new technology? Copy out three examples of words, phrases, or sentences that show his bias.

STYLE AND CONVENTIONS

3. a) An article has its own set of "conventions" or rules to follow. **Reread** the article and make a list of conventions for magazine articles. Use your general knowledge, the conclusions you can draw from the **graphic features**, as well as information you have learned from others classes and this book.
   b) Find a partner and talk about your list. Be sure that you can prove your ideas by referring back to the article. You may be asked to read your list to the class.

CRITICAL THINKING

4. a) With a partner, **brainstorm** a list of gadgets you'd like to see invented. One example might be a machine that allows you to be in two places at once.
   b) Choose one of your ideas and develop it, using the subtitles from the article ("Why It's Cool," "Bonus," "The Next Step").
   c) Be prepared to present your new gadget to the class.

short story

PURPOSE
- To **visualize** what you read
- To understand story elements

BUBBLE CHAMBER
Tania Nepveu

> TEST SUBJECT #GEH00792

> FINAL DNA TEST COMMENCING

> RELEASE GAS

> VENTILATING CHAMBER

BEFORE Reading

Predicting is a strategy used by readers, especially when the reading is difficult. Look at the graphic that accompanies the text and at the title. As a class, **brainstorm**, on the board, some predictions you can make about this story.

AS YOU READ

You will be asked several times to make a prediction. Write your predictions in your notebook. After you have read the story, look back at your predictions to see which ones were accurate.

(1) The clear dome rose around and over him. Lights shone dimly above casting just enough for him to see.

(2) To his left, computer screens flashed on and off, scrolling information. The rhythmic beep of a cardiovascular monitor and the soft drone of human speech echoed faintly on metallic walls.

(3) He could feel wires attached to him. To his temples, his chest, his back. The head of a needle was embedded in his skin, securely taped to the back of his hand.

(4) He shivered. There was no source of warmth here. He crouched and curled his tail about him. It was a curious thing, really, he looked human, yet wasn't. Well … not anymore.

◀ Predict: What happened in the past to this creature to make him look part human and part animal?

Bubble Chamber | SHORT STORY 201

AS YOU READ

(5) They'd done this to him. They had taken away his identity. His name was GEH00792.

(6) That's what They called him. They, with Their white coats, monotone voices and Their constant tests and evaluations. He was nothing more than an experiment to Them. That's all he was. A genetically engineered mutation.

(7) They'd done this to him.

(8) But there was one thing They hadn't managed to do. He still had feelings, he still had a soul.

(9) Unconsciously he scratched at the tattooed bar code on his left arm. It identified him as a lab rat, an experiment. He loathed Them for it.

(10) A woman wearing a white lab coat approached. She held a clipboard in one hand, pens tucked carefully in her breast pocket. Her other hand was hidden in her hip pocket.

Predict: Who are "They" and what experiments were they doing to him?

> **But there was one thing They hadn't managed to do. He still had feelings, he still had a soul.**

(11) She scrutinized him with a bored expression. He bared his teeth at her, his tail uncoiling itself and starting to twitch behind him.

(12) Early on in his training, he'd overheard them talking about the changes the animal DNA had made to his body. He'd grown a tail that was slim and puffed out at the end. His ears and eye colour had also changed. He remembered his eyes being darker in colour … not the sickly yellowish-green they were now. From the discussions he'd overheard, these were all characteristics of the DNA they'd injected into his system. He knew he had barely survived the change.

(13) No one knew They were doing this to children and no one would find out.

(14) He vaguely remembered his days before the lab. War had ravaged the land. No one knew who had won. The only difference in his life was that the bombing stopped. Now he knew it had been Them.

(15) The faces of other kids flickered in his mind. Some had disappeared long before he had. Children vanished regularly but no one cared about homeless, orphaned children. Now he knew why they were disappearing. Because They wanted them for illegal genetic research.

(16) He was one of the unfortunates, and, according to Their conversations, the only one to survive to date. His DNA had been crossed with that of a feline. Drugs, gases, and chemical solutions had been tested on him time and time again. He had been trained like an elite soldier.

Predict: What is he going to do about his situation?

(17) He knew They thought They were close to achieving Their goal: The making of the perfect weapon. But he also knew They had already succeeded.

(18) "Begin the final testing," the woman said and retreated into the all-encompassing darkness.

(19) He flinched at the voice of his tormenter. Again he scratched at the bar code. His tail continued twitching nervously back and forth. The beep of the cardio monitor sped its rhythm.

(20) A vaporous blue gas hissed from grates on the floor. This was it. If he made it look real, maybe he could escape. They weren't the only ones who had been observing. He knew what to do. He inhaled the vapor, choked and went down on all fours, the blue cloud slowly asphyxiating him. Desperately, he threw himself at the clear walls of the dome, trying to scratch and claw his way out. The humans stepped back. It was working … it must be looking real.

(21) Eventually he succumbed to the gas, slumping to the cold floor. The heart monitor cried out in stress skipping a few beats, slowing then stopping.

(22) "Ventilate the chamber immediately! Get him out of there and revived." Even in his comatose state he was aware of what was happening around him. People scrambled to obey the orders. He closed his eyes.

(23) Lab workers rushed in, picked him up and put him on a stretcher, already at work at revitalizing his heart. He felt Them working on him as They wheeled him out of the dome and he grinned at his cleverness.

(24) Yes, They had definitely taught him too much.

(25) His heart started beating again. That's when he sprang.

AS YOU READ

◀ Predict: What is the perfect weapon?

◀ Predict: What does he do?

◀ Predict: What happens next?

AFTER Reading

CHECKING FOR UNDERSTANDING

1. a) Reread the prediction notes you made.
   b) As a class, compare each of your predictions. Talk about what made you decide on those predictions.
   c) This story doesn't have an ending. As a class, make up some possible endings.

PURPOSE / AUDIENCE / FORM

2. The short story has a specific form: **introduction, conflict, rising action, climax, falling action (denouement)** (see The Reference Shelf, page 248). Match one event in the story to each of these parts of a short story.

STYLE AND CONVENTIONS

3. Rewrite one to three paragraphs from the story in **first person** from the boy's point of view. Decide which point of view you think is more effective (**third person** or first person), and be prepared to read your revised portion to the class.

CRITICAL THINKING

4. a) As a class, review the following terms (see The Reference Shelf, page 287):
      Camera shots: extreme close-up; close-up; medium shot; long shot
      Camera angles: bird's eye; worm's eye; eye level
      Camera movement: zoom in; zoom out; pan
   b) With a partner, use a chart like the one below to create a shooting **script** for one scene.
   c) Write your shooting script and post it in the classroom. Be prepared to talk about your scene in front of the class.

Scene Description:

Camera angle(s)	Camera shot(s)	Camera movement	Script
1.			
2.			
3.			

graphic text

PURPOSE
- To study vocabulary associated with technology
- To study **graphic features** of a text

New Science of Body Measurement

Computer systems using biometrics—the scanning and measuring of a person's physical or behavioral characteristics—are being developed to help security and law enforcement agencies verify people's identities. A look at some of those technologies:

BEFORE Reading

Draw a chart like the one below for each of these terms: *biometrics, digital, database*.

Definition	What is its **root word(s)**?
Examples	Where did it come from?

Fill in as much information as you can. As you read, add to your charts. What helped you find more information as you read?

■ **Face Recognition**
Video camera and scanner locate several dozen features, such as tops of eyes, corners of mouth, sides of face and calculates their relationship; in most cases, only one person has exactly that combination of features

■ **Digital Fingerprinting**
Person puts thumb on a small scanner; computer translates the thumbprint's curving ridges into a numerical code

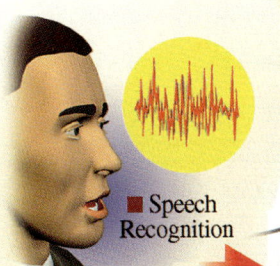

■ **Speech Recognition**
Person speaks into a microphone; voice recorded and its sound characteristics analyzed and recorded

Central Database

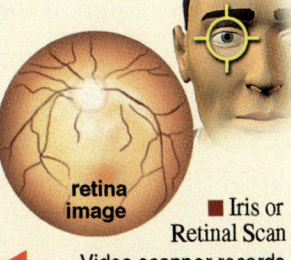

■ **Iris or Retinal Scan**
Video scanner records unique patterns in colored ring surrounding pupil (iris) or blood vessels in back of eyeball (retina)

retina image

An essential part of any biometric data system
Scanners send information to a secure central computer, where it is analyzed and compared to similar information on file

Practical applications
Currently used in some prisons and airports; other proposed uses:
■ Criminal investigation
■ Distribution of government benefits
■ ATM and computer passwords
■ Automobile security keys

■ **Hand Geometry**
Hand is put on flat surface with fingers resting against raised bumps; video system records finger length, width and curvature

■ **Handwriting**
Person writes signature on digital tablet; computer analyzes structure of letters and words and other characteristics of writing

© 2001 KRT   Source: Biometric Consortium, Michigan State University
Graphic: John W. Fleming, Detroit Free Press

AFTER Reading

CHECKING FOR UNDERSTANDING

1. Form a group of four. Assign one of the words that you defined in the Before Reading section to each person in your group Starting with *database* and moving clockwise, each person will share his or her chart with the group. Group members will compare what they have in their charts to the presenter's chart, and will help fill in any section left incomplete. When all the groups are finished, the class will discuss any problems groups had with their words.

PURPOSE / AUDIENCE / FORM

2. List four graphic features that make finding information in this text easier, and explain how they do so.

STYLE AND CONVENTIONS

3. Refer to the section in the Reference Shelf on **tone** and formality (page 262). **Reread** "New Science of Body Measurement" and describe the tone of this graphic piece. Defend your choice.

CRITICAL THINKING

4. *Biometric* is made up of two **root words**: *bio* and *metric.* List as many words or phrases as you can think of that have grown from *bio.* Do the same for *metric.* As a class, combine your lists and post them in the classroom.

magazine article + cartoon

PURPOSE
- To learn some strategies for dealing with new words
- To write a **summary** of the article

BEFORE Reading

1. Survey your class to find out how many people own a cell phone, and to find out how many people use the text messaging feature. Record the results.

2. In a group of four, make a list of all the text messaging short forms and emoticons you can think of. In a **round robin**, each group will give one answer without repeating anything that has been said before. Add to your own list as you hear answers you did not include with your group.

TECH TALK

TED KRITSONIS

AS YOU READ

You will see underlined words that may be new to you. Write them in your notebook. In the same sentence as each of these words, you will find another word or phrase that gives you a clue to the meaning of the underlined word. Find that clue and write it next to its matching word in your notebook.

(1)   If u were messaging on your cell would u key in words properly or use the shortcuts like most ppl do? Abbreviated sentences have become the standard lingo for communication through electronic means. Whether it's chatting online or sending text messages, cryptic acronyms like TTYL (talk to you later) and BTW (by the way) are changing the way people approach the English language in its written form.

(2)   It may be far too early to tell whether or not the dotcom era will bring any real change to the language as we know it, but when considering all the ways the language has <u>evolved</u> over the last 100 years, we might be using TTYL and BTW a lot more often than we think.

Text Messaging | MAGAZINE ARTICLE + CARTOON | 207

(3)   In 1904, it would have been hard to imagine saying "would've" instead of "would have" or "doesn't" instead of "does not" but we do it without hesitation now. Why? Because language evolves to reflect changes in society as a whole. It's probably safe to say that we're not as uptight as people might've been back then, and a century is plenty of time for a society and language to evolve. The examples are all over the place.

(4)   Take slang in the spoken word, for instance. It's been around forever, and has even taken on a life of its own in some circles: ebonics or "Black English" is considered a dialect of sorts in the United States, thanks to inner-city black youth and music like rap and hip-hop.

(5)   On the written side of things, businessmen and politicians set the standard for <u>acronyms</u> long ago by shortening their company and political party names so they could make it easier for customers and voters to remember them. And if it weren't for the Internet and wireless communication, "tech talk" would probably never be what it is today. Throughout this <u>linguistic</u> evolution, technology has played a key role in driving language to new heights. <u>Cryptanalysts</u> during the Second World War (1939–1945) used the world's first computers to decipher German and Japanese military codes, and militaries all over the world soon started using their own languages of cryptic **euphemisms** and acronyms to operate with security, which continues to this day through computers and telecommunications.

(6)   The online boom of the last 10 years has created an entirely different way for people to express themselves, though the real key to it all is the speed that goes with it. The convenience of shortening words or combining them with acronyms is hard to resist, especially in a day and age where time is a precious resource.

… if it weren't for the Internet and wireless communication, "tech talk" would probably never be what it is today.

(7)   Using shortened variations of words and phrases has been an accepted practice for a long time, and that won't change anytime soon. But it's the technology of the online era that has provided the

speed with which to do it easily and efficiently. What might take 20 seconds to type with normal spelling could take as little as eight seconds with all the right abbreviations. That's a significant drop, and amounts to a lot of time saved when you start factoring in the minutes, hours, and days we spend text-messaging and e-mailing.

(8) Still, regardless of how powerful online lingo has become, it hasn't penetrated all circles yet, and may have a tough time doing so. The business world may have helped give acronyms the role they have today, but would a corporation endorse the practice of using LMK (let me know) and LOL (laugh out loud) in the near future? It may also take some time before résumés, formal letters, and newspapers use tech talk, which seems hypocritical, like a big double-standard, after all, what makes ASAP any different from LMK, or OK any better than U 2?

(9) The ? is, will ppl run with it, or will it B just another fad 2 4get about?

Zits By Jerry Scott and Jim Borgman

AFTER Reading

CHECKING FOR UNDERSTANDING

1. a) With a partner, compare the clues you found for each word. Be prepared to explain to the class how the clues helped you understand the new words.
   b) Writers use many ways to help readers figure out the meanings of words. Record these techniques in your notebook: including a definition, giving an example, including a word or phrase that is similar or means the same, adding information. Which techniques did the writer of "Tech Talk" use? Be prepared to discuss your decisions with the class.

PURPOSE / AUDIENCE / FORM

2. What is some evidence that proves both "Tech Talk" and *Zits* were written for students your age? Consider the content, language, and the visual features You can use a chart to organize your thoughts.

STYLE AND CONVENTIONS

3. Quotation marks (" ") are used for two different purposes in the article, "Tech Talk." Look at each time quotation marks are used, and make up two rules for using quotation marks in your own writing. As a class, discuss the rules. Add any other rules you know about quotation mark.

CRITICAL THINKING

4. This article could be shortened to about four main points. Individually, make **jot notes** of those four points in your notebook. With a partner, compare your points and make a final list of four points you can agree upon. Together, write a topic sentence that could be used to introduce your four points, write your four points in sentences, and add a concluding sentence to form a complete summary paragraph. Be prepared to read your summary to the class.

5. Inferred messages are not directly stated but are suggested by the author. What inferred messages about our modern society are suggested by both the *Zits* cartoon and "Tech Talk"?

graphic text

PURPOSE
- To understand the reasons for using **graphic features** and specific **text features**
- To create a **narrative** from a non-fiction text

Best Advice: Handle with Care

BEFORE Reading

As a class, discuss and then record the types of features (for example, bolding) that help you know what information you should pay attention to when you read an informational text.

Treat the plastic discs well and they will last longer, if not forever. Here are some handling tips for CDs and DVDs, including the recordable versions, from the U.S. National Institute of Standards and Technology.

Do:
- Handle discs by the outer edge or the center hole. Your fingerprints may be acidic enough to damage the disc.
- Use a felt-tip permanent marker to mark the label side of a CD. The marker should be water-based or alcohol-based. In general, these will be labeled "nontoxic." Stronger solvents may eat through the thin protective layer to the data.
- Keep discs clean. Wipe with cotton fabric in a straight line from the centre of the disc toward the outer edge. If you wipe in a circle, any scratches may follow the tracks of the CD, rendering them unreadable. Use CD/DVD-cleaning detergent, isopropyl alcohol, or methanol, to remove stubborn dirt.

AS YOU READ

*Make **jot notes** of the features of this text that help you notice the information that is important.*

Best Advice: Handle with Care | GRAPHIC TEXT

- Return discs to their plastic cases immediately after use.
- Store discs upright (book style) in their cases.
- Store discs in a cool, dry, dark place with clean air.
- Open a recordable disc package only when you are ready to record.
- Check the disc surface before recording.

Do not:
- Touch the surface of the disc.
- Bend the disc. This may cause the layers to separate.
- Use adhesive labels, since they can warp the disc or unbalance it.
- Expose discs to extreme heat or high humidity. Don't leave them in sun-warmed cars, for instance.
- Expose discs to extremely rapid temperature or humidity changes.
- Expose recordable discs to prolonged sunlight or other sources of ultraviolet light.

For CDs especially:
- Don't scratch the label side of the disc. It's more sensitive than the transparent side.
- Don't use a pen, pencil, or fine-tip marker to write on the disc.
- Don't try to peel off or reposition a label. Again, you risk unbalancing the disc.

The fragile lives of compact discs

User care is the best way to keep CDs functioning, but even the best kept CD can eventually rot and lose data.

Label
This thin layer stands between the elements and a CD's fragile data. Even minor scratches can eliminate vital data.

Lacquer
If this sheer seal is poorly applied or damaged, oxygen and moisture can reach the data layer.

Data layer
This ultra-thin layer of aluminum is subject to oxidation.

Cover
The laser passes through this thick, clear plastic before reading the data. Deep scratches or warping can disrupt the laser making the data unreadable

SOURCE: National Institute of Standards and Technology   Dan DeLorenzo·AP

AFTER Reading

CHECKING FOR UNDERSTANDING

1. a) As a class, compile the list of text features you found in this text. Add any that you were missing to your own list.
   b) How does the diagram of the CD add to your understanding of the text?

PURPOSE / AUDIENCE / FORM

2. a) On a scale of 1 to 3, rate this text, where 1 means "It's really hard," 2 means "It's kind of easy," and 3 means "Anyone could read this!"
   b) **Scan** the text and pick out three words that might be hard to understand. Write the words and a definition for each one in your notebook. Compare the lists you have made with a partner. Choose any words you had in common and write them and their definitions on the board. Write a sentence for each word that will help you remember its meaning.
   c) As a class, talk about who the intended **audience** is for this text. Scan the text to find the information that helped you make your decision.

STYLE AND CONVENTIONS

3. When should you use a **bulleted list** and when should you write in paragraphs? Make up a rule to use in the class for future writing and note taking that you do.

CRITICAL THINKING

4. a) International symbols are designed so that a person does not have to be able to read to understand them. Make a list of international symbols that you see on a regular basis.
   b) Create **thumbnail sketches** (see The Reference Shelf, page 285) for international symbols that could represent three items on the "Do" list and three items on the "Do not" list from the "Best Advice" text. Have a partner look at your sketches and determine whether or not they could be easily understood by someone who is not familiar with how to handle a CD. Create final sketches for these symbols. Post them around the classroom.

Best Advice: Handle with Care | GRAPHIC TEXT | 213

graphic fiction

PURPOSE
- To **predict** what will happen in the story
- To study camera shots and angles in the story

THE TOYNBEE CONVECTOR

original story written by **RAY BRADBURY**

adapted by **RAY ZONE** and **CHUCK ROBLIN**

GOOD! GREAT! BRAVO FOR ME!

ROGER SHUMWAY REVVED THE ROTOR AND DRIFTED HIS DRAGONFLY SUPER-6 HELICOPTER ON THE SUMMER SKY SOUTH TOWARD La JOLLA. HE WAS ON HIS WAY TO AN INCREDIBLE MEETING.

BEFORE Reading

1. Look closely at the title page of this **comic**. From this panel, determine when this story is taking place. Support your answer with specific references to the illustration.

2. Read this **visual story** aloud as if it were a play. You will need four readers:
   - Roger Shumway
   - Craig Bennet Stiles
   - the narrator
   - someone to make the sound effects and voices from television (one person)

As you are reading, think about how the artist indicates when someone or something other than the main characters are speaking.

214 UNIT 6 | TECH TALK

AS YOU READ

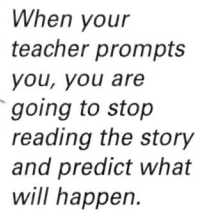

When your teacher prompts you, you are going to stop reading the story and predict what will happen.

THE OLD MAN WAS WAITING FOR HIM ON THE ROOF OF THE TIME LAMASERY.

I CAN'T BELIEVE I'M HERE.

YOU ARE, AND NONE TOO SOON!

CRAIG BENNET STILES, FOR ALL HIS 130 YEARS WAS NOT OLD. HIS BRIGHT FACE WAS A SUNBURST CELEBRATING ITS OWN BIRTHDAY.

The Toynbee Convector | GRAPHIC FICTION | 215

WHAT DO YOU WANT TO KNOW?
FIRST, WHY HAVE YOU BROKEN SILENCE AFTER A HUNDRED YEARS?
SECOND, WHY TO ME? THIRD, WHAT'S THE BIG ANNOUNCEMENT YOU'RE GOING TO MAKE THIS AFTERNOON?
THOSE ARE THE QUESTIONS.
YOU SHALL HAVE YOUR ANSWERS. ALL IN GOOD... TIME.

The Toynbee Convector | GRAPHIC FICTION

"YOU REPORTED BY SATELLITE FEED AROUND THE WORLD TO BILLIONS OF VIEWERS AND TOLD THEM THEIR FUTURE."
WE MADE IT! WE DID IT!
THE FUTURE IS OURS!
WE REBUILT THE CITIES.
WE STOPPED THE WARS.
WE COLONIZED THE MOON, MOVED ON TO MARS, THEN ALPHA CENTAURI.
WE CURED CANCER AND STOPPED DEATH.

THE WORLD WENT MAD WITH JOY. IT RAN TO MEET AND MAKE THAT FUTURE.

NOW THE TIME MACHINE IS ON EXHIBIT. DIGNITARIES WILL BE ARRIVING HERE SOON FROM EVERY COUNTRY IN THE WORLD.

AT FOUR O'CLOCK TODAY YOUR YOUNGER SELF IS DUE TO ARRIVE FROM THE PAST.

"FOR A BRIEF MOMENT, YOU WILL APPEAR IN TWO PLACES."

WHEN YOU WENT AHEAD IN TIME, DID *NO ONE* SEE YOU ARRIVE?

DID ANYONE AT *ALL* HAPPEN TO LOOK UP AND SEE YOUR DEVICE HOVER IN THE MIDDLE OF THE AIR, HERE, OVER CHICAGO, NEW YORK, AND PARIS? *NO ONE?*

The Toynbee Convector | GRAPHIC FICTION | 219

I DON'T SUPPOSE ANYONE WAS EXPECTING ME! I WAS CAREFUL NOT TO LINGER TOO LONG!
"I NEEDED ONLY TIME TO PHOTOGRAPH THE REBUILT CITIES, THE CLEAN SEAS AND RIVERS, THE FRESH, SMOG FREE AIR, THE UNFORTIFIED NATIONS, THE SAVED AND BELOVED WHALES. I MOVED QUICKLY, PHOTOGRAPHED SWIFTLY AND RAN BACK DOWN THE YEARS HOME."
WOULD YOU LIKE TO SIT IN THE TIME MACHINE?
TESLA
THERE. GO. SIT.
DON'T BE AFRAID. I WON'T SEND YOU ON A JOURNEY.
I WOULDN'T MIND.

The Toynbee Convector | GRAPHIC FICTION

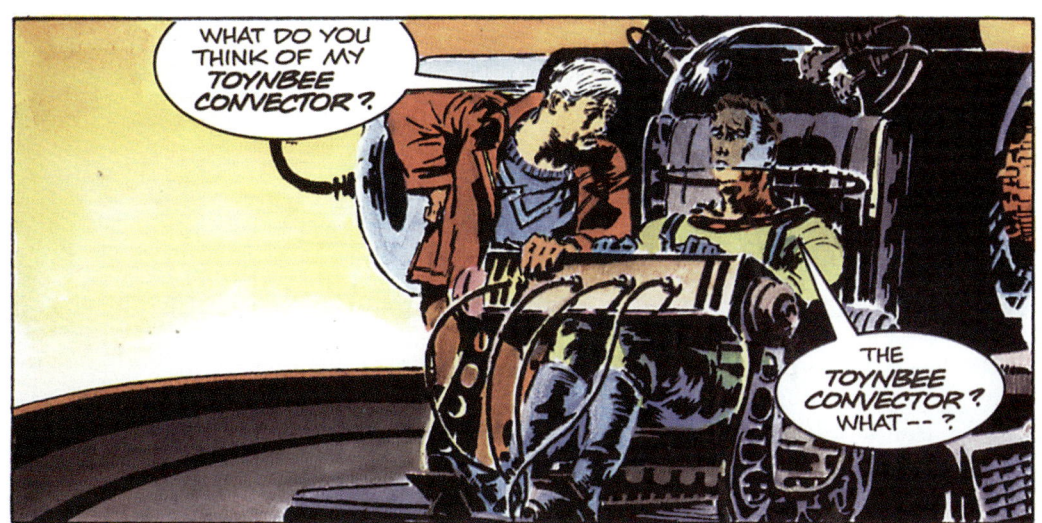

BACK ON THE ROOF, THEY LOOKED DOWN AT THE GARDENS.
ALL THIS, MY GOD, FOR *ME*.
TEN MINUTES TO FOUR AND COUNTING.
OUR OWN PRIVATE TOAST AND OUR OWN PRIVATE CELEBRATION. WHAT TIME DO YOU HAVE ?
POP!
ONE MINUTE AND COUNTING.
"NINE.
"EIGHT.
"SEVEN...
"SIX, FIVE..."

The Toynbee Convector | GRAPHIC FICTION   223

NO.!
Oh, BUT YES. I NEVER WENT ANYWHERE. I STAYED, BUT MADE IT SEEM I WENT.
BUT WHY?. WHY?.
TURN ON THE TAPE RECORDING BUTTON ON YOUR LAPEL. I WANT EVERYONE TO HEAR THIS.
"I WAS BORN AND RAISED IN A TIME WHEN PEOPLE HAD STOPPED BELIEVING IN THEMSELVES.
"EVERYWHERE, I SAW AND HEARD DOUBT. EVERY-WHERE WAS PROFESSIONAL DESPAIR.

The Toynbee Convector | GRAPHIC FICTION

"AREN'T I SOMETHING? I MADE MACHINES, BUILT MINIATURE CITIES, TALKED TO DOLPHINS, FAKED TAPES. IT TOOK YEARS OF SWEATING WORK AND SECRET PREPARATION BEFORE I ANNOUNCED MY DEPARTURE, LEFT, AND CAME BACK WITH GOOD NEWS."

QUICKLY NOW. HERE ARE THREE MORE TAPES WITH FULLER DATA. HERE'S A HISTORY OF MY WHOLE INSPIRED FRAUD AND A FINAL MANUSCRIPT.

CRACK!

QUICKLY!

CRACKLE!

YOU SEE THE POINT, DON'T YOU, SON? WHAT SEEMS A LIE IS A RAMSHACKLE NEED WISHING TO BE BORN.

The Toynbee Convector | GRAPHIC FICTION

After Reading

CHECKING FOR UNDERSTANDING

1. a) Think back to the predictions you made. What happened to the accuracy of your predictions as you got closer to the end?

PURPOSE / AUDIENCE / FORM

2. a) Create and complete a **frames** chart like the one below.

Shot	Angle/View	Page	Frame #	Effect of the Shot and Angle
Long shot	Bird's eye	215	1	We see the impressive lamasery from Shumway's **point of view** as he flies toward it in his helicopter.
Close-up	Eye level			
Medium shot	Bird's eye			
Medium close-up	Worm's eye			
Extreme close-up	Eye level			
Long shot	Bird's eye			

b) With a partner, compare your charts. Check that your explanations are complete. Help each other improve any explanations that are incomplete.

STYLE AND CONVENTIONS

3. a) Write the comic book artist's **conventions** for showing that a character is speaking, showing that a character is thinking, and showing that a **narrator** is speaking
   b) Look for other conventions and write a rule for each.

CRITICAL THINKING

4. a) With a partner, talk over what might happen next in this story. Plot out the events for the next scene.
   b) Write the next scene using one of the following forms: **comic, narrative,** or **drama**.
   c) Exchange scenes with another pair of students. Read their scene, and write questions to help them improve it.
   d) Return the scene to the other pair. Answer the editors' questions before you revise your scene for your final draft.
   e) Be prepared to read the scene aloud and to comment on others' scenes.

228 UNIT 6 | TECH TALK

UNIT 6 Activity

For your project for this unit, you will be evaluated using a rubric your teacher will discuss with you before you start. You will be expected to keep any process work and submit it with your final product.

Choose one of the following activities to complete.

1. a) Choose one selection (for example, a story, an article, a cartoon, or a graphic text) from this unit.
   b) Use cue cards or sticky notes to record as many ideas from the reading as you can. These ideas can be directly stated or implied. Record only one idea per card or note.
   c) When you have recorded all of your ideas, look at them carefully and start arranging the notes into three piles according to the way the author sees technology: "Positive," "Negative," "Neither Positive nor Negative." Label each of the piles.
   d) Write a **summary** of the author's opinion of technology starting with the sentence, "The author believes technology is _____." Use the details from your cards or notes to complete your summary.

2. a) Choose one of the selections that shows technology could be dangerous ("Bubble Chamber" or "The Toynbee Convector"). For the selection you have chosen, create and fill in the chart below.

The Real Problem Is ...		
The **facts** as we know them are: (identify facts from the selection you have chosen)		
So the real problem is: (summarize the problem)		
A solution might be ...	A solution might be ...	A solution might be ...
But the consequences are ... (Think of the plusses and minuses of the solution above.)	But the consequences are ... (Think of the plusses and minuses of the solution above.)	But the consequences are ... (Think of the plusses and minuses of the solution above.)

(Source: Beers, Sue; Howell, Lou. *Reading Strategies for the Content Areas.* Alexandria, VA (USA): Association for Supervision and Curriculum Development, 2003)

   b) Choose the best solution and, in a well-written paragraph, explain why you chose that solution.

3. a) How has technology affected the way we communicate with each other? **Reread** at least <u>two</u> of the selections from this unit. Fill out a chart like the one below.

Positive ways	Write your question here	Negative ways
Find proofs from the selections that show positive effects.		Find proofs from the selections that show negative effects.
Your personal opinion after filling out the chart.		
The reasons for your opinion in a well-written paragraph.		

4. a) How does technology affect our privacy? Using ideas from the selections you have read, imagine a story about the way technology affects a person's privacy. Use a graphic organizer like the one below to help plan the story.

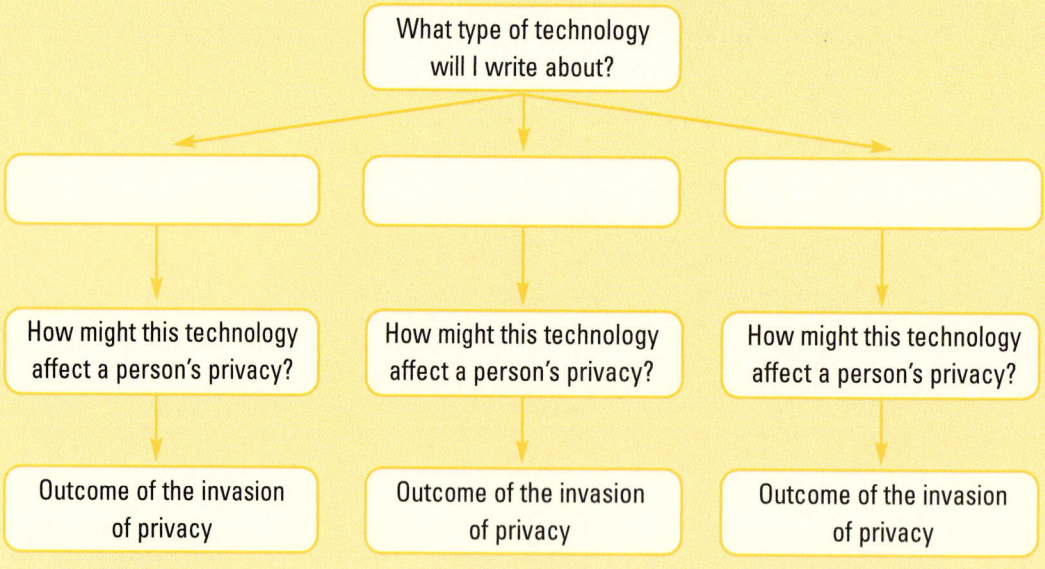

```
                    What type of technology
                      will I write about?
           ┌──────────────────┼──────────────────┐
           ▼                  ▼                  ▼
      [          ]       [          ]       [          ]
           │                  │                  │
           ▼                  ▼                  ▼
   How might this       How might this       How might this
   technology affect    technology affect    technology affect
   a person's privacy?  a person's privacy?  a person's privacy?
           │                  │                  │
           ▼                  ▼                  ▼
   Outcome of the       Outcome of the       Outcome of the
   invasion of privacy  invasion of privacy  invasion of privacy
```

b) Summarize the idea you think would make the best story. Write a short **explanation** paragraph about how one of the selections you read gave you the ideas for your story. Refer to specific parts of the selection in your explanation.

The REFERENCE SHELF

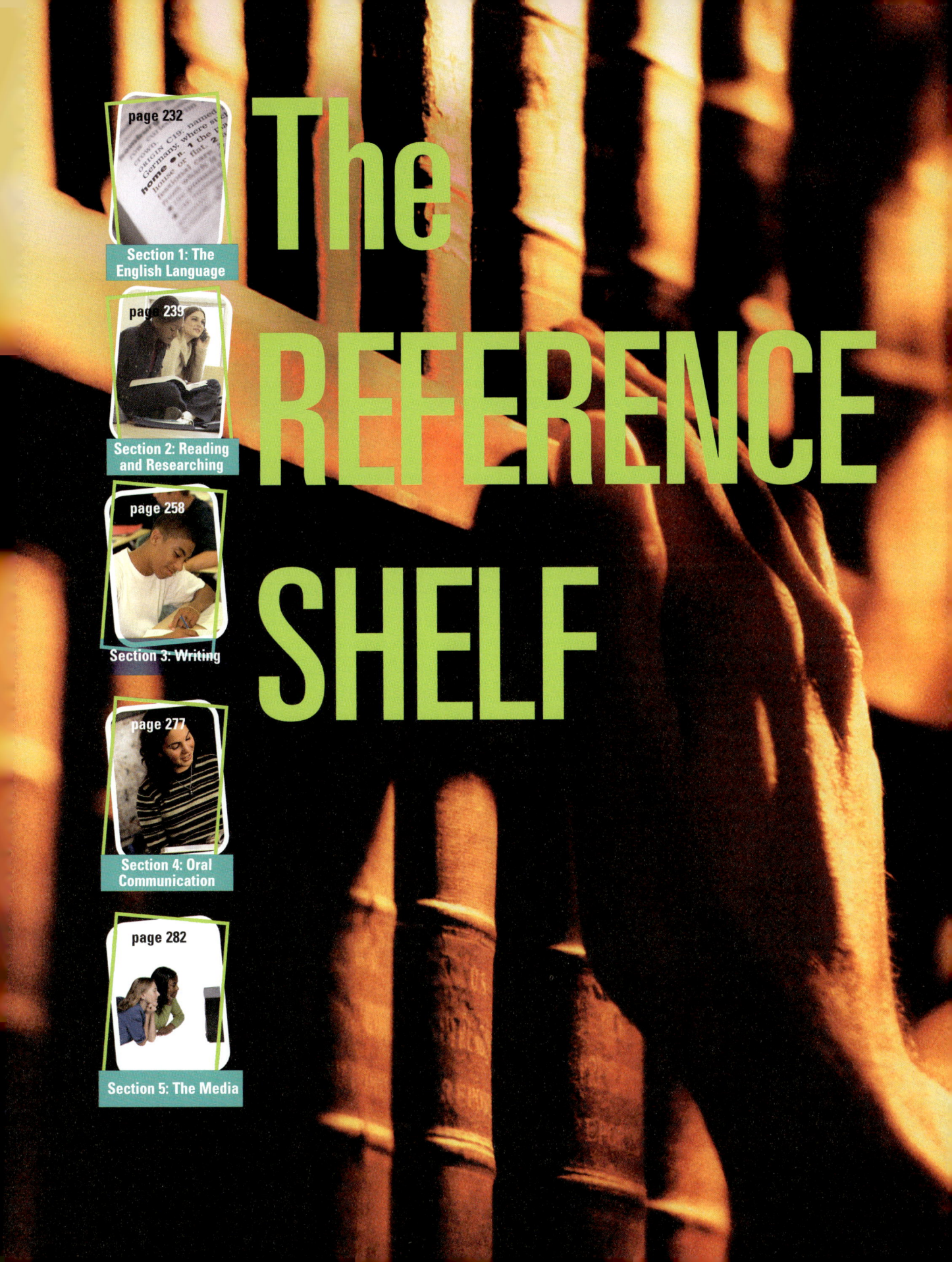

page 232
Section 1: The English Language

page 239
Section 2: Reading and Researching

page 258
Section 3: Writing

page 277
Section 4: Oral Communication

page 282
Section 5: The Media

SECTION 1

The English language

Modern English is continually changing and adding new words to its vocabulary. Many of these words are the result of inventions (e.g., fibre optics, biodegradable plastics), evolving technology (computers, digital video disks), and globalization (gyros, haiku, tea). It borrows words from many cultures, popularizes technical terms, and finds new uses for old words.

GO! In this section you will find information about spelling, punctuation, and grammar.

| Levels of Language page 232 | Parts of Speech page 232 | Parts of Sentences page 234 | Sentence Variety page 235 | Sentence Errors page 236 | Punctuation page 238 |

LEVELS OF LANGUAGE

- **Slang** is very informal and usually short-lived vocabulary and language patterns used by particular groups or in special informal contexts. It is usually not appropriate to use slang in formal written work, but it is often used in fiction to show character and create mood.
- A **colloquialism** is an informal, conversational expression that is often inappropriate to use in formal written work. Many dictionaries will tell you whether an expression is considered slang or colloquial.
- **Jargon** is specialized vocabulary used by a profession, trade, or group. Jargon must be used carefully in oral and written work. Sometimes it is used to obscure meaning. Good writing uses simple, clear language—called plain English—and avoids the use of slang, colloquialisms, and jargon.
- **Dialect** is a local version of language, with its own vocabulary and sentence structure.
- **Standard Canadian English** is the oral and written English used by a broad range of Canadian society (including government, medicine, law, science, business, and the media). Standard Canadian English follows accepted rules and practices of grammar, usage, spelling, and punctuation.

PARTS OF SPEECH

- A **noun** names a person, place, or thing. There are five types of nouns:
  - **common** (book, pen)
  - **proper** (Canada, Mary)
  - **collective** (class, team)
  - **concrete** (desk, chair)
  - **abstract** (love, honesty)

232 | THE REFERENCE SHELF

- A **pronoun** replaces a noun. The noun that the pronoun replaces is called the antecedent.
  - The pronoun must agree in number (*it*—the book, *them*—the books) and in gender (*he*—the boy) with its antecedent, and it must play the same role in the sentence as its antecedent. (The girl hit the ball. *She* hit *it*. Dan scored the goal. *He* scored *it*. Mahalia read the books. *She* read *them*.)
  - Pronouns can be **possessive** (my, her, your) or **relative** (that, which, who, whom, whose).
- An **adjective** describes a noun or pronoun (Mrs. Lee drives a *red* car. Thomas likes *chocolate* doughnuts.)
- A **verb** identifies the action (The child *grabbed* the cookie.) or state of being (The sky *seemed* dark. "Foul Shot" *is* a poem about basketball.).
- An **adverb** describes a verb (The teacher spoke *loudly*.), an adjective (The grass is *emerald* green.), or another adverb (The horse raced *very* quickly down the road.).
- The **verb tense** tells when the action took place. The three verb tenses are **present** (Ashur *eats* his lunch.), **past** (Ashur *ate* his lunch.), and **future** (Ashur *will eat* his lunch.). If the event is happening in the present, all verbs should be in the present tense. If the event happened in the past, all verbs should be in the past tense.
- An **infinitive verb** uses "to" in front of it. (The place *to visit* is Niagara Falls. The basketball player jumped *to shoot*.)
- A **conjunction** joins words or groups of words:
  - The conjuctions *for, and, nor, but, or, yet, so* link equal main ideas. (I was sick so I didn't go to school. I wanted the doughnut but my brother ate it.) TIP: Use FANBOYS (for, and, nor, but, or, yet, so) to remember these conjunctions.
  - Subordinating conjunctions such as *after, before, although, because, even though, until, unless* link a main idea and a less important idea. (Neela isn't allowed to go to the party *unless* she cleans up her room.)
- A **preposition** shows the relationship between a noun or pronoun to some other word in the sentence. Some prepositions are *at, behind, by, in, into, near, of, on, to, through, under, with, out*. (The cat slipped *out* the door.)
- An **interjection** expresses emotion or thought but is not essential to the sentence. Examples are *alas, hey, oh dear, oops, ouch, well, wow, yikes*. *Oh dear*, they will never find their dog in this storm. *Ouch*, that hurt!)

The English Language

PARTS OF SENTENCES

Sentences are words joined together to make sense. A sentence begins with a capital letter and ends with a period, question mark, or exclamation mark. A sentence contains at least one verb.

Here are the parts of a sentence:

PART OF SENTENCE	EXAMPLE
subject • tells who or what is doing the action	*Mahima* worked on the computer. The *printer* was not working.
predicate The verb is in the predicate. • tells what the subject is doing or being	The soccer coach *kicked the ball.* Biajo *seems proud of his marks.*
object • receives the action of the verb	Black bears eat *blueberries.*
subjective completion • comes after the verb and describes the subject	Mr. Elliot is *the principal.* Joanne looks *healthy.*
prepositional phrase • starts with a preposition, may have an adjective, and ends with a noun • can act like an adjective and describe a noun or pronoun (prepositional adjective phrase) • can act like an adverb and describe a verb, an adjective, or an adverb (prepositional adverb phrase)	The kitten *in the tree* can't get down. The flowers *on the table* are for you. He swam *in the pool* everyday.
principal clause (independent clause) • is the main idea of the sentence • makes complete sense on its own	I did not go to school. (makes sense alone)
subordinate clause (dependent clause) • is the less important idea of the sentence • does not make complete sense on its own	I did not go to school *because I had a dentist appointment.* ("because I had a dentist appointment" does not make sense alone)

THE REFERENCE SHELF

Activity

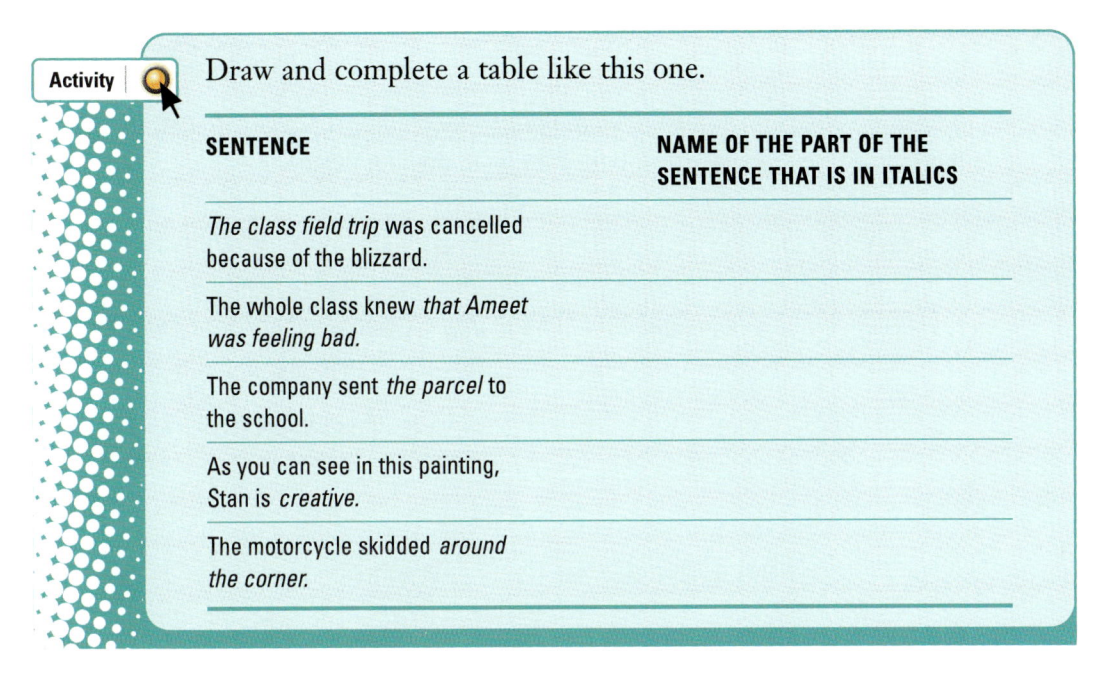

Draw and complete a table like this one.

SENTENCE	NAME OF THE PART OF THE SENTENCE THAT IS IN ITALICS
The class field trip was cancelled *because of the blizzard*.	
The whole class knew *that Ameet was feeling bad*.	
The company sent *the parcel* to the school.	
As you can see in this painting, Stan is *creative*.	
The motorcycle skidded *around the corner*.	

SENTENCE VARIETY

Your writing will be more interesting if you use different types of sentences.

Some types of sentences have different purposes.
- An **assertive** sentence makes a statement. (The temperature is 25 degrees today.)
- An **interrogative** sentence asks a question. (Where does that boy live?)
- An **imperative** sentence makes a command. (Give that to me! Bring her some water.)
- An **exclamatory** sentence expresses strong emotion. (This was the best holiday I've ever had!)

The order of the parts of a sentence can be different.
- In the **natural** order, the subject comes first, followed by the predicate. (The *train* left the station on time.)
- In the **inverted** order, the predicate comes first, followed by the subject. (*Behind the gentle smile* was a monster.)
- In the **split** order, part of the predicate comes before the subject (or between the subject and the verb) for emphasis. (*No matter how you get there*, you will enjoy your visit to the farm.)

The English Language | SECTION 1 | 235

The English Language

SENTENCE ERRORS

Here are the mistakes writers make most often when writing sentences. Use the **Fix-It Tips** when you edit your own sentences.

PROBLEM	FIX-IT TIP
fragment • looks like a sentence because there is a capital and a period, but the verb does not sound complete Example: Desperately running to catch the bus.	Add the missing pieces so that the sentence is complete. Example: *Maya was* desperately running to catch the bus.
run-on • too many complete sentences or thoughts joined together as one sentence Example: Kaiya went to the school dance with Lee Brad brought her home.	Add a conjunction to join the thoughts into one sentence. Example: Kaiya went to the school dance with Lee *but* Brad brought her home.
comma splice • using a comma instead of a period to separate two complete thoughts Example: Gina likes reading mystery stories, she thinks she would like to write one someday.	Replace the comma with a period if the two sentences can stand alone as complete sentences. Example: Gina likes reading mystery stories. She thinks she would like to write one someday. or Add a conjunction to join the two thoughts. Example: Gina likes reading mystery stories *and* she thinks she would like to write one someday.
subject-verb disagreement • subject and verb don't match Example: Joe and Juan is playing on the team.	Decide whether your subject is singular or plural. Example: Joe and Juan *are* playing on the team.
pronoun-antecedent disagreement • pronoun and its antecedent don't match in gender, number, or person Example: Gordon borrowed my CD and she never returned it.	Decide whether the antecedent is masculine or feminine, singular or plural, first, second, or third person. Example: Gordon borrowed my CD and *he* never returned it.

THE REFERENCE SHELF

SPELLING

Accurate spelling is important to communicate your ideas and information effectively. Incorrect spelling will distract and even confuse your reader.

Here is a list of common spelling problems.
- words that sound the same but have different spellings (*there*, *their*, and *they're* or *wear* and *where*)
- placement of apostrophe *do'nt* for *don't*, *her's* for *hers*, *it's* for the possessive *its*
- easily confused words (*accept* and *except*)
- new and specialized terms (*colloquial, euthanasia, parliament*)

> **-- Technology Tip --**
>
> Spell checkers can be useful tools. They can help you pick up obvious mistakes, but the computer does not know what word you really mean. It cannot know when you have used *there* instead of *they're*, or *right* instead of *write*.

If you are not sure how to spell a word, try these strategies.
- Sound out the word slowly while you write out all the syllables.
- Think of other words that you do know how to spell and that sound like the difficult word.
- Write the word the way you think it is spelled. See if it looks right. If it doesn't, try writing it a different way.
- Look up the word in a dictionary or check it on the spell checker.

If you cannot find a word in a dictionary, there might be a different way to spell one of the sounds in the word. For example, the "k" sound can be made by "k" as in kick, "c" as in candy, "ch" as in chemistry, and "q" as in quiche.

You can become a better speller by
- keeping a list of misspelled words so you don't have to keep looking them up.
- making up and using rhymes and phrases that will help your memory. For example, "i before e except after c or when sounded like "a" as in neighbour and weigh."

The English Language | SECTION 1

The English Language

PUNCTUATION

All sentences end with a **period (.)**, a **question mark (?)**, or an **exclamation mark (!)**.
- A period ends a statement. (The tickets go on sale tomorrow.)
- A question mark ends a question. (Where did you work last year?)
- An exclamation mark ends a sentence expressing strong emotion. (Stop! Surprise! Wow! I love that song!)

Use a **comma (,)** in the following situations:
- to separate items in a list (I bought apples, cheese, and bread.)
- after an introductory word, phrase, or clause (Then, I was so tired.)
- after the introduction to direct speech (Tony said, "My favourite snack is potato chips.")
- to make the meaning of the sentence clear (*I went on vacation with my sister and my brother, and my father stayed home*, or *I went on vacation with my sister, and my brother and my father stayed home*. Without the comma, the reader does not know who stayed home.)

Quotation marks (" ") show the reader when someone is speaking.

Direct speech (the actual words of the speaker) requires quotation marks. ("Do you know the escape route?" Toby asked. "I think we are trapped.")

Indirect speech does not require quotation marks. (Toby asked if I knew the escape route. He thought we were trapped.)

Quotation marks are also used for titles of short poems, stories, and articles. (The poem "Foul Shot" is about basketball.)

Use the **colon (:)** in the following situations:
- to introduce a list after a complete sentence (You will need the following items: scissors, paste, and pencils.)
- after a sentence that introduces a quotation (Our school motto is carved over the door: "Respect and Responsibility.")
- after a sentence that introduces an explanation (She realized what she loved about him: how kind he was, how patient he was with her children.)
- with expressions of time (10:45)
- in a **script** to show that a character begins speaking (Rufus: Hand me the axe. I will destroy this castle door.)

| THE REFERENCE SHELF

SECTION 2

Reading and Researching

Reading is a skill; it is something you learn how to do. And like any skill, there are ways to get better at doing it. When you become a more effective reader, reading will be more pleasurable and more useful to you. Reading is an active process. For effective readers, understanding does not happen all at once at the end of reading a selection—it is built along the way.

GO! In this section you will find information about reading strategies and researching skills.

| Reading Strategies page 239 | Elements of a Narrative page 246 | Reading Drama page 251 | Research Strategies page 253 |

| Using the Internet page 255 | Reading for Pleasure page 256 |

READING STRATEGIES

Before You Read

Decide on Your Purpose for Reading a Selection.

Why you are reading tells you *how* to read. When you read for research, you probably sit at a table in a quiet place. You read more slowly, sorting out what information you need and perhaps stopping to take notes. You can read for pleasure almost anywhere and you probably read faster.

Scan

Move your eyes quickly over the entire reading selection to pick up a few words and get an overview of the topic and the layout. This method helps you plan the most effective way to "get inside" the selection.

Here are some sentence starters to help you scan before you read:
- What kind of a selection is this? A story? A poem?
- What is the topic? What do I already know about this topic?
- Do any words stand out because they are in **italics** or bold?
- How difficult will this selection be for me to read?
- What strategies should I use to understand this selection?

Predict (Before You Read)

Ask yourself these questions:
- What do you think this reading selection is about?
- How do you think you are going to react to it?

Reading and Researching | SECTION 2 | **239**

- What aspects of this selection will be easy and what aspects will be more difficult for you to understand?

Activate Prior Knowledge

Everyone understands a reading selection a little differently because each person has had different experiences in life. What knowledge and experience do you have that can help you understand this selection better?
- What do you already know about the topic and the author?
- What do you already know about the type and **format** of the selection?
- How is the selection similar to and different from anything else you have read before?

Here are some sentence starters to help you make predictions and activate prior knowledge before you read:
- I predict that …
- The title makes me think that …
- I bet that …
- I'm guessing that …
- I imagine that …
- I think that …
- I wonder if …
- What might happen is …
- Based on … (something already read) I think …
- If … (predict something) … then …

Activity

Apply the pre-reading strategies to the reading selection "Unbalanced," page 141. Although you are not really going to read this selection right now, assume that you are going to read it for pleasure.
1. Notice the story's title, where the story came from, and the section of your textbook where it is located. What kind of a story do you think "Unbalanced" might be? What characteristics do you expect in a story of this type?
2. Scan the first page of the story. What can you guess about the story based on just this page? (Where is the story taking place? Who are the key characters? What seems to be the problem? What do you think is going to happen?
3. Are you familiar with the words "on pointe" and "in arabesque" (paragraph 6)? What do you think they mean? (They refer to a ballet step.) What kind of a connection can you make between ballet and crime investigations?

THE REFERENCE SHELF

While You Read

Visualize

Try to see and hear the selection as if you were watching a movie. Reading out loud can help to do this. Use your imagination to fill in details.

Here are some sentence starters to help you visualize as you read:
- I see …
- I imagine …
- I have a picture of …
- I saw something like this on TV.
- In art I saw …
- I saw a photograph that …
- This colour reminds me of …
- If I could draw this it would look like …

Predict

Think ahead about what might happen next. When your prediction doesn't fit, it might mean you have misunderstood what you have read. Instead of ignoring an incorrect prediction, try making a new prediction, or go back to reconsider your earlier reading.

Question

Ask questions and think about what is happening in the selection as you go along. You can also ask questions to help you understand vocabulary. You can do this alone by writing in your notebook or in a journal. However, many people like to talk to a partner. The important thing is to ask questions and react along the way, not all at the end.

Not all the answers you need will come from the selection alone, especially for "how" and "why" questions. You may need to draw connections from various parts of the text or from your own life experiences.

Here are some sentence starters to help you ask questions as you read:
- Why did…?
- Who will…?
- Where might…?
- What happened when…?
- Who is…?
- What does this word mean?
- How does this work?
- Which…?
- What is this author talking about?

Reading and Researching | SECTION 2

Reading and Researching

You can use a Q-chart like the one below to help you ask questions. Start with a word in the first column, and pair it with a word from the top row.

- If you want to learn a **fact**, use a word from the first column and a word from the top row that meet in the yellow section, for example, "*What did* Grimm do to make Mother Goose put him outside?" (*Mother Goose and Grimm*, page 11).
- If you want to make a prediction, use two words that meet in the blue section, for example, "*What might* happen to Linda after her fall?" ("Unbalanced," page 141).
- If you want to analyze or examine the text, use two words that meet in the green section, for example, "*How does* Leonid Stadnik feel about his height?" ("Tallest Man Feels Lowly at the Top," page 96).
- If you want to make connections or apply the text to something else, use two words that meet in the orange section, for example, "*Why would* the sister wish for gold from the magic sieve?" (*The Magic Sieve*, page 102).

	IS/ARE	DOES/DID	CAN	WOULD	WILL	MIGHT
WHAT						
WHERE		Q1–FACTS			Q2–PREDICTION	
WHEN						
WHO						
WHY		Q3–ANALYSIS			Q4–SYNTHESIS/ APPLICATION	
HOW						

Notice Print Conventions

Paying attention to the appearance of the text adds to your understanding. Writers use format tools such as italics, bold print, font size and style, and capitalization to make key words stand out and to give the reader a sense of how the selection might sound. Punctuation also gives you important signals. For example, quotation marks set off direct speech, and an exclamation mark indicates excitement.

Find the Pattern

Knowing how a selection is structured will help you understand it. A newspaper report is organized differently from a short story. An essay is organized differently from a scripted play.

Clarify Vocabulary and Confusing Ideas

When you come to an unfamiliar word, try these ideas to find out what it means.
- Say the word out loud. You may have heard the word before but have never seen it.
- Look at the way it is used in the sentence. Read the words around it. Try to substitute another word for the unfamiliar word.
- Does it contain a **root word**, a prefix, or a suffix that you know?
- Use a glossary. Sometimes the word is highlighted in the margin.
- Look up the word in a dictionary.

Here are some sentence starters to help you clarify as you read:
- Now I understand …
- I get the sense that …
- I think this means …
- First I thought … but now I understand that …
- What this part is saying …
- If I replace this word for that one, I see it means …

Change Your Reading Speed

Like good drivers who adjust their speed according to road conditions, good readers slow down when something is difficult or new. How fast or slowly you read depends on your purpose and how familiar you are with the topic, with the type of selection, and its vocabulary.

Comment

Good readers often write down their thoughts as they read. Writing a **summary**, a response, or even just point-form **jot notes** helps you understand a reading selection.

Here are some sentence starters to help you comment as you read:
- I never noticed that …
- I'm confused about …
- This is the best part because …
- I like the part that …
- I think that …

Connect

How does the selection connect to your own life experiences? When you read, all your memories, personal experiences, knowledge about the subject, structure, and **style** of the selection can contribute to your understanding.

Here are some sentence starters to help you connect as you read:
- This reminds me of …
- This is like the time …
- This is helping me think about …
- This person is like …
- This **setting** reminds me of …
- This also happened to another character when …
- I saw something like this on TV. It was …

Infer

Sometimes all the information you need is stated right there "on the line." But often a reader has to make connections among pieces of information that are not said directly. This is called **making an inference** or "reading between the lines." You are doing this when you make your own conclusions based on clues and evidence the author has given you.

When the answers to your questions aren't on the page, ask yourself:
- Where am I getting confused? What information is missing for me? Is that information in my head or in the reading selection?
- Were any clues given to me along the way?

Reread

Rereading a chunk of the selection can give you clues to the meaning of unfamiliar words or ideas. Rereading an entire selection allows you to focus on a different aspect of it. You can use your additional knowledge to understand it better. Even if you read the selection only five minutes ago, by rereading it, you will experience it in a different way than you did the first time.

Here are some sentence starters to help you reread more effectively.
- Where did I start getting confused?
- What is confusing me?
- Does it help if I reread more slowly or out loud?

After You Read

Effective readers know that the thinking about the reading is not done when they come to the end of the selection.

Retell

By retelling the selection orally or in writing, you select the important parts and organize them in the best way for someone else to understand what you have understood. Retelling helps you know whether your understanding is accurate and complete.

Reflect

While you were reading, you were inferring, questioning, commenting, and connecting. Now that you have read the entire selection, you have a bigger picture, which means that you might have to change your earlier thoughts and feelings.

You could use some of the following questions to help you reflect:
- What did I get out of reading this selection?
- What would I have done if…?
- What else could have happened?
- How do I know that…? What proof do I have that…?
- What would have happened if…?
- I wonder if the writer…?

Reformulate

Consider the reading selection in a different form. For example, imagine a short story as a **news report** or a novel as a movie. Consider what changes you would have to make and why.

Here are some sentence starters to ask yourself:
- What would I want to include or leave out?
- How would I show…?
- What performer should play the part of…?
- Who would be the **audience** for…?

ELEMENTS OF A NARRATIVE

Point of View

When you hear the **narrative** (story) in your mind, you are hearing the "voice" of the **narrator** or storyteller. The narrator can tell the story from different **points of view**. The narrator could be a character in the story itself (**first-person** point of view) or an observer outside the story (**third-person** point of view).

In first-person point of view, the narrator is a character in the story.
- The narrator uses "I" to describe the action. ("Although merely a form letter … I could hardly read it and trembled as tears of joy blurred my vision." "A Fly In A Pail Of Milk," page 66)
- First-person narration can make the reader feel very personally involved because the reader is inside the head of the character telling the story. However, a first-person narrator does not always have to be involved in the story. He or she could be someone who is observing what is happening to people he or she knows. (I watched my brother's shoulders droop and his smile fade as he heard Jinah's words. I knew his life was changing forever.)

In **third-person point of view**, the narrator has a "bird's eye view" of the action and characters without being a character in the story.
- Third-person narration is sometimes less personal but it gives the reader a wider view of events and characters because the narrator can get inside the head of every character. ("The money Shichiri gave the burglar could not be stolen, because it was a gift. The samurai was so generous that he wanted to give the thief an even greater gift, the ability to appreciate the beauty of the moon, the wonder of the things we see around us everyday that have a value beyond money." "The Gift That Could Not Be Stolen," page 132)
- Some stories have a **limited narrator**. The limited third-person narrator can sound very personal, almost as if the narrator were the character that he or she is describing. It's like the narrator is a camera sitting on the character's shoulder. The reader sees exactly what the character sees. ("He shivered. There was no source of warmth here. He crouched and curled his tail about him. It was a curious thing, really, he looked human, yet wasn't. Well … not anymore." "Bubble Chamber," page 201)

THE REFERENCE SHELF

Activity

Work with a partner.
Partner A tells a joke in the third person. Partner B retells the joke in the first person. Then switch roles.

Here's an example.

PARTNER A TELLS THE JOKE IN THE THIRD PERSON	PARTNER B RETELLS THE JOKE IN THE FIRST PERSON
A duck walks into a bar. He's all dressed up, looking very wealthy He says to the bartender, "It's my birthday. I want to buy everyone a drink." The bartender says, "Well, how do you propose to pay for this?" The duck replies, "Just put it on my bill."	**Version 1 from the bartender's point of view:** I was really busy working the bar last night. Suddenly, the door opened and in walked a duck. He said, "It's my birthday. I want to buy everyone a drink." I looked at him, thinking he's pretty dressed up and rich-looking, but he's a duck after all, so I said, "How are you going to pay for all those drinks?" The duck looked at me and said, "Just put it on my bill!" **Version 2 from the duck's point of view:** It was my birthday and I was feeling a little depressed because no one had a party for me, so I decided to make a party for myself. I got dressed up and went downtown to a bar. I said to the bartender, "It's my birthday. I want to buy everyone a drink." The bartender looked at me suspiciously. I guess he doesn't serve ducks very often because he said to me, "How are you going to pay for all those drinks?" Trying not to be insulted by his rudeness, I said, "Just put it on my bill!"

Plot

Plot is the sequence of events that make up the "action" of the story. A traditional story plot is focused on **conflict**.

There are several types of conflict. See the web on page 248 for descriptions of the different types of conflict.

Reading and Researching

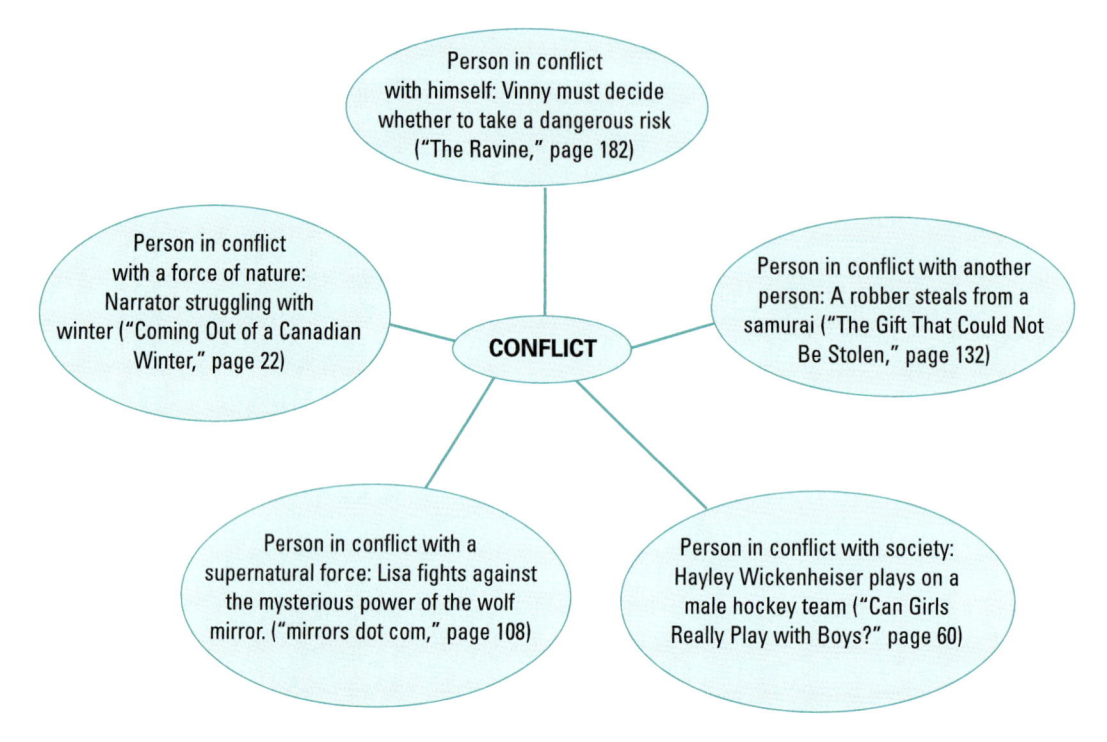

CONFLICT

- Person in conflict with himself: Vinny must decide whether to take a dangerous risk ("The Ravine," page 182)
- Person in conflict with a force of nature: Narrator struggling with winter ("Coming Out of a Canadian Winter," page 22)
- Person in conflict with another person: A robber steals from a samurai ("The Gift That Could Not Be Stolen," page 132)
- Person in conflict with a supernatural force: Lisa fights against the mysterious power of the wolf mirror. ("mirrors dot com," page 108)
- Person in conflict with society: Hayley Wickenheiser plays on a male hockey team ("Can Girls Really Play with Boys?" page 60)

A story usually begins by setting up the situation and the characters. The plot develops **suspense** as the reader learns about the conflict and waits to see how it will be resolved. The **climax** occurs at the highest point of tension. The writer could use **foreshadowing** to give hints about what is going to happen. Suspense builds as the story progresses until the climax.

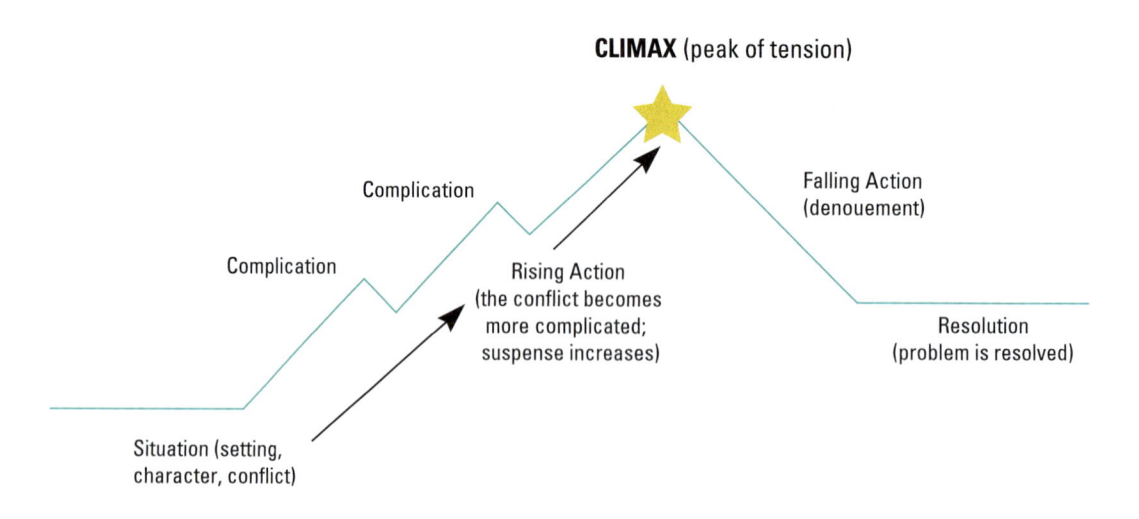

CLIMAX (peak of tension)

- Situation (setting, character, conflict)
- Complication
- Complication
- Rising Action (the conflict becomes more complicated; suspense increases)
- Falling Action (denouement)
- Resolution (problem is resolved)

248 | THE REFERENCE SHELF

Language

A writer shows how he or she feels about a topic through the choice of words. **Tone** means the writer's attitude towards his or her topic and **diction** means word choice. Writers choose words carefully to communicate ideas accurately and expressively. For example, "self-confident" sounds positive but "arrogant" sounds negative even though both words mean a similar **character trait**. Depending on the writer's purpose, **language** can range from very formal and proper to very informal and conversational. A reader can tell a lot about a character, including the narrator, by the way the character uses language. For example, a writer might have a grandmother in a story use the old-fashioned slang expression "the cat's meow" to show that she grew up in a time period in the past.

Atmosphere

Atmosphere is the feeling that the reader experiences while reading. In a film or television show, music is used to create mood or atmosphere. In literature, the writer chooses expressive words and tells about the events in a particular order to create atmosphere. The atmosphere of a story, poem, or play could be lighthearted, eerie, frightening, sad, and so on. For example, by mentioning the dead boy's body at the beginning of "The Ravine," the author, Graham Salisbury, makes the reader feel uneasy. That tension increases each time the character Vinny remembers how the boy died.

Character

Characters are the people, animals, and even objects that behave like humans in a story. A writer wants a reader to identify with a character, to feel connected to a character, and to care about what happens to that character. Major characters are most important; minor characters are less important. The **protagonist** is the main character. His or her main opponent is called the **antagonist**.

See the webs on page 250 for ways the personality of a character can be shown.

CHARACTERIZATION

- What the character looks like (character's appearance)
- Narrator's information (what the narrator tells us)
- The character's actions (what the character does)
- The character's words (what the character says)
- The character's thoughts (what and how the character thinks)
- Other characters' reactions (what other characters say and think about the character)

CHARACTER: LINDA

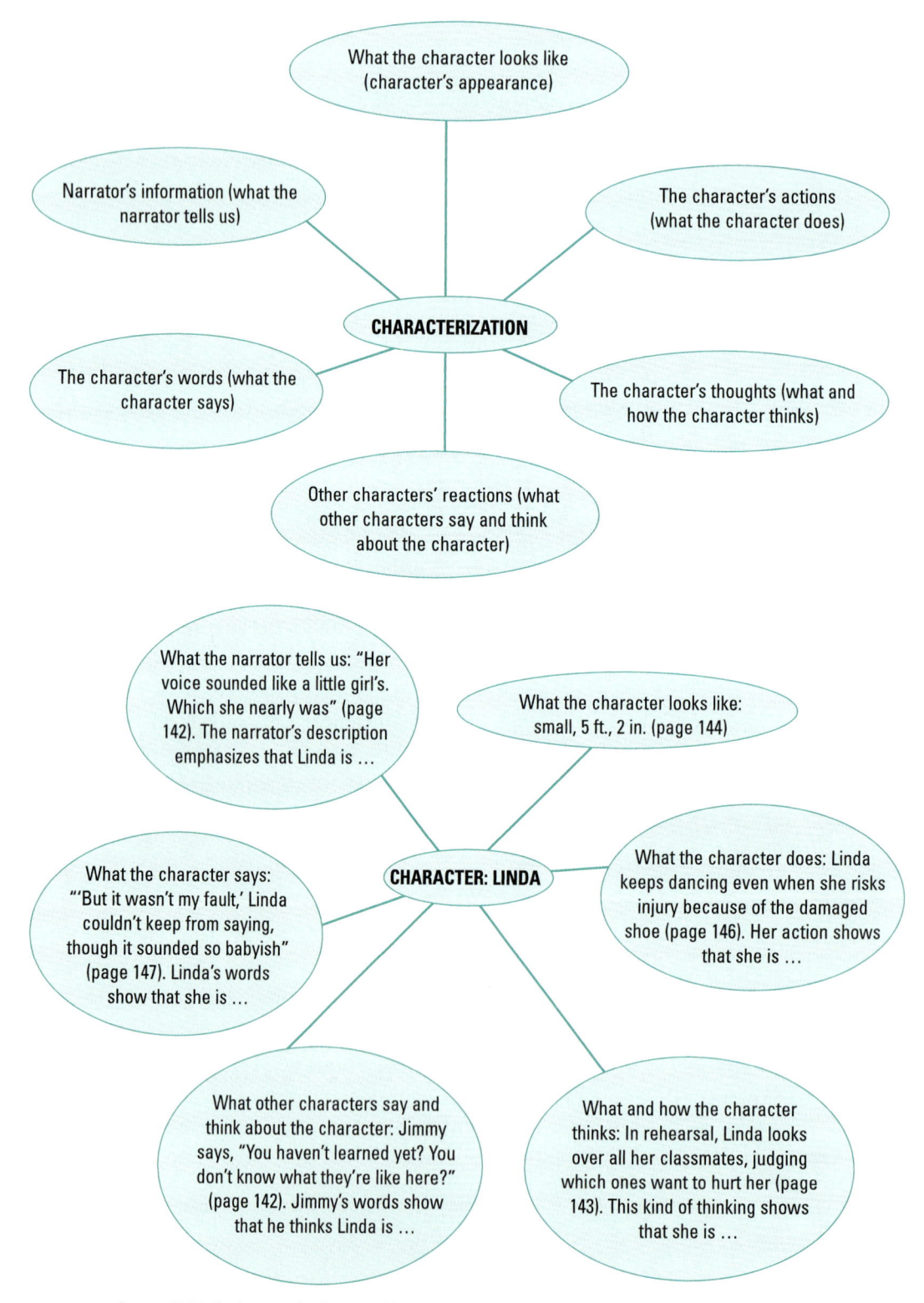

- What the narrator tells us: "Her voice sounded like a little girl's. Which she nearly was" (page 142). The narrator's description emphasizes that Linda is …
- What the character looks like: small, 5 ft., 2 in. (page 144)
- What the character says: "'But it wasn't my fault,' Linda couldn't keep from saying, though it sounded so babyish" (page 147). Linda's words show that she is …
- What the character does: Linda keeps dancing even when she risks injury because of the damaged shoe (page 146). Her action shows that she is …
- What other characters say and think about the character: Jimmy says, "You haven't learned yet? You don't know what they're like here?" (page 142). Jimmy's words show that he thinks Linda is …
- What and how the character thinks: In rehearsal, Linda looks over all her classmates, judging which ones want to hurt her (page 143). This kind of thinking shows that she is …

from "Unbalanced" by William Sleator (page 141)

Setting

Setting is the time and place in which the story takes place. A writer can manipulate time by including a flashback from the past or foreshadowing a scene from the future. Settings can be real or imaginary.

Theme

Theme is different from **plot** or **subject**. Plot is the storyline, the events or action of a story. Subject is the topic, what the writing piece is about. Theme is how the reader understands the overall message that the writer is saying. For example, a story about a soldier (character) who kills an enemy (plot) in a World War II battle (setting) shows the horror of war (overall message). The author may be saying that the horror of war causes a loss of innocence for a young person who is seeing death and destruction for the first time (theme). The author may also be saying that the only way a person can show true bravery and patriotism is by experiencing the horror of war (theme). To express the theme, try starting your sentence with "The author is saying that …" For example, "You Never Know (Tish)" (page 24) tells the story of a complicated friendship that ends in tragedy. Through the plot events (the kiss, the mock wedding, sending the letter, and so on), we see how the girls' friendship changed. A reader may feel that the author is saying that even though someone risks rejection, she has to be honest with friends and hope they will accept her as she is. This statement is the theme.

READING DRAMA

Purposes of Acts and Scenes

- Show the setting (time and place).
- Introduce or develop the conflict.
- Introduce or develop the characters.
- Give background information. (for example, flashback)
- Introduce or develop an important image or symbol.

Differences in Types of Drama

	FILM	TELEVISION	STAGE	RADIO
ACTS AND SCENES	• smooth movement from scene to scene	• smooth movement from scene to scene; cuts may occur for commercials	• scene changes are obvious through changes to sets, lighting, intermission	• scene changes are obvious through sound effects or narrator's comments
PLOT	• story is shown through actions and words • voice-over narrator may fill in gaps	• story is shown through actions and words • voice-over narrator may fill in gaps	• story is shown through actions and words • chorus or actor as narrator may fill in gaps	• story is shown through words • voice-over narrator may fill in gaps
SETTING	• very flexible—easily changed by camera shots and editing	• very flexible—easily changed by camera shots and editing	• less flexible than film or TV; shown by changes of sets, props, lighting, costumes	• less flexible than film or TV; shown by sound and dialogue
ACTORS	• wide range • multiple takes allow actors to get the performance right	• wide range • multiple takes allow actors to get the performance right	• human, puppets, with or without sound • live performance means actors get one chance to get the performance right	• human voices, synthesized sound • multiple takes allow actors to get the performance right
DIALOGUE	• action, voice, camera work, sound, special effects add to dialogue	• action, voice, camera work, sound, special effects add to dialogue	• action, voice, sound, use of props, lighting, and sets add to dialogue	• sound, sound effects, and voice adds to dialogue
SPECIAL EFFECTS	• limited only by current technology	• limited only by current technology	• more limited than film and TV	• limited to sound and dialogue
AUDIENCE IMAGINATION	• picture and sound can provide detailed information so imagination can be limited	• picture and sound can provide detailed information so imagination can be limited	• fewer details are provided so there is more room for imagination	• a lot of imagination is needed

RESEARCH STRATEGIES

PLAN before you begin to search.

- Figure out what your assignment really asks you to do. A 10-minute oral presentation to your class needs a different amount and kind of information than a 250-word letter to the editor.
- Figure out what you already know about the topic and what you need to know for the purpose of your assignment. Make a list of questions that you want answered.
- Calculate how much time you can put into the research stage of the assignment. Remember that you will need time to work on the final product too.
- Think about resources. Which kinds of resources will be most useful (books, magazines, films, human resources, the Internet, and so on)? Where are they located? When can you get to them?

Here is an example of the way one student named Kita researches for a 15-minute oral presentation on an endangered animal in Canada.

At First ... Initial Thinking and Research

Kita thinks: *What do I know already?*

Maybe I could do my presentation on whales. I know there are whales in Canada because I've heard of tourists who go whale-watching on the west coast. I know whales are endangered but I don't know if Canadian whales are in trouble.

What do I need to know?

Where do whales live? Are Canadian whales endangered? If so, by what and where?

Where could I look for information?
- *encyclopedias*
- *atlases*
- *non-fiction books*
- *the school or public library*
- *the Internet using "whales in Canada" as key words*

Then Later ... Narrowing the Topic and the Research

Kita thinks: *Wow, there is way too much information on whales in Canada and the problems they have. Those beluga whales are cute.*

I'll focus on them.

What do I need to know now?

What is harming beluga whales? What is being done to help them? Could I join an environmental group to help save them?

Where could I look for information?
- *newspaper articles*
- *recent magazine articles in vertical files*
- *the school or public library*
- *the Internet using "beluga whale" as key words*
- *an interview with a representative of an environmental group*

FIND your resources.

It helps a lot if you know your way around a library and if you have used electronic search engines before. A librarian can help you learn these skills.
- Start with general resources such as dictionaries, encyclopedias, atlases, and indexes. These resources can be in hard copy and electronic format.
- Move to more specific sources such as books, magazines, newspapers, CD-ROMs, videotapes, audiotapes, and Web sites.
- Skim the tables of contents and indexes to see if your topic is listed.
- Scan articles and scroll through Web sites for headings, illustrations, and key words related to your topic.
- Skim-read to see if the resource is going to be useful to you.
- Save resources and bookmark Web sites that look as if they have the information you want.
- Notice that you are not taking notes at this stage.

SORT your resources.

Not every resource you found will be useful to you and you may have gaps that need to be filled in with further research. You must decide what to keep, what to toss, and what to keep looking for.

Keep information that is
- on your topic.
- clearly written and understandable to you.
- up-to-date.
- included in at least one other source (so you can trust that it is true).

Toss information that is
- off topic or over-general.
- written above or below your age, grade, and reading levels.
- mostly **opinion** and without **facts**.
- prejudiced, one-sided, racist, sexist, or homophobic.
- out-of-date.
- found only in one source, especially an Internet source.

RECORD your information.

- Take **jot notes** rather than notes in full sentences.
- Use your own words to be sure you understand the ideas and to avoid plagiarism.*
- Organize your notes as you go along. Use cue cards, a graphic organizer, a special section of your notebook, or an electronic file.
- Keep accurate notes, including page numbers, of your sources.

* **Plagiarism** means presenting someone else's words and ideas as if they were your own. Quoting from a reliable and expert source of information shows you have done your research well. But it is lying to your reader and unfair to the original writer if you copy his or her words without saying where they really came from.

USING THE INTERNET

There are many reliable resources online including journals and sites set up by universities and serious organizations. However, you have to be careful when it comes to trusting the accuracy of information and the reliability of online sources. The Internet is a rich source of valuable information but not everything on the World-Wide Web is true.

Here are a few guidelines to help you use the Internet effectively:
- **Do not rely on Internet resources only.** You should check the accuracy of information against information from other print sources.
- **Narrow your research topic before logging on.** Before you start searching, decide on exactly what you are looking for. Choose key words that will narrow your search.
- **Keep a list of all the sites you visit.** List each site as useful or not. It is a good idea to bookmark useful sites as you search. Your tracking list allows you to return quickly to the good sites and prevents you from

Reading and Researching | SECTION 2 | 255

wasting time returning to the bad ones. It also helps you identify the sites you have used when you write your bibliography.

- **Record the useful information that you find.** Record only what you really need and to identify the site that the information came from. Record the information exactly as it appears, and use quotation marks. To avoid plagiarism, you will need to include the source for anything you copy from someone else's writing.
- **Double-check the accuracy of all addresses you have included in your assignment.** It is easy to make mistakes with complicated Internet addresses, and a small typo will make your references useless.

READING FOR PLEASURE

Reading for pleasure could mean reading a science fiction fantasy to escape the pressure of exams one day, and reading a "how-to" book for information about a hobby the next day.

Try this self-assessment of your reading preferences. Do you like to read
- novels, short stories, magazines, manuals, newspapers, Web sites?
- certain types of books and magazines?
- work by a particular writer?
- things with lots of illustrations and photographs?

Do you like to read about
- certain topics such as playing the guitar or fashion?
- made-up or real events and people?
- events, issues, and people today, or events and people in the past or future?
- familiar or far away places?
- boys or girls as the main characters?

Here are some ways to start your search.
- Ask a friend, a librarian, or a teacher for a recommendation.
- Browse the bookshelves and magazine racks of your classroom, school, and public libraries, and stores selling new and used books.
- Skim the front and back covers and a page of a possible book or magazine for a quick taste of what is inside.
- Use the card catalogue to locate books and magazines.
- Check whether an author you like has written other books.
- Check out other books in a series or other issues of a magazine you enjoyed.

256 | THE REFERENCE SHELF

- Look in a category you like. Some libraries group books by genre (mysteries, romance, science fiction) and by reader (young adult).
- Look for the print version of a movie you enjoyed.
- Read reviews in newspapers, in magazines, and online about subjects that interest you.
- Join a book club.

Activity
- Create a bulletin board of book recommendations that identify the title, author, reader, and reasons for each recommendation.
- Interview three Grade 11 students. Ask what they remember reading two years ago that was interesting.
- Take a class excursion to a public library or used book store. Come back with some selections to read and share.

SECTION 3

Writing

The writing process is not a set of rules; it's a set of possibilities. You won't go through the same steps in the same order every time you write. You'll have to decide what's the best approach for each piece of writing you do.

GO! In this section you will find information about types of writing and ways to improve your writing skills.

| Types of Writing page 258 | Tone and Purpose page 261 | Methods of Development page 264 | Graphic Organizers page 269 |

| Edit and Revise page 272 | Constructing a Portfolio page 275 |

TYPES OF WRITING

Narrative

A **narrative** tells a story that is made up (fiction) or real (non-fiction). Some forms of non-fiction that can be narrative are biography, autobiography, and historical accounts. A narrative is often told in **chronological order**, the order in time in which the events happened, but writers use flashbacks to go back into the past and foreshadowing to suggest the future. The short story "The Ravine" (page 182) and the play *The Magic Sieve* (page 102) are examples of narrative. Graphic organizers that show the organization of a narrative are the **plot** diagram (page 248) and the timeline (page 271).

Explanation

An **explanation** answers the questions: Who? What? When? Where? How? Why? One of the questions answered by "Superpoopers" (page 83) is What? (What does a penguin do when nature calls?) Another example of an explanation is "Why Do People Yawn, and Why Are Yawns Contagious?" (page 90). The graphic organizer on page 272 can help you write an explanation.

| THE REFERENCE SHELF

Report

A **report** is an **objective**, factual account of information. Some reports, such as a laboratory report, require specific headings. If no headings are given, organize your report into three main parts like this:

INTRODUCTORY PARAGRAPH
- identifies the topic
- explains the **purpose** of the report

BODY • each paragraph is about one aspect of the topic • uses research, facts, quotations, examples to develop main idea of each paragraph • may include charts, diagrams, tables, graphs, footnotes	1st body paragraph
	2nd body paragraph
	3rd body paragraph

CONCLUSION
- refers back to purpose
- summarizes key findings and key ideas
- may make recommendations

An example of a report is "Spittin' Mad? That'll Be $155" (page 136). Graphic organizers to use when writing a report are prewriting clustering (page 269) and a concept web (page 270).

Procedure

A **procedure** describes the sequence of steps necessary to perform an operation. An example of a procedure is the article, "Fix That Flat!" (page 41). Numbers clearly show the order of steps to take. Graphic organizers that help you write a procedure are the timeline and the sequence flow chart on page 271.

Supported Opinion

A **supported opinion** presents a point of view on an issue and backs it up with reasons, examples, facts, and quotations. An editorial is an example of a supported opinion. A useful graphic organizer for outlining a supported opinion is on page 8.

Summary (Retell)

A **summary** is a short version of an original document, and contains the main idea and important details in as few words as possible.

When writing a summary,
- read the whole selection before making any notes.
- identify the main idea.
- identify the important supporting details.
- leave out unnecessary words, examples, and unimportant details.
- use one general word to replace several specific words.
- follow the original selection's order of ideas.

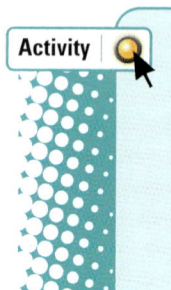

Activity

Create an organizer like the one below to summarize the selection "Tiny Bubbles? Fish May Be Talking" (page 85).

Main Idea:

Supporting Details:
-
-
-

Conclusion:

Description (Comparison)

A **description** uses words to "paint a picture" of an object, a person, a place, an event, a feeling, or an idea. A writer of a description wants to create a strong feeling or impression in the reader by

- choosing words that are powerful and accurate.
- choosing details that appeal to the reader's senses.
- using **similes** and **metaphors** that help the reader's imagination.
- organizing details according to time, spatial location, or thematic idea.

The opening section of "Future Watch" (page 197) is a description organized chronologically by time.

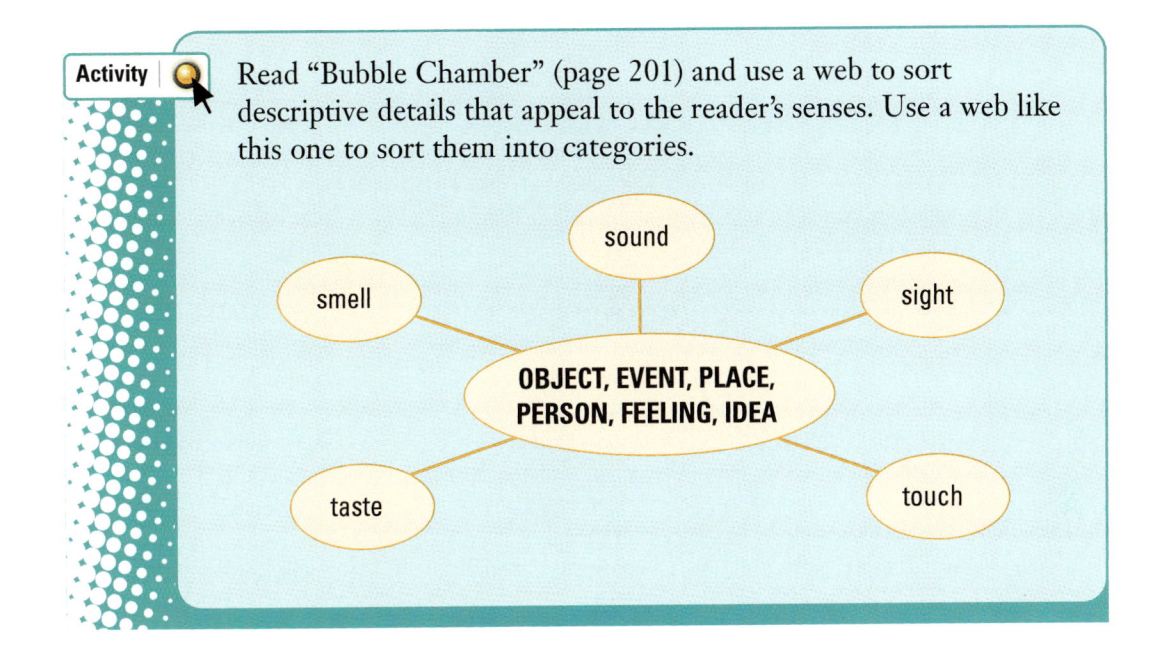

Activity 🔍 Read "Bubble Chamber" (page 201) and use a web to sort descriptive details that appeal to the reader's senses. Use a web like this one to sort them into categories.

- sound
- smell
- sight
- taste
- touch

OBJECT, EVENT, PLACE, PERSON, FEELING, IDEA

Reflection (Metacognition)

Reflection gives us a chance to think about the way we think. This process is called "metacognition." On your first reading about the Youth Criminal Justice Act ("You Have the Right to Remain … Informed," page 125), you may have asked yourself, "What is this act? What does it do?" On your second reading, you knew that information. Now you might think, "Is this act a good idea? Would I want this act applied to me if I were the offender or the victim of a crime? What does my reaction to this act show about my own attitudes to youth crime?"

TONE AND PURPOSE

The language you use in your writing will depend on why you are writing (your **purpose**) and your **audience**. **Tone** means your attitude towards the topic you are writing and towards your audience. See the table on page 262 for a description of the different levels of language and the tone each achieves.

LEVELS OF LANGUAGE	FORMAL →	MODERATE	← INFORMAL
TONE	• impersonal; instructions and information	• varies depending on purpose and audience	• casual, sounds like everyday speech
VOCABULARY AND WORD CHOICE	• longer, less common words, specialized terms • little or no slang • no contractions • rarely uses pronouns like *I* and *you*	• large and small words • some slang • some contractions • sometimes uses pronouns like *I* and *you*	• shorter, simple, everyday words • often slang • often contractions • often uses pronouns like *I* and *you*
SENTENCES AND PARAGRAPHS	• longer, complicated sentences and paragraphs • always correct grammar	• combination of complicated and simple sentences and paragraphs • usually correct grammar	• shorter and simple sentences and paragraphs • usually correct grammar but can include deliberate grammar errors
EXAMPLES (See the chart on page 263.)	• letter applying for a job	• serious letter to the editor	• letter to a friend

Example of Formal Level of Language

"No matter what you have been told, there is no law requiring a waiting period before reporting a missing child to the police or before entering the data into the CPIC (Canadian Police Information Centre)." ("Talk Before They Run," page 3).

This example shows the traits of formal language because it
- provides information about reporting a runaway.
- uses long words ("requiring") and specialized terms ("data," "Canadian Police Information Centre").
- does not use contractions ("you have been told," "there is").
- uses long and complicated sentences.

Example of Moderate Level of Language

"Avoid foods high in fat, protein, and fibre, as they're tougher to digest and make you feel sluggish. Take a pass on anything greasy, spicy or unfamiliar—this is not the time to experiment with new foods. And hey, eat foods you actually like!" ("Chew on This," page 43).

This example shows the traits of moderate language because it uses
- long ("unfamiliar," "experiment") and short ("this is not the time") words.
- popular expressions ("take a pass" "and hey").
- contractions ("they're").
- short and long sentences.

Example of Informal Level of Language

The bell rang. History class was starting but I didn't care. I sat in a stall and thought about the word *dump*. I had been *dumped*. *Dumped* where people *dump*" ("You Never Know (Tish)," page 24).

This example shows the traits of informal language because it uses
- everyday speech and everyday words.
- popular expressions ("out of my life") and slang ("where people dump").
- contractions ("didn't").
- short simple sentences ("The bell rang.").
- sentence fragments (Dumped where people dump).

Form and Purpose

This table shows some forms, their purposes, and the appropriate level of language.

FORMS OF WRITING	PURPOSE	APPROPRIATE LEVEL OF LANGUAGE
Personal Writing • diaries and journals • notes and lists • letters	• expresses personal thoughts	• informal, casual
Creative Writing • letters • poems and song lyrics • stories and scripts • autobiographies	• amuses and entertains • makes audience think and feel	• ranges from informal to formal • uses descriptive language
Informational Writing • essays and reports • business letters • instructions • news articles • textbooks • biographies	• summarizes information based on research and analysis • describes how to put something together • interprets information, sometimes using charts and graphs • argues and persuades	• ranges from moderate to formal • may be in point form, especially in a chart or diagram • may use specialized terms especially if the audience is a particular group

Writing

→ METHODS OF DEVELOPMENT

Whether you are writing a single paragraph or a series of several paragraphs as a report or essay, you want to organize your details effectively for your reader. The best organizational structure will depend on your purpose and the information you have.

1. Development by Example

Specific examples help make a general idea clearer, especially if the example can connect to the reader's personal experience and knowledge.

> **Activity**
> With a partner, make up a specific example to support one of the following general ideas:
> - Participation in sports teaches important lessons in life.
> - People do not make good use of their leisure time.
> - Television offers good entertainment.

2. Development by Comparison

One way to explain something is to show how it is similar to (comparison) or different from (contrast) something else. A Venn diagram (page 270) can help sort out similarities and differences. When you write up your comparison, you can organize your information in different ways.

Here is Sasha's Venn diagram comparing Niagara Falls and Windsor:

NIAGARA FALLS
- tourist attractions: Butterfly Garden, The Falls, parks
- smaller, permanent population
- few industries, several factories closed

(overlap)
- in Ontario
- border cities (beside USA)
- popular tourist destinations (museums, natural beauty)
- problems (border-crossing security)

WINDSOR
- tourist attractions: Underground Railway museums, Science Centre, Pelee Island Bird Sanctuary close by
- large, permanent population
- university
- many industries, especially car-making
- pollution

THE REFERENCE SHELF

Here are two ways Sasha could organize the presentation of her information.

	METHOD A: DEVELOPING FEATURE BY FEATURE	**METHOD B:** DEVELOPING ONE CITY AT A TIME
Paragraph 1 **Introduction**	• How Niagara Falls and Windsor are similar (border cities in Ontario, tourist destinations) Transition sentence—But Niagara Falls and Windsor are also different in many ways.	• How Niagara Falls and Windsor are similar (border cities in Ontario, tourist destinations) Transition sentence—But Niagara Falls and Windsor are also different in many ways.

Paragraph 2	• Size of permanent and tourist populations of Niagara Falls
	• Size of permanent and tourist populations of Windsor
		• Description of Niagara Falls
		  • population (permanent and tourist)
		  • tourist attractions
		  • problems

Paragraph 3	• Tourist attractions of Niagara Falls
	• Tourist attractions of Windsor
		• Description of Windsor
		  • population (permanent and tourist)
		  • tourist attractions
		  • problems

Paragraph 4	• Problems with Niagara Falls • Problems with Windsor	
Conclusion	The two cities are similar, but each city has its own character.	The two cities are similar, but each city has its own character.

Activity

1. With a partner, discuss the advantages and disadvantages of each method.
2. Practise developing a comparison by creating a Venn diagram and then an outline chart like the one above for one of the following pairs:
   - two sports such as hockey and tennis
   - two animals such as a cat and a dog
   - two foods such as a doughnut and pizza

3. Development by Cause and Effect

Cause and effect tells why something happened. You can
- start with a cause and show its effect (for example, playing loud music and wearing headphones damages hearing).
- start with an effect and explain its cause (for example, hearing loss is the result of playing music too loudly while wearing headphones).

CAUTION: Just because one event follows another does not mean that the first event is a cause of the second. For example, you might think, *Whenever my grandmother comes to visit, it rains.* But your grandmother's visit cannot cause the weather to change.

A web (see page 270) can help organize cause and effect.

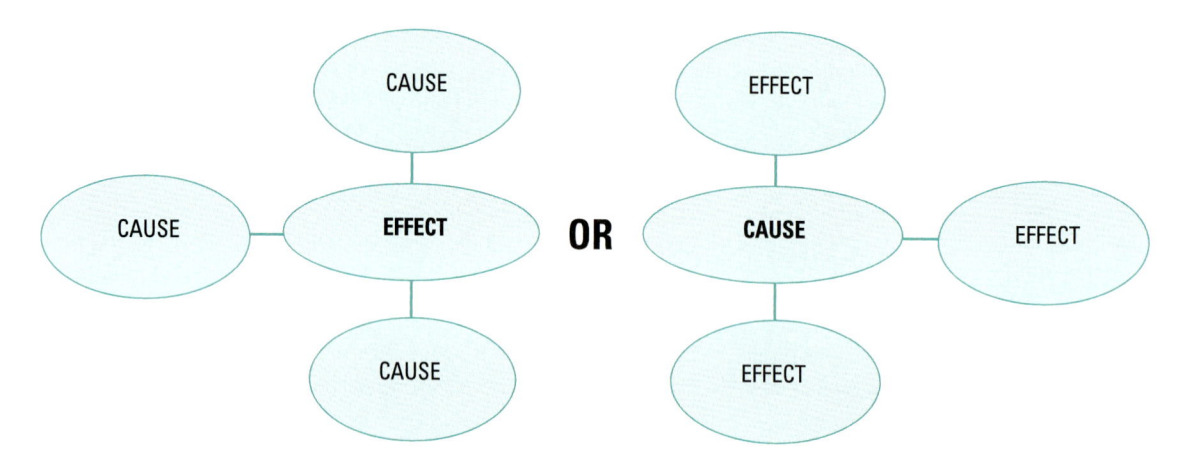

```
    CAUSE                    EFFECT
      |                        |
CAUSE—EFFECT    OR    CAUSE—CAUSE—EFFECT
      |                        |
    CAUSE                    EFFECT
```

Activity

Read the following paragraph. Create a web to show the reasons why (causes) the Royal Canadian Mounted Police was formed.

The Royal Canadian Mounted Police was first formed in 1873. Railroad construction had opened Canada's western territories to new settlers who wanted the security of an official police agency. Lawless fur traders poisoned wildlife and stole from the Aboriginal people. The RCMP was meant to establish law and control these traders. In addition, the RCMP was to ensure that the increasing number of American settlers did not take over Canadian land and claim it for the United States. Today, the RCMP continues to maintain the peace and enforce the law.

4. Development by Classification

Classification is used to show how something does or does not fit into a category. Your paragraph or essay might show how *The Blind Hunter* (page 16) fits into the category of "legend."

FEATURES OF THIS CATEGORY	HOW YOUR TOPIC FITS INTO THIS CATEGORY	HOW YOUR TOPIC DOES NOT FIT INTO THE CATEGORY
Feature A		
Feature B		
Feature C		

Transitions

Transitions are like bridges that link one idea to another. They make writing flow smoothly and logically. Transitions are used to connect sentences in the same paragraph and paragraphs in a longer writing piece. Here are some ways to link ideas.

Repetition

Repetition of a word or phrase from one sentence or paragraph to the next reminds the reader of the idea. Be careful though. The writing can sound repetitive and boring if this technique is overused.

Activity Which sample uses repetition effectively?

Sample A
Several species of wild birds live in Ontario. Some species of wild birds live in Ontario all year round, and other species of wild birds live in Ontario only during the warmer months. The species of wild birds that do not live in Ontario all year round migrate south for the colder months.

Sample B
Several species of wild birds live in Ontario. Some live there all year round, and others live there only during the warmer months. The species that do not live in Ontario all year round migrate south for the colder months.

Substitution (Pronouns, Synonyms)

Using a pronoun to replace a noun and using synonyms (two words that have the same meaning) links ideas and avoids too much repetition.

Example:

The Beatles and *The Rolling Stones* were two English bands. *Both* became popular in the 1960s. *The first* played music from the American rock tradition while *the other* was influenced by Black American blues.

However, you must be sure that the meaning of your substitution is clear.

For example: "Many popular music groups today like to play *Beatles* and *Rolling Stones* songs, not just listen to them. *It* is inspiring." (What does the word "it" refer to, the playing or the listening?)

Connecting Words and Phrases

Connecting words and phrases shows relationships between ideas. Here are some examples.

To add ideas	and, in addition, similarly, too, likewise, again, in the same way, besides, moreover, furthermore, further
To show cause and effect	as a result, consequently, therefore, accordingly, thus, hence, for this reason, it follows that
To show similarity (to compare)	similarly, likewise, in the same way
To show differences (contrast)	but, however, nevertheless, otherwise, on the other hand, on the contrary, by contrast, yet, still, conversely
To introduce examples	for example, for instance, such as
To show order	first (note: not firstly), in the first place, to begin with, next, in conclusion
To show time	now, then, currently, at present, later, thereafter, eventually, at the same time, meanwhile, during
To show location	here, there, to the right, above, below, in between, to the left, farther away, straight ahead, in the distance

GRAPHIC ORGANIZERS

Generating Ideas

It can be difficult to get started writing. To overcome writer's block, try **brainstorming** on paper with a strategy called **quick write**. You may have a topic in mind or your teacher may give you a topic related to a reading or to an assignment. Write non-stop for one to two minutes, without judging and without lifting your pen off the page. Not everything you write will be useful, but this strategy gets the mental wheels turning and helps you get ready for the next stage—organizing ideas.

Graphic organizers are visual diagrams of organizational patterns. Different organizers suit different types of writing, but all will help you group ideas so they can be presented logically and effectively.

Clustering

Clustering is a way of recording, and later connecting, ideas and information as you read. Put the key concept in the centre of the page. In the surrounding circles, jot down words that come to you. After reading, draw lines to show how ideas could be linked together. Below is an example of this strategy.

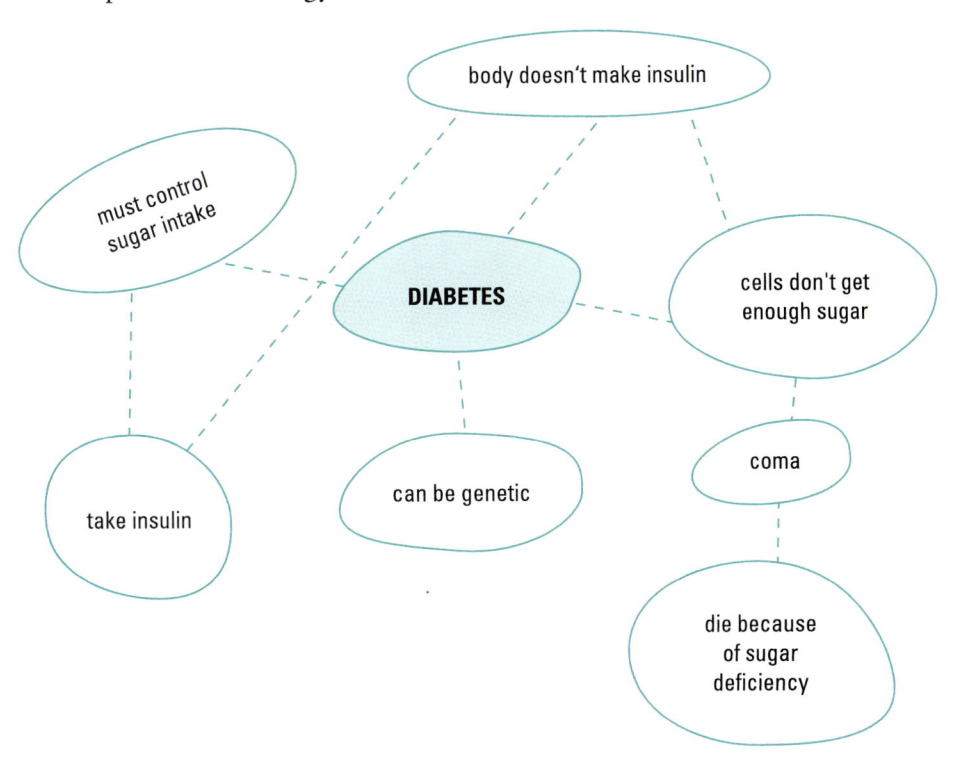

Webs

Sometimes your cluster circles (page 269) give you enough organizational structure to begin writing. But sometimes you need to reorganize or sort out ideas and make the connections more clear. This is when you can use a web. The main topic or concept is placed in the centre and the subtopics are placed around it. Details are grouped around the subtopics. An example of a web is below.

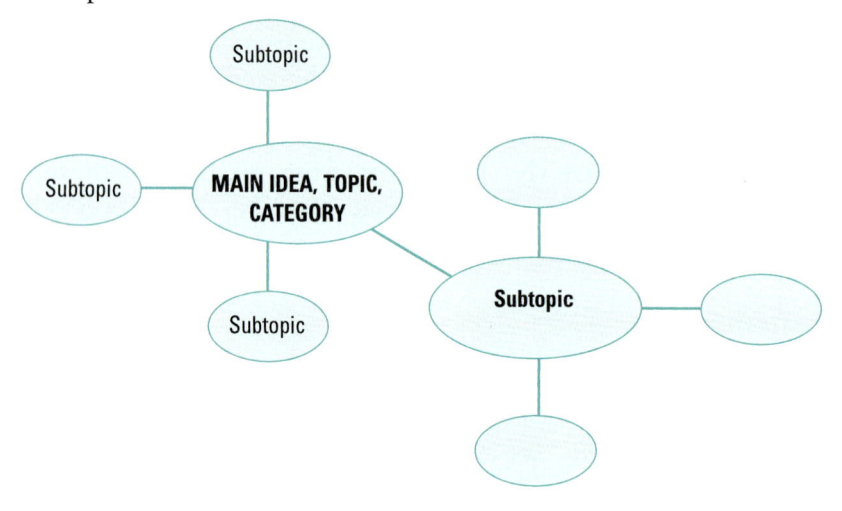

Mind Maps (Drawing)

Drawing a mind map works well for people who think more in pictures than in words. Do not worry about your artistic ability. The drawings are symbols to represent your thoughts. As each thought comes to you, draw a diagram or picture or write a key word to capture it. Afterwards, look for patterns and connections.

Venn Diagrams

Use a Venn diagram when you want to show how two or more things are similar and different. This graphic organizer is useful to prepare a comparison.

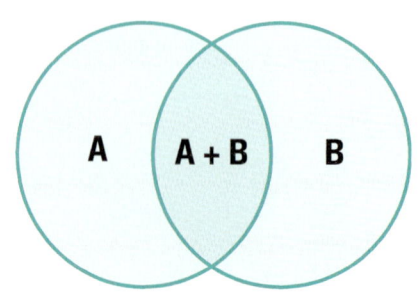

Timelines

A timeline shows the sequence of events in the order in which they happened. A timeline is especially useful to untangle a story or biography that has many flashbacks or that does not use chronological order.

History of the Basketball

1891
James Naismith invents the game of basketball, and writes the original 13 basketball rules. A soccer ball and two peach baskets are used to play the game

1935
Milton Reach, who worked at Spalding, patents a moulded ball built around a thin hollow sphere.

1939
James Naismith dies.

1950
Milton Reach's ball becomes the official ball used for the sport.

1890
James Naismith graduates from McGill University in Montréal and enters the YMCA Training School in Springfield

1896
Spalding Sporting Goods publishes the "Official Basket Ball Rules" and makes their own 18–20 ounce ball the standard.

1936
Basketball is added to the Olympics.

1946
The National Basketball Association (NBA) is formed.

A variation of the timeline is a sequential **flow chart**. A flow chart is a useful organizer to prepare step-by-step instructions or procedures where it is important to follow the correct order.

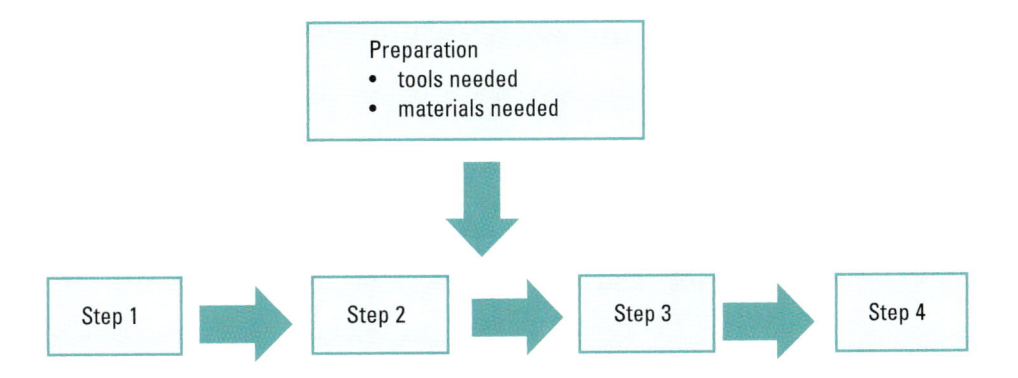

Preparation
- tools needed
- materials needed

Step 1 → Step 2 → Step 3 → Step 4

Writing | SECTION 3 | 271

Expositions

This graphic organizer helps you write a report, an essay, or an explanation.

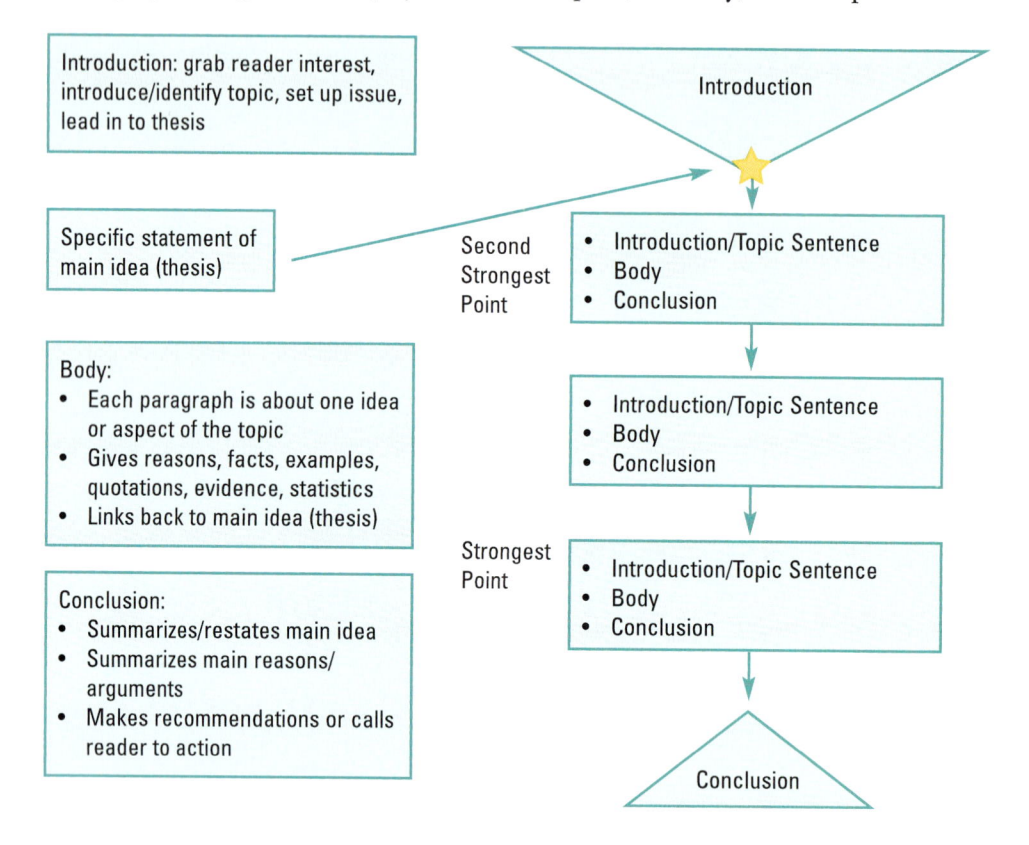

Introduction: grab reader interest, introduce/identify topic, set up issue, lead in to thesis

Specific statement of main idea (thesis)

Body:
- Each paragraph is about one idea or aspect of the topic
- Gives reasons, facts, examples, quotations, evidence, statistics
- Links back to main idea (thesis)

Conclusion:
- Summarizes/restates main idea
- Summarizes main reasons/arguments
- Makes recommendations or calls reader to action

Introduction

Second Strongest Point
- Introduction/Topic Sentence
- Body
- Conclusion

- Introduction/Topic Sentence
- Body
- Conclusion

Strongest Point
- Introduction/Topic Sentence
- Body
- Conclusion

Conclusion

EDIT AND REVISE

Revising Your Work

To help you decide if your ideas are complete, clearly expressed, and well organized, use RADS (Reorder, Add, Delete, and Substitute).

R—Reorder

❒ Does each idea flow clearly and logically to the next one?
❒ Are there any ideas out of place?
❒ Are my ideas organized in the best way

A—Add

- ❏ Have I included enough information and examples, reasons, or proof?
- ❏ Should I add description to make my writing more interesting?
- ❏ Should I add imagery to strengthen the effect I want to create?
- ❏ Should I add more transitions to link ideas more clearly?
- ❏ Will my readers react to my writing the way I want them to?

D—Delete

- ❏ Do I have any ideas that are not connected to my topic?
- ❏ Do I have any ideas that do not strengthen the point I'm trying to make?
- ❏ Have I repeated words or ideas unnecessarily?

S—Substitute

- ❏ Are other facts or ideas better than those I have included?
- ❏ Is my language appropriate for my purpose and audience?
- ❏ Could I find better words to capture the feeling I want to express?
- ❏ Are there linking words that are not working?

Editing and Proofreading

When you are editing your own or someone else's work, try to answer these questions:

Ideas

- What is your main idea?
- How many ideas have you included? Are they enough?
- What details did you use to support your ideas?
- Have you used the best details to support your ideas?
- How do your ideas relate to the reading or research you did?
- Have you used **facts** or **opinions** to support your ideas?
- Are there ideas you can get rid of?

Organization

- Have you written in the form you were asked for?
- How have you made the beginning of your writing interesting?
- How do you know you stayed on topic?
- Is there a better order you could put your ideas in?
- (For poetry) Are there other forms that might be better for your ideas?
- Show me your beginning, middle, and end.

- (For narratives) Have you used all the parts of a story?
- How have you followed the **conventions** of the form you have used?
- How do the details in your paragraph develop your topic sentence?
- What transitions have you used?

Voice

- Have you used the **point of view** asked for in the instructions?
- Why have you changed your point of view?
- Is this the best point of view to use?
- How does this writing sound like … (put in the writer's name)?
- Can you describe the tone of your writing?
- How does the tone suit your audience?
- How does the tone suit your purpose for writing?

Word and Sentence Choice

- Who is your audience?
- What words have you used that suit your audience?
- Have you chosen words that express your meaning and feeling?
- How formal is your language? Does it suit the purpose and audience?
- What different types of sentences have you used?
- Have you avoided racist, sexist, and homophobic language?

Punctuation

- Could you have used a period here?
- Have you used periods and capital letters where you need them?
- Could you have used a question mark here?
- Have you used commas and **dashes** correctly?
- Why did you use a comma here instead of a period?
- Have you checked and corrected comma splices?
- Have you used quotation marks around direct speech?

Grammar and Usage

- Are all verb tenses correct?
- Do pronouns agree in number and gender with the words they replace?
- Is this a complete sentence?
- Why are these ideas run together?
- Have you checked and corrected run-on sentences?

Spelling

- Have you used the Spelling and Grammar feature on the word processor? (Note: Even if your answer is yes, do not depend on this tool as your only check.)
- Have you checked all your **homophones** such as *their/there/they're, know/no, it's/its?*
- Have you checked for missing letters?
- Have you used apostrophes correctly?
- Have you included capital letters where needed?
- Have you checked the spelling of specialized vocabulary?
- How do you spell…?

Sources

- Have you used quotation marks around all words that have come from someone else's writing?
- Have you named the source of those words in a footnote and/or a bibliography?

Constructing a Portfolio

A portfolio is a collection of work developed over a period of time. Your portfolio showcases your skills for other people to see. Usually each item has an explanation with it, telling why it has been included in the portfolio. For example, you might say, "This item shows how much better I became at …," or "This item shows that I learned how to …" The purpose of your portfolio will determine what you want to include in it. See the chart on page 276 for tips on how to set up a sample writing portfolio.

PURPOSE OF PORTFOLIO	CRITERIA FOR CHOICES	SAMPLE PORTFOLIO INCLUDES ...	USE THE PORTFOLIO ...
• to demonstrate the highest level of your skills to date • to show off your capabilities	• samples of your best work • a variety of items that show a range of **styles** and forms, to show simple and complex work	• a short story, an essay, a poem, a script, a letter, a lab report, a news article, and an instructional diagram	• to apply for a job or for a placement in a course or college
• to demonstrate a process, to show how something developed over time • to show that you know how to do something from start to finish • to show that you know how to apply strategies to complete a project effectively and efficiently • to prove that your work is not plagiarized	• samples of different stages of one assignment or samples of different stages of work from different assignments • sample items from all the stages of the writing process for an assignment	• the final copy of a persuasive essay along with its prewriting idea web, its two different point-form outlines, the first draft covered with peer- and self-editing comments, and all later drafts showing revisions and editing	• to teach someone else the skills you already have • to apply for a job or project • when submitting an assignment
• to show the growth in your learning and skills • to show how much your work has improved	• before and after samples of work for similar assignments • Items should be good quality if not best quality	• two short stories: one written in September and a better one written in December	• to demonstrate your ability to learn • to apply for a course at a higher level
• to showcase "you": your personality, your interests, and skills	• items chosen mostly for their ability to represent your personality • a variety of items that show a range of styles and forms, to show simple and complex work	• a funny poem you wrote, a speech you gave at a friend's birthday, a thank-you note to your peer mentor, a letter of application for an award	• to apply for a job

SECTION 4

Oral Communication Skills

Most people feel nervous and lack confidence when they speak in front of others. But making an oral presentation is a big part of everyday life. A person uses oral communication skills when meeting new people, working in a group, participating in an interview, delivering a speech, performing, and making formal and informal presentations.

GO! In this section you will find information about ways to improve your presentation and listening skills.

| Good Listening Skills | Oral Presentations | Cooperative Learning |
| page 277 | page 277 | page 280 |

GOOD LISTENING SKILLS

Here are some things you should and should not do as a listener. When it is your turn to be the speaker, you will appreciate an audience that acts according to the DO list.

DO ...	DON'T ...
• look at the speaker (eye contact).	• make a quick judgment of the speaker based on appearance or delivery.
• ignore outside noises and distracting behaviours.	• tune out or let your mind wander especially when difficult ideas are being discussed.
• think about what the speaker is saying (go back over the speaker's facts and ideas).	• interrupt the speakers or make side comments to others in the audience.
• participate, if invited, in questioning and discussion.	• let distractions break your concentration.
• take notes.	• let your own opinions interfere with your understanding of the presentation.
• pay attention to non-verbal communication such as gestures, facial expressions, and posture.	
• pay attention to aids such a slides, photographs, charts, and diagrams.	

ORAL PRESENTATIONS

Activity

With a partner, **brainstorm** five situations in which you are likely to need strong oral communication skills <u>outside of school</u> within the next ten years. Here are a few examples to get you started:
- making a speech at a wedding or funeral
- accepting an achievement award
- making a presentation at your job

Planning Your Oral Presentation

You will feel more confident and your presentation will be more effective if you think about your **purpose**, **audience**, and message.

Know Your Purpose

What do you want your oral presentation to do?
- inform
- persuade
- motivate

Know Your Audience

Who will be listening to your presentation?
- reason they want to hear your presentation
- interests and characteristics of the audience
  - age and attention span
  - interest in topic
  - amount of knowledge the audience already has on the topic
- ways you can involve your audience

Know Your Subject

What is the message you want to communicate in your presentation?
- Research to gather accurate information on topic.
- Decide on the key ideas you want to communicate.
- Select appropriate information.
- Organize information.
  - Get rid of information that does not add to your presentation, is unimportant, or might bore audience.
  - Add information to fill in gaps.
  - Replace weak points with strong points.
  - Emphasize key ideas.
  - Put information in logical order.
  - Start with a hook to get your audience interested in your topic.
  - End with a powerful conclusion.
  - Plan ways for your audience to participate.
- Prepare a handout for your audience if it is appropriate.

Some General Tips for Presenting

Rehearsal

- Write your key points on numbered cue cards.
- Practise making your presentation in front of a mirror, in front of friends or family members, into a tape-recorder, or on videotape. Ask for feedback about the variety in your voice and your body language.
- Go over your presentation many times aloud. Rehearse the pronunciation of unfamiliar words.
- Practise with audio-visuals aids and be sure to cue them before presenting.
- Time the delivery of your presentation to be sure it fits within your given time frame. You may need to add or remove information.

On Stage

- Be yourself; act natural. Smile and relax a little.
- Look at your audience. Make your audience feel like you care about their interest.
- Let your own enthusiasm for your topic show.
- Make it clear to the audience at the start why your presentation is important to them (and to you).
- Glance at your notes, but do not read them word-for-word.
- Speak slowly, clearly, and loud enough so your audience can hear and understand you. Put expression in your voice.
- Hook your audience through an appeal to their emotions and needs.
- Use humour if appropriate and effective.
- Use audio and visual aids such as writing on the board, posters, overheads, slides, video clips, and presentation software (for example, Microsoft PowerPoint). Remember to have all the equipment on hand and cued.

Stage Fright

- Be prepared. The actual presentation is just a small part of the total job. If you have researched your subject, organized your information logically, and rehearsed your delivery, you will feel in control and the presentation will flow easily.
- Focus on the audience, not on yourself. You are giving something—information or entertainment—that your audience wants.
- Move around. Facial expressions and hand gestures use up some of that extra energy and may stop nervous and distracting behaviours.

Oral Communication Skills

COOPERATIVE LEARNING—WORKING IN A GROUP

Activity

In a small group, list as many situations you can think of in which individuals work together. All members of your group must agree with the idea before you can list it on your page.

Read the description of an effective group member below. Now think about the way your group performed the task. Did your group demonstrate effective group work skills? Share your opinion with your group members.

Skills and Attitudes of an Effective Group Member

AN EFFECTIVE GROUP MEMBER ...	BY SAYING ...
• respects the opinions and contributions of others	"Your idea is really different from mine. Maybe we could combine the two."
• accepts responsibility	"Okay, I'll volunteer to give the oral presentation. Someone else can make the posters."
• participates willingly	"Let's get started. I'll take the first turn at note taking."
• listens closely to others	"This is what I think you are saying: ..."
• encourages others	"We haven't heard from Marcia yet."
• asks questions to clarify understanding	"I don't understand what you mean. Could you please go over that point again?"
• disagrees without being disagreeable	"If you look at this issue from a different **point of view**, you can see that ..."

Groups work best when each member clearly understands the
- task—What is the group supposed to accomplish?
- timeframe—How much time does the group have to complete the task?
- roles—Who does what? How will each person contribute to the task?

THE REFERENCE SHELF

ROLE	BY SAYING ...
The Leader	
• keeps the group focused on the task	"We're getting off topic. Let's get back to our task."
• keeps the big picture in mind	"What about doing this in another way?" "If we focus on that one part, we won't be doing the whole task that we've been assigned."
• ensures that all group members contribute	"Does everyone understand what each person is doing?"
The Manager	
• ensures that all parts of the task are completed	"This is what I think we should do first."
• organizes materials	"We will need a tablecloth, a basket, and a red hat for the skit on Monday. Who can bring them to school?"
• watches time	"We have 10 minutes left and we haven't looked at question #3 yet."
The Note Taker/Recorder	
• writes down ideas and information	"Have a look at what I've written so far and tell me if I've got it all down accurately."
• makes sure that the group understands what members are saying	"When you say ..., do you mean that...?"
• summarizes key ideas	"This is what I'm writing down to summarize your idea."
The Reporter/Presenter	
• speaks for the group	"How do you want me to show that we didn't all come to the same conclusion?"
• presents the group project or task to others	"What is the best way to share our information with everybody else?"
The Supporter/Encourager	
• helps group members interact effectively and respectfully	"This discussion is getting a little tense. Let's not take things so personally." "That's a really good point."
• makes sure no one interrupts or puts down another group member	"Peter, you have some good ideas but you need to give other people a chance to speak."
• makes sure all members are able to contribute	"Let's hear from ... before we decide."

(Source: adapted from *Think Literacy Cross-Curricular Approaches, Grades 7–12*. Published by the Ontario Ministry of Education, page 160; ISBN 0-7794-5426-X; 03-252)

SECTION 5

The Media

The ability to analyze and understand the media and its affect on us is becoming increasingly important. Understanding how media creators and advertisers create their works, how they address the needs of the audience, and the techniques they use is an important aspect of understanding the world around us. By understanding these things, we are able to create our own media works as well.

GO! In this section you will find information about creating and understanding media texts.

| Graphic Texts | Creating Visual and Media Works | Production Elements |
| page 282 | page 284 | page 280 |

➤ GRAPHIC TEXTS

Cartoons, **comics**, and graphic stories often include words, but the visual aspect of them is most important. Here are some considerations to help you "read" visual texts more effectively.

Central Focus

The artist draws your attention to one part of the drawing.
- making the focus larger
- putting the most important image in the centre of the **frame** or by itself
- including more details in the drawing of the central focus
- using stronger or different colours for emphasis
- using strong lines to point to the central focus (for example, someone pointing to it, lines from other objects leading the eye to it)

Point of View

A cartoon is like a frame in a film, and the artist's **point of view** is like a camera. The artist draws the action from a point of view and distance. Look at the sections Camera Angle and Camera Distance (page 288) for more information.

Use of Text

The appearance of the text is important. Font style and size are important visual clues to information and emotional meaning.

| THE REFERENCE SHELF

A character's spoken words and thoughts are shown in bubbles. The design of the bubble often expresses emotion.

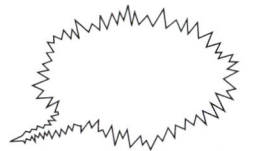

A zigzagged edge on a bubble might indicate anger.

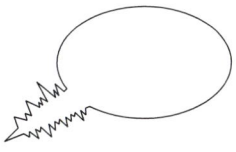

A jagged pointer of the speech bubble can indicate that these words are being spoken on a telephone or electronically.

Thoughts are distinguished from speech by a series of small circles from the character to the text.

Speech bubble

Font style is also used for expression, especially for sound effects. Because text is meant to add to, but not overwhelm, the visual presentation, the artist must choose words carefully. Writers of graphic text make use of **onomatopoeia** for sound effects. Onomatopoeia means that the word imitates the sound. Examples are "BAM," "POW," and "ZOOM."

Movement

To suggest movement, the artist can use various techniques. A gesture partway through the action such as a person in mid-step or an arm partly raised lets us know that a character is moving. Details in the drawing such as "speed lines" can show movement.

Unity

In a single frame cartoon such as a political cartoon in a newspaper, unity is achieved by the emphasis on the central focus. In a comic strip or graphic story that is made up of a series of frames, unity is achieved by
- repetition of images
- placing one object so that a line or edge of it continues to another shape
- extending an image from one frame into the next frame (for example, chimney smoke from one frame is shown in the following frame as a cloud)
- using text to provide background information or narrative links

Activity

1. Using frames from "The Toynbee Convector" (page 214), find examples of each of these concepts.
   - central focus
   - use of text
   - unity
   - point of view
   - movement

2. Create a classroom display of cartoons, comic strips, and photocopied pages from graphic stories (comic books, graphic novels). Choose one and comment on the way it demonstrates the idea of central focus, point of view, use of text, movement, or unity.

CREATING VISUAL AND MEDIA WORKS

Posters, storyboards, collages, book covers, and brochures are all examples of visual or media works. Creating visual media works requires similar steps to the ones you take when writing.

Research

- Get ideas and background images by looking through books and magazines and viewing videos. Photocopy print images that you like for reference, but never cut up a book that is not your own.
- Take your own photographs or make your own sketches from your own observations.

Choose a Focus

- What is the main idea or aspect of the topic that you want your final product to show—the **characters**? the **setting**? an event or action? a symbolic object?

THE REFERENCE SHELF

- What should be in the foreground, middle ground, and background?
- How can you use size and colour to emphasize important ideas?

Create Thumbnail Sketches

- A **thumbnail sketch** is a small sketch, drawn quickly inside a frame. It is done to experiment with ideas for content and composition, like an outline is used for a writing assignment. It does not contain details, only the rough main idea.
- Make many thumbnail sketches to capture your different ideas about content, arrangement, colour, and sizing.
- Use your research pictures for inspiration, but avoid copying them. Most pictures belong to the artist (see Plagiarism, page 255) and your work should be uniquely your own.
- Spread out your sketches to look at them. Choose the best two or three to work from for the rough sketch.

Create Rough Sketches

- A **rough sketch** is usually larger and more detailed than a thumbnail.
- The rough sketch is in proportion to the final product if it is not the same size.
- Check over your finished rough sketch.
  - Does your sketch communicate the message you want to send?
  - Is there a definite centre of interest that emphasizes your main ideas?
  - Have you used **graphic features** such as size, colour, and layout effectively?
  - Are all words spelled correctly?

Final copy

When you are satisfied with your design, create a final, full-sized version.

Creating a Collage

A **collage** is a collection of visual materials that, grouped together, express an idea, a **theme**, or a mood. Pictures, photographs, words, and symbolic objects are all used in collages to provide visual interest.

Here are some suggestions to help you make your collage expressive, interesting, and thoughtful.

Create a Background with Depth

- Let the background colour suit the mood of the collage.
- Materials on a similar subject collected from magazines, such as pictures of sports events, city skylines, country landscapes, or celebrity faces, can be used as the background. Placing other visuals on top of them will create some depth to your collage.

Create Areas of Focus

There are various ways to establish the focus of your collage. One is to use one very strong image or object as the central focal point and arrange other images around it. Another way is to divide your collage into sections, with each section saying something different about your main idea.

Create Variety Within the Main Idea

Although all your images relate to the main idea, try to create variety by
- using visual similarities (for example, wheels on a toy truck, a Ferris wheel, a steering wheel)
- using contrasting images (for example, pictures of a baby's face and an old person's face)
- using contrasting textures or materials (for example, a yellowed newspaper article and a glossy, colourful magazine advertisement)
- connecting unrelated things by putting them together

Use Repeated Images

Repetition reinforces an idea. For example, many pictures of pairs of eyes along with a few simple visuals and text would make a powerful collage on the theme of guilt.

Use Words Creatively

Many collages combine pictures and words in a balanced way.
- Try using quotations from various sources.
- Look for, or make, the words in different font sizes and styles.
- Cut up words and arrange them in new ways.

PRODUCTION ELEMENTS

People who make television programs, videos, and films pay attention to the visual (picture) and the audio (sound) elements.

Visual Elements

The picture elements of a media production include the following:
- film footage
    - original live-action
    - interviews
    - dramatizations and reenactments
    - stored footage, either footage shot in the past (archival) or footage from other films
- still photographs
- titles, headlines, **subtitles**
- cartoon and other graphics
- special effects

Audio Elements

The sound elements of a media production include the following:
- live recordings made at the same time as the visuals (for example, on-the-street interviews, music at a live concert)
- sound recorded separately, on its own, and dubbed onto the film or tape
- voice-over commentary, usually scripted and spoken by a **narrator**, recorded separately, and then dubbed onto the film or tape
- music
- sound effects
- background noise
- silence
- ambient noise (for example, street sounds, birds, farm animals)

Camera Terms

Camera Distance

- extreme close-up: for example, person's eyes
- close-up: for example, person's whole face
- medium close-up: for example, person's head and shoulders
- medium shot: for example, person's body from the waist up
- medium long shot: for example, person's complete body
- long shot: for example, full body and some of the surrounding environment
- extreme long shot: for example, person is in the distant background; a lot of the surrounding environment can be seen

Camera Angle

- high—the bird's eye view
  - camera placed well above normal eye level—viewer looks down on subject
  - subject can appear to look victimized or alone
- low—the worm's eye view
  - camera placed below eye level—viewer looks up at subject
  - subject can appear to be more powerful or in control

Camera Movement

- tilt—camera moves up or down
- pan (panorama)—camera moves right to left or left to right
- dolly—camera moves towards or away from the subject in a straight line
- truck—camera moves right or left in a straight line
- zoom—camera lens focuses in on the subject or moves back from the subject

Creating a Storyboard

A **storyboard** is a series of sketches used to prepare for filming. A storyboard sketch shows
- content of scene
- camera distance
- camera angle
- camera movement
- audio
- length of shot

The storyboard below shows a series of three shots.

Sample Storyboard

1. description of shot contents: person approaching mall entrance
2. camera distance: long shot
3. camera angle: eye level
4. camera movement: pan left as subject enters doorway
5. audio: traffic and footsteps
6. shot duration in seconds: five seconds

1. person carrying a shopping bag
2. medium shot
3. eye level
4. pan right as subject walks to bus stop
5. footsteps
6. two seconds

1. shopping bag
2. close up
3. eye level
4. (no movement)
5. (no audio)
6. three seconds

> > > Glossary

alliteration: Alliteration is a group of words that begin with the same sound. Alliterations can help you remember the writing and reinforce meaning. Examples are: perfect pancakes, super spicy samosas, chocolate chip cheesecake

antagonist: The antagonist is the character in a story who goes against the main character; he or she may be the villain.

atmosphere: Atmosphere is the feeling in a piece of writing. It is created through word choice, descriptive details, and vivid imagery. For example, a horror story writer might create atmosphere by saying, "The heavy black door slowly creaked open. A gust of cold air hit Misha's face as she peeked inside. Her heart started to beat faster, and she felt a shiver go down her back. Suddenly, she was blinded by a flash of light."

audience: Audience is the group of people for whom a piece of writing, film, television program, and so on, is intended. When trying to figure out who the audience is, consider things like the author's word choices, and the age, gender, cultural background, clothing style, interests, and level of education of those people featured in the piece.

bias: Bias happens when only a specific viewpoint is shown. Authors show bias when they present only one side of an issue, such as showing only the advantages or disadvantages of an issue.

brainstorm: Brainstorming is a writing strategy used to create ideas about a topic. When brainstorming, you should write down <u>all</u> the ideas given, even if they don't seem correct. When you've finished brainstorming, you can sort your ideas to decide which ones you want to use.

bulleted list: A bulleted list gives small amounts of information. The following are some characteristics of a bulleted list:
- incomplete sentences (point form)
- bullets at the start of each point
- general information (not detailed)

character: Characters are the people who are in a story. The story involves things that happen to these people (the plot). In myths or **legends**, the characters might be animals, monsters, or gods.

character traits: Character traits describe the personality of a character in a story. For instance, a character may be kind or cruel, funny or dull, warm and caring, or cold and insensitive. Character traits can also be physical, such as hair or eye colour or body type. You can discover characters' traits by how they act, by what another character says about them, what they say about themselves, what a narrator says about them, and how they respond to others.

chronological order: Chronological order is the order in which events actually happen. For example, this morning, you had to wake up, get out of bed, get ready for school, the bell rang, and classes began.

climax: Climax is a part of the plot of a story. It is the point at which the conflict is resolved. It is usually the point of greatest interest in the story.

collage: A collage is a combination of various items and materials that makes a visual statement about an idea or a theme.

comic: A comic is a story told in picture format. The story can be funny or serious. The story is divided into frames, and characters' speech and thoughts are shown in bubbles. Actions are shown using lines to suggest movement, and also by the changes in the characters' positions from frame to frame. Tone of voice is shown using different types of speech bubbles and fonts.

conflict: Conflict is a struggle between characters, forces, or emotions, usually between the protagonist and someone or something else. Some examples of conflict are person versus person, person versus nature, person versus technology, person versus himself or herself, person versus circumstance.

conventions: This word has two meanings in this book. 1. Conventions of language are spelling and grammar. 2. Conventions of a text are features that are specific to that type of text. For example, comics use speech bubbles to show speech or thought, and lines to show movement; film uses sound, images, and camera angles to tell a story.

dash: A dash is a punctuation mark that looks like this — . It is used to show emphasis or an interruption. For example, to show emphasis, a dash might be used like this: "Money, fame, and fast cars—those are his goals in life." To show interruption, a dash may be used like this: "According to the teacher—but not me—the assignment was difficult."

direct address: Direct address is used when you write or speak directly to someone. For example, the introduction to this book is written in direct address. The authors are speaking directly to the readers of this book.

drama: Drama is a story written in the form of a dialogue that is meant to be acted out in front of an audience. It has the same elements as a story, including plot, character, conflict, setting, and theme.

euphemism: A euphemism is a word or phrase used to hide an unpleasant reality. Examples include saying "pre-owned vehicle" instead of "used car" or "washroom" when you mean "toilet."

explanation: An explanation makes an idea clear and understandable by giving detailed information. For example, your explanation about why you were late for class might include the following: you couldn't get your locker open, you couldn't find your books, and the halls were too crowded to allow you to move quickly.

fact: A fact is something that is known to be true. For example, it is a fact that the Earth circles around the sun.

falling action (denouement): Falling action is sometimes called denouement. It is a part of the plot of a story. Falling action happens after the climax. In the falling action, most of the unanswered parts of the plot are answered or the problems are worked out.

figure of speech: A figure of speech uses words in ways that go beyond their ordinary meaning. Some examples of figures of speech are metaphor (this class is a zoo), simile (he looked like a weasel), personification (the walls have ears), and hyperbole (I've waited 700 years to see this movie).

first person: First person is usually used to refer to the type of narrator for a story. A first-person narrator may tell his or her own story, and refers to himself or herself as "I." A first-person narrator may also be observing and telling the reader about someone else's life but will still tell the story from the "I" point of view. (See The Reference Shelf, page 246.)

flow chart: A flow chart is a graphic organizer that shows a step-by-step method of solving a problem or completing a task. Usually, simple questions are answered by "yes" or "no," and, depending on your answer, you move to the next step in the process. (See The Reference Shelf, page 271.)

folktale: A folktale is a story originating among the common people (the folk) and handed down, usually orally, from generation to generation.

foreshadowing: Foreshadowing is a technique that authors use to give clues about what is going to happen later in the plot. Foreshadowing is used to build suspense and curiosity, and help prepare the reader to accept events that occur later in the story.

format: Format is the way a piece of writing looks. Format could refer to things like the number of columns used in a magazine, the amount of white space left around text and pictures, the size of font, and the space between lines.

frames: Frames are used in comics or storyboards (storyboards are used for ads, TV, and film). Each frame is usually a square shape and shows action and speech in the story. Comics and storyboard pictures are drawn within the frames.

gist statement: A gist statement is an educated guess (prediction) about what you think a story will be about, based on the clues given to you. It is usually written in one sentence.

graphic features: Graphic features are found in visual texts. Examples include: pictures, diagrams, coloured font, different styles of font, size of font, illustrations, titles, subheadings, and background colour.

graphic organizer: A graphic organizer can be a chart, graph, Venn diagram, or other visual means used to record, organize, classify, analyze, and assess information.

homophone: A homophone is a word that sounds the same as another word but has a different meaning. Examples include: to, too, two; hear, here; red, read; their, there, they're.

introduction: The introduction is at the beginning of the paragraph or piece of writing. It tells the reader what he or she will be reading about.

italics: Italics are used as a computer font or graphic feature in a text. Italics look like this: *italics*. They are used to add emphasis to a speaker's voice, point out something important to the reader, or show what a character is thinking. Italics are also used when quoting the name of a book, play, or comic.

jot notes: Jot notes are also called point-form notes. When writing jot notes, you only record the most important information. Jot notes are usually not written in complete sentences. To jot-note this definition, you might say:
- also called point-form notes
- only record most important information
- don't have to be complete sentences

language: Language is the way we communicate with each other. In writing, language refers to the particular words we use to describe something or explain our ideas. For example, you might say, "It's sunny" or "The sun is beaming down on us in golden splendour." When writing, you need to use language appropriate for your audience and the type of writing you are doing.

legend: A legend is a story that is about real or historical people. There is usually a small amount of truth in a legend that could be researched and found to be fact. For example, King Arthur is a legend because there is a real historical king who could be the basis for the King Arthur stories. There are sometimes supernatural characters and events in a legend.

limited narrator: A limited narrator is sometimes called a limited **omniscient narrator**. This narrator knows and shows the thoughts of only a few characters. This type of narrator is not the main character in the story.

metaphor: A metaphor is a **figure of speech** that makes a comparison between two seemingly unlike things without using words such as *like* or *as*. Examples include: this class is a zoo, this room is a pigsty, her eyes are moonbeams.

narrative: Narrative is another word for story.

narrator: The narrator is the person or character who tells the story.

news report: A news report is a truthful retelling of an event or issue. The title of a news report is usually a brief sentence, and the report itself contains short paragraphs. The most important information appears first in a newspaper article so that the reader can stop reading once he or she has sufficient information on the topic.

objective: Objective has several meanings:
1. When you act or think objectively, you deal with situations without being influenced by your emotions. For instance, you buy a new car because it holds all six members of your family, rather than buying a tiny sports car that seats two people.
2. When you have a goal in mind, it can be called an objective. For example, the objective of a video game is to beat the villain and score the most points.

omniscient narrator: An omniscient narrator knows the thoughts of all characters. This type of narrator is not the main character in the story.

onomatopoeia: An onomatopoeia is a word that sounds like its meaning. Examples are *buzz, zip, pow, crack*.

open-ended: If a story is open-ended, it has many possible endings and the reader must imagine an appropriate ending. If a question is open-ended, it means it must be answered with more than a "yes" or "no" answer. Open-ended questions usually include the words *explain* or *why*.

opinion: Your opinion is what you think of a topic, even though you might not know all the facts about it. For example, your opinion might be that you should be able to watch movies at the theatre that are rated above your age group, but the fact is, it is illegal for you to do so.

organization: When writing or reading, organization refers to the way the piece is structured. For example, paragraphs are organized by topic sentence, detail sentences, and conclusion sentence. A story is organized to have a beginning, middle, and end.

outcomes: Outcomes are the results or consequences of a person's actions or words.

plot: The plot of a story is the events of the story. The plot may be simple or complicated.

point of view: Point of view is the perspective from which a story is told. It depends on who is narrating the story. See The Reference Shelf, page 246, for more information.

preview: Previewing is a reading strategy that you use before you read a piece of text. When you preview, you look over a piece of text to help you see what you will be reading about. Previewing also helps give you clues about what information will be important. When previewing, look for things like titles, subheadings, how the piece is laid out, use of colour, illustrations, and bold, italicized, or underlined type.

protagonist: The protagonist is the main character in a narrative. The audience focuses most of their attention on the protagonist. The main character may or may not be the narrator.

pun: A pun happens when a word has more than one meaning. For example, turn to page 247 of The Reference Shelf. The duck joke is a pun on the word *bill*, where "bill" is your charge at a bar or restaurant, and "bill" is another word for the beak of certain birds.

purpose: The purpose of a piece of writing is the reason it was written; sometimes the purpose is also called the goal or aim of a piece of writing. The purpose may be to inform, to entertain, to teach, to explain, and so on.

quick write: Quick writing is a writing strategy that is similar to **brainstorming**. To do a quick write, you write down all the things that come into your head in response to a topic, picture, or quotation. You do not plan this writing and you don't have to worry about spelling, grammar, or repetition. You don't stop writing to fix mistakes.

reader's theatre: Reader's theatre is a technique used for reading a piece of writing out loud. When creating or performing a reader's theatre, you should use the original script or create a script from the original piece of writing. You use few props in reader's theatre; instead, you use your voice, body movement, and repetition to emphasize what is happening in the story.

rhythm: Rhythm is the pattern of sound created by stressed and unstressed syllables. A piece of writing, such as a poem, that has a clear rhythm will make your voice rise and fall (almost like singing) when you are reading it.

rising action: Rising action is a part of the plot of a story. It happens before the climax. Rising action is the series of events that lead to the climax.

root word: A root word is the base word from which other words are formed. For example, the root word *aqua*, which means water, forms the root of words such as aquarium, aquatics, and Aquarius.

rough sketch: A rough sketch is an unpolished drawing of something. It is done quickly to get an idea of size, layout, and use of colour.

round robin: In a round robin each person in a group takes turns speaking.

script: A script is the text written for a play, video, film, or radio or television broadcast. It includes dialogue, sound effects, stage directions, and so on.

setting: Setting is the time and place of a story, play, or poem. For time, a piece of writing could be set in the past, present, or future. Place could be a specific country, city, or town.

simile: A simile is a **figure of speech** that makes a comparison between two unlike things using a word such as *like* or *as*. For example: She's as light as a feather; He looks like he just saw a ghost; The baby is as pretty as a picture.

stage directions: Stage directions are the instructions in a play. They are used to describe the stage setting and to tell actors when to exit or enter the stage, how to deliver their lines, and so on. Stage directions may appear in brackets or italics so you know they are not lines to be read.

stanza: A stanza is a set number of lines grouped together to form units in poetry. Sometimes it is called a verse.

storyboard: A storyboard is a series of panels with sketches and dialogue, representing the shots in an advertisement, film, television program, and so on. It is used to plan a work on film or video.

style: Style is the particular way in which a writer expresses himself or herself in writing. Style is created by the author's choice of voice, vocabulary, and sentence structure, and use of devices such as imagery, onomatopoeia, and rhythm.

subheading: A subheading is a small title used in a piece of long writing. It titles a section or part of the writing; the main title explains what the whole piece of writing is about.

subject: The subject of a piece of writing is the topic the writing is about.

subtitle: A subtitle is an additional title for a piece of writing. The subtitle gives the reader more information on what the piece is about. For example, the title of an article by Anne McIlroy is "Tiny Bubbles?" and the subtitle is "Fish May Be Talking."

summary: A summary is a brief description of a piece of writing that gives only the most important points of a story or article. (See The Reference Shelf, page 260.)

supported opinion: A supported opinion piece of writing tells your opinion on a topic. You support your opinion with evidence from a text or your real life. (See The Reference Shelf, page 259.)

suspense: Suspense is what you feel when you aren't sure about how something will end. Often you feel anxious, scared, or nervous. Suspense is used by writers to create tension, excitement, or anxiety.

T-chart: A T-chart looks like a very large lower-case "t." It is used to show different views on the same topic. For example, if you were asked to create a T-chart about whether students should be allowed to eat in class, it might look like this:

Yes	No
Students need energy to learn.	It makes a mess.
Many students skip breakfast.	It is distracting to learning.
Some students eat lunch very early or late in the day.	It attracts bugs and rodents.

text features: Text features help you make your way through a textbook. The common text features designers include are table of contents, colour, illustrations, pictures, charts and graphs, type features like bolding, italics, underlining, different fonts for different purposes, titles and subheadings, margin notes, glossary, and index.

theme: Theme is a statement of the main idea of a piece of writing or film; it is often referred to as the message the author is trying to send. Theme is implied rather than directly stated. To make a theme statement, you can begin by saying, "The author is saying that …" (See The Reference Shelf, page 251.)

third person: Third person is a type of narrator used in a story. This narrator is not a part of the story but can see all the events that are happening. (See The Reference Shelf, page 246.)

thumbnail sketch: A thumbnail sketch is a small drawing that doesn't have much detail. It is used to plan larger drawings or illustrations.

tone: Tone is the attitude a writer expresses toward his or her subject. The tone of writing may be formal or informal, personal or impersonal, angry or cheerful, bitter or hopeful, and so on. Tone is created by the words the author uses.

transitions: Transitions are links between ideas that help the reader understand how ideas relate to each other. Transitions can be specific words, such as *next*, *first*, *second*, *third*, *finally*, *but*, *yet*, *however*, *for example*, *for instance*, *therefore*, and *then*. Transitions can also be made by repeating a word (or a synonym) between sentences or paragraphs to make sure the reader knows he or she is still on the same topic. You can create a transition by referring back to a previous idea. You can also create transitions by using pronouns like *it*, *they*, *her*, and so on. Be careful when using pronouns. The reader must know what noun the pronoun refers to (called an antecedent).

visual story: A visual story is a story told either entirely with pictures, or with pictures and text. Comic books are visual stories.

voice: Voice is the way a piece of writing uses language. An author creates voice by the words he or she chooses, whether the piece is formal or informal, use of a narrator, and use of descriptive language.

> > > Index

Actors, 252
Acts, in drama, 251
Adjectives, 15, 66, 233, 234
Adverbs, 233, 234
Agreement, 20
"All Ears" (Gorrell), 12–14
Alliteration, 83, 84, 87
Antagonists, 249
Antecedents, 233, 236
Assertive sentences, 235
Atmosphere, 16, 249
Audience, 116, 245. *See also* Readers
   adults as, 3, 8, 87
   of autobiographies, 71
   of drama, 252
   of graphic texts, 213
   of informational texts, 3, 41, 42, 47
   of magazine articles, 84
   of newspaper articles, 87, 167
   of oral presentations, 278
   of plays, 193
   of poems, 10, 181
   for quizzes, 178
   of television shows, 149
   tone and, 261
   young people as, 149

Bar graphs, 159, 162
Barlow, Steve, 150–153
"Best Advice: Handle With Care," 211–212
Bias, 96, 98, 136
The Blind Hunter (Watts), 16–20
"Blue Eyes" (Wafer), 99–100

Body
   of paragraphs, 65
   of reports, 259
"Bones" (de la Mare), 93
Borgman, Jim, 209
Bradbury, Ray, 214–227
Brainstorming, 269
   about characters, 118
   about poetry, 9, 10
   about power, 193
   about procrastination, 175
   adjectives, 15
   editing an opinion piece, 192
   good communication, 38
   inventions, 200
   of knowledge, 83, 84
   predictions regarding a story, 201
   subjects of play, 20, 107
   subjects of poems, 181
   thoughts about height, 98
   visual methods, 162
Broadcasts, 140
   news, 156
Brochures, 38
"Bubble Chamber" (Nepveu), 201–203
Bulleted lists, 213
Burke, L.M., 46–47

Camera
   angles, 214, 288
   distance, 287–288
   movement, 288
   shots, 214

"Can Girls Really Play with Boys?" (Ross), 60–63
Carnegie, Herb, 66–70
Cartoons, 89
Cause and effect, 266
   effect-and-cause charts, 46, 47
Characters
   in comic books, 228
   in drama, 16, 251
   in first-person narrative, 246
   in graphic fiction, 214
   in narratives, 248, 249–250
   in opinion paragraphs, 37
   role playing, 156
   in script, 38
   in short stories, 78
Character traits, 107, 150, 154, 249
Charts, 131, 136, 150, 154, 205
"Chew on This!" (Law), 43–44
Child Find Ontario, 3–7
Chronological order, 191, 258
Classification, 267
Climax, 248
Clustering, 269
Colbourne, Scott, 170–173
Collages, 285–286
Colloquialisms, 232
Colons, 238
Comics, 214, 228
"Coming Out of a Canadian Winter" (Gill), 22
Commas, 236, 238
Comma splices, 236
Commenting, 245
Comparisons, 260, 264–266
Conclusion, 15, 65
   of reports, 259
Conflict, 247–248, 251
Conjunctions, 233
Connecting words/phrases, 268
Connections, 108, 132, 242, 244, 245

Contractions, 262
Conventions, 115, 136, 200, 228, 274
   print, 242
Conversations, 121
Cooperative learning, 280–281
Creative writing, 263
Cue cards, 124, 229, 255

Dashes, 92
Debates, 65
Decision making, 15, 182, 191
de la Mare, Walter, 93
Department of Justice Canada, 125–130
Dependent clauses, 234
Description, 260
Design, 3
Dialects, 232
Dialogue, 252
Dictionaries, 59
Direct address, 45
Directions, for procedures, 41, 42
Direct speech, 238
Drama, 107, 154, 228, 251–252. *See also* Plays
"Dream Variation" (Hughes), 9

Editing, 15, 37, 59, 79, 92, 116, 178, 273–274
Examples, 264
Exclamation marks, 238, 242
Exclamatory sentences, 235
Explanation paragraphs, 230
Explanation reports, 118
Explanations, 258
Expositions, 272

Facts, 66, 255
   editing for, 273
   opinions *vs.*, 60, 64
   in Q-charts, 242
   research, 118
   sorting into categories, 11, 15
Films, 101, 252

Fineday, Wes, 72–77
"Fingerprinting the Dead" (Owen), 121–122
Finton, Nancy, 83
First-person point of view, 204, 246
"Fix That Flat!" (Hayhurst), 41
Flashbacks, 251, 258
Flow charts, 59
"A Fly in a Pail of Milk" (Carnegie), 66–70
Folktales, 102, 135
Font, 8
Foreshadowing, 248, 251, 258
Formality, 206
Formal language, 21, 249
Format, 98, 162
   procedure, 178
   reflection, 194
   sentences, 174
"Foul Shot" (Hoey), 49–50
Fragments, 236
Frames charts, 228
Future tense, 233
"Future World" (Smith), 197–199

"The Gift That Could Not Be Stolen"
   (Konzak), 132–134
Gill, Lakshmi, 22
Gist statements, 16, 20
Glossaries, 131, 243
Gorrell, Gena K., 12–14
Grammar, 169, 274
Grammar and spell check computer program,
   59, 274
Graphic features, 8, 205, 206, 211, 285
Graphic organizers, 95, 255, 259, 269–272
   for characters, 174
   for decision making, 191
   to sort lists of words, 87
   of theme statements, 107
Graphic texts, 282-284
"Gross Out?" (Norlander), 94

Groups
   working in, 20, 280–281
Guilt (Barlow, Skidmore), 150–153

Hayhurst, Chris, 41
Headlines, of news reports, 136
"Helping Kids Make Sense of the Media,"
   163-166
"The Hockey Game" (Fineday), 72–77
Hoey, Edwin A., 49–50
Homophones, 88, 89, 275
Howarth, Lesley, 108–114
Hughes, Langston, 9

Ideas
   editing for, 273
   interesting *vs.* important, 90, 92
Imperative sentences, 235
Independent clauses, 234
Indirect speech, 238
Inferred messages, 210
Inferring, 93, 244
   about magazine article, 43
   about newspaper articles, 140
   meanings of words, 88, 93, 179
   theme of story, 24
   while reading, 46, 85, 87
Infinitive verbs, 233
Informational writing, 263
Interjections, 233
International symbols, 213
Internet, 255–256
Interrogative sentences, 235
Interviews, 71, 80, 125, 131
Introductory paragraph, 259
Inuktitut, 169
Inventions, 170, 174, 197
   words from, 232
Inverted order of sentences, 235
"Is Skateboarding a Crime?" (Burke), 46–47
Italics, 36, 95, 109, 115, 192, 242

Jargon, 232
Jot notes, 243

"Kendra Ohama: Wheeling and Shooting Her Way Around the World" (Robinson), 52–58
King-Smith, Dick, 88
Kritsonis, Ted, 207–209
Konzak, Burt, 132–134

Ladder organizers, 140
Language, 249. *See also* Vocabulary
   and audience, 41, 42
   clear, 178
   of drama, 16
   formal, 21, 261, 262
   informal, 261, 263
   levels of, 232, 261, 263
   moderate, 261, 262
   power in, 179
Languages, 179
Law, Jaclyn, 43-44
Lee, Susan, 180
Letters to the editor, 253
Lewis, Wendy A., 24–35
Limited narrators, 246
Listening, 277
"Looking Like a Kid" (Mayer, Colbourne), 170–173

The Magic Sieve (Watts), 102–106
Mayer, André, 170–173
McIlroy, Anne, 85-86
MacLennan, Robin, 136–139
Media, 163, 282–289
Media productions, 284–289
Menlichuk, Anna, 96–97
Metacognition, 261
Metaphors, 260
Mind maps, 65, 270
"mirrors dot com" (Howarth), 108–114

Mother Goose & Grimm (Peters), 11
"Mother Tongue" (Lee), 180

Narratives, 258
   creating from non-fiction texts, 211
   drama *vs.*, 154
   elements of, 16, 141, 148
   suspense in, 101
   and voice of narrator, 246
Narrators, 246, 249, 250
   in comic books, 228
   main characters as, 78
   in role playing, 21, 118
Natural order of sentences, 235
Nepveu, Tania, 201–203
News broadcasts, 156
"New Science of Body Measurement," 205
Newspaper articles, 140
News reports, 52, 59, 132, 135, 136, 245
Norlander, Britt, 94
Nouns, 232

Objective writing, 259
Objects, 234
Onomatopoeia, 283
Open-ended questions, 71
Opinion paragraphs, 8, 51, 98
Opinions, 255. *See also* Supported opinions
   changes of, 154
   of characters, 107
   editing for, 273
   examples from text to support, 45, 98, 123
   facts *vs.*, 60, 64
   identifying writer's, 46, 47
   summaries of, 229
   supported, 259
Oral communication, 277–282
Oral presentations, 170, 174, 253, 278–279
Oral reading, 10, 95
Organization
   of articles, 59

editing for, 273–274
in news reports, 136
Outcomes, 16, 194
Owen, David, 121–122

Panel discussions, 155
Paragraphs, 59. *See also* Opinion paragraphs
    explanation, 230
    introduction to, 65
    introductory, 259
    and levels of language, 261
    opinion, 98
    of reports, 259
    supported opinion. *See* Supported opinions
    writing, 15
Past tense, 233
Patterns, 243
Periods, 236, 238
Personal writing, 263
Peters, Mike, 11
Phrases, connecting, 268
Plagiarism, 255
Plays, 214. *See also* Drama
    creation of, 193
    performance of, 21
Plots, 16, 247–248, 251, 252
Points of view, 16, 149, 246–247, 274, 282
Portfolios, 275–276
Possessive pronouns, 233
Posters, 178
"The Praying Mantis" (King-Smith), 88
Predicates, 234
Predicting, 36, 201, 239, 241, 242
Prepositional phrases, 234
Prepositions, 233, 234
Present tense, 233
Principal clauses, 234
Prior knowledge, 240
Procedure format, 178
Procedures, 41, 42, 95, 259
Procrastination, 175, 178

Pronoun-antecedent disagreement, 236
Pronouns, 233, 268
Proofreading, 273–274
Protagonists, 249
Punctuation, 238, 242, 274
Puns, 174
Purpose, 239, 253
    of articles, 45
    of autobiographies, 71
    of bolded words, 166
    of folktales, 102
    form and, 263
    of italics, 115
    of oral presentations, 278
    of poems, 89
    of reports, 259
    tone and, 261–264

Question marks, 238
Questions, 241–242, 245, 258
    different types of, 72
    for interviews, 80
    to understand reading, 8, 78
Quick write, 52, 269
Quotation marks, 210, 238, 242

Radio, 252
RADS (reorder, add, delete, substitute), 51, 272
"The Ravine" (Salisbury), 182–190
Readers. *See also* Audience
    attention of, 43
Reader's theatre, 10, 95
Reading
    aloud, 214
    drama, 251–252
    for pleasure, 256–257
    speed, 243
    stopping to check word meanings, 23
    strategies, 121, 123, 239–245
Reflection, 245, 261

Reformulating, 245
Rehearsals, 279
Reordering, 272
Repetition, 267
   in collages, 286
   of words, 10
Reporters, 156
Reports, 140, 259
   body of, 259
   conclusion of, 259
   explanation, 118
   final copy of, 84
   news, 52, 59, 132, 135, 136, 245
   paragraphs of, 259
   rough draft of, 84
   topics of, 259
   writing, 79
Rereading, 244
Research, 83, 84, 118, 140, 170, 174, 253–255, 284
Resources, 253, 254–255
Retelling, 50, 58, 90, 92, 115, 169, 245, 247, 260
Revising, 15, 59, 79, 92, 116, 124, 140, 272–275
Rewriting, 21
Rhyme, 49
Rhythm, 10, 49, 95
Roach, Jody, 168
Robinson, Laura, 52–58
Robinson, Maija, 52–58
Roblin, Chuck, 214–227
Role playing, 21, 118, 156, 197, 200
Root words, 89, 205, 206, 243
Ross, Oakland, 60–63
Rough sketches, 285
Run-on sentences, 236

Salisbury, Graham, 182–190
Scanning, 239
Scenes, 228, 251–252

Scott, Jerry, 209
Scripts
   characters in, 238
   shooting, 204
   for television shows, 149
Script writing, 38, 154, 156
Sentences, 234
   choice of, 274
   errors in, 236
   format, 174
   and levels of language, 261
   parts of, 234–235
   short, 101
   starters, 243, 244, 245
   types of, 23
   variety of, 235
Sequence flowcharts, 259
Setting, 16, 244, 251, 252
Similes, 102, 260
Skidmore, Steve, 150–153
Skimming, 131
Skits, 38
Slang, 232
"slang tongue twist" (Wabegijig), 179
Sleator, William, 141–148
Smith, Michael N., 197–199
Sources, 275
Special effects, 252
Speech, parts of, 232–233
Speech writing, 121, 124
Spelling, 237, 275
"Spittin' Mad? That'll Be $155" (MacLennan), 136–139
Split order of sentences, 235
Stage, 252
Stage directions, 154
Stage fright, 279
Standard Canadian English, 232
"State of the Teen Nation" (Youth Culture Group), 159–161
Storyboards, 99, 101, 289

Story tellers. *See* Narrators
Style, 9, 22, 59, 132, 135, 244
Subheadings, 64, 84
Subjective completion, 234
Subjects
   of oral presentations, 278
   of plays, 107
   of poems, 181
   of sentences, 234
   themes *vs.*, 20, 36
Subject-verb disagreement, 236
Subordinate clauses, 234
Subordinating conjunctions, 233
Subplots, 251
Substitution, 268, 273
Subtitles, 8, 21, 66, 174
Subtopics, 118
Summaries, 162, 243, 260
"Superpoopers" (Finton), 83
Supported opinions, 37, 96, 108, 117, 118, 192, 259
Surveys, 159, 162, 179
Suspense, 99, 248
Synonyms, 268

"Talk Before They Run" (Child Find Ontario), 3–7
"Tallest Man Feels Lowly at the Top" (Menlichuk), 96–97
T-charts, 3, 8, 37, 98, 107, 108, 117, 192
"Tech Talk" (Kritsonis), 207–209
Technology, 197, 229, 230
   vocabulary of, 205
   words from, 232
Television, 252
Text features, 95, 211, 213
Themes, 251
   as "big idea", 72, 78, 181
   statements, 20, 78, 107, 181, 193
   subjects *vs.*, 20, 36
Third-person point of view, 246–247

Thumbnail sketches, 149, 213, 285
Timelines, 259, 271
"Tiny Bubbles? Fish May Be Talking" (McIlroy), 85–86
Title page, 214
Tone, 9, 22, 206, 249, 261–264
Topics, 251, 253
   of reports, 259
   researching, 84, 170
Topic sentence, 15
"The Toynbee Convector" (Bradbury, Zone, Roblin), 214–227
Transitions, 267–268
Translations from other languages, 168, 169
Tree organizers, 8

"Unbalanced" (Sleator), 141–148
Usage, 274

Venn diagrams, 149, 150, 270
Verbs, 233, 234, 236
   action, 49
   description, 49
   lists of, 51
   tenses, 233
Visual and media works, 284–286
Visual displays, 193
Visualization, 88, 89, 201, 241
Visuals, 162
Visual stories, 214
Vocabulary, 243, 261. *See also* Language
   for adult audience, 3
   specialized, 125
   of technology, 205
Voice, 274

Wabegijig, Vera, 179
Wafer, Meghan, 99–100
Watts, Irene N., 16–20, 102–106
Webs, 270
"What Are You Waiting For?" 175–177

"What Dreams May Come" (Roach), 168
"Why Do People Yawn, and Why Are Yawns Contagious?" (Wollard), 90–91
Wollard, Kathy, 90–91
Words
   checking meanings of, 23
   choice of, 59, 249, 260, 261, 274
   in collages, 286
   combinations of, 23
   connecting, 268
   formal *vs.* informal, 167
   from globalization, 232
   from inventions, 232
   meanings of, 210
   new, 207, 210
   plays on, 174
   root, 89, 205, 206, 243
   from technology, 232
   thinking, 192
   unfamiliar, 243

Word webs, 23, 85, 116, 141, 150
Work habits, 175, 178
Writing
   creative, 263
   development methods, 264–268
   forms of, 263
   informational, 263
   personal, 263
   types of, 92, 93, 174, 258–261

"You Have the Right to Remain Informed" (Department of Justice Canada), 125–130
"You Never Know (Tish)" (Lewis), 24–35
Youth Culture Group, 159–161

Zits (Scott and Borgman), 209
Zone, Ray, 214–227

> > > Acknowledgements

Text

9 From the *Collected Poems of Langston Hughes*, by Langston Hughes, copyright © 1994 by The Estate of Langston Hughes. Used by permission of Alfred A. Knopf, a division of Random House, Inc.; **11** © Grimmy Inc., Reprinted with special permission of King Features Syndicate; **12** Taken from *Working Like A Dog*, ©2003 by Gena K. Gorrell, published by Tundra Books; **16** Reprinted by permission of the author, Irene N. Watts; **22** Reprinted by permission of the author, Lakshmi Gill; **24** Reprinted by permission of Red Deer Press; **41** "Fix That Flat!," from *Mountain Biking! Get on the Trail*, by Chris Hayhurst. (New York: The Rosen Publishing Group, Inc. copyright 2000); **43** "Chew on This," by Jaclyn Law from *Fuel* Magazine, September 2003. Reprinted by permission; **46** "Is Skateboarding a Crime?" from *Skateboarding: Surf the Pavement* (from the Extreme Sports Collection) by L.M. Burke. ©2002 by The Rosen Publishing Group. Reprinted by permission; **49** Reprinted by permission of Weekly Reader Corporation; **52** "Kendra Ohama: Wheeling and Shooting Her Way Around the World," by Laura Robinson, from *Great Girls: Profiles of Awesome Canadian Athletes*. Published by Harper Collins Publishers Ltd. Copyright © 2004 by Laura Robinson. All rights reserved; **60** Reprinted with permission – Torstar Syndication Services; **66** Excerpt from *A Fly in a Pail of Milk: The Herb Carnegie Story*, by Herb Carnegie with Robert Payne. Reprinted by permission, Herb Carnegie; **72** Reprinted by permission of the author, Wes Fineday; **83** From SCIENCE WORLD, March 22, 2004. Copyright © 2004 by Scholastic Inc. Reprinted by permission of Scholastic Inc.; **85** Reprinted with permission from The Globe and Mail; **88** Used with permission of A.P. Watt Ltd. On behalf of Dick King-Smith; **90** copyright © 1993 by Kathy Wollard; **93** The Literary Trustees of Walter de la Mare and the Society of Authors as their representative; **94** From SCIENCE WORLD, March 8, 2004. Copyright © 2004 by Scholastic Inc. Reprinted by permission of Scholastic Inc; **96** Reprinted with permission of The Associated Press; **99** "Blue Eyes" by Meghan Wafer, first appeared in the *Toronto Star*, September 21, 2003. Reprinted by permission of the author; **102** Reprinted by permission of the author, Irene N. Watts; **108** Reprinted by permission of the author, Lesley Howarth; **121** Reprinted by permission of Quintet Publishing Limited, United Kingdom; **125** Reprinted by permission of WHAT! Publishers Inc. publishers of *What* Magazine; **132** Taken from *Samurai Spirit* © 2002 by Burt Konzak, published by Tundra Books; **136** Reprinted by permission of Robin MacLennan; **141** UNBALANCED, copyright © 2000 by William Sleator. First published in ON THE EDGE: STORIES AT THE BRINK, Aladdin Paperbacks. All rights reserved. Used with permission of Sheldon Fogelman Agency, Inc.; **150** *Guilt*, from *Send in the Clones* by Steve Barlow and Steve Skidmore. Reprinted by permission of Harcourt Education; **159** "State of the Teen Nation," from *Fuel* Magazine, April 2004. Reproduced by permission; **163** "Helping Kids Make Sense of the Media," by Terry Price, President of the Canadian Teacher's Federation, first appeared in the *Toronto Star*, November 19, 2003; **168** NIGHT IS GONE, DAY IS STILL COMING: STORIES AND POEMS BY AMERICAN INDIAN TEENS AND YOUNG ADULTS. "What Dreams May Come," Copyright © 2003 by Judy Roach. Reprinted by permission of the author. All rights reserved. Translations Copyright © 2003 by Jean Kusagak. All Rights reserved. Introduction Copyright © 2003 by Simon J. Ortiz. Collection Copyright © 2003 Annette Piña Ochoa, Betsy Franco, and Traci L. Gourdine. Reproduced by permission of the publisher Candlewick Press, Inc., Cambridge, MA.; **170** Reprinted by permission of the author André Mayer; **175** "What Are You Waiting For?" from *Verve* Magazine, Back to School Issue, 2003. Reprinted by permission; **179** "slang tongue twist," by Vera Wabegijig from *Breaking the Surface* (Victoria: Sono Nis Press, 2000). Reprinted with permission of the author, Vera Wabegijig; **180** "Mother Tongue," by Susan Lee from *Where Are You Really From?* Anthologized and Edited by Hazelle Palmer (Toronto: Sister Vision, 1997.) Reprinted by permission; **182** Reprinted by permission, The Flannery Agency; **197** "Future World: What Your Life Could Be Like in 2025," by Michael N. Smith, from *National Geographic Kids*,

March 2004. Reprinted by permission of National Geographic; **201** "Bubble Chamber," written and illustrated by Tania Nepveu from *What If?* Magazine (Guelph: What If? Publications, 2004) Reprinted by permission; **205** Copyright, 2004, Knight Ridder/Tribune. Reprinted with permission; **207** Reprinted by permission of *Faze Magazine*; **209** © Zits Partnership. Reprinted with special permission of King Features Syndicate; **211** Reprinted with permission of The Associated Press; **214** Reprinted by permission of Don Congdon Associates, Inc. Copyright © 1988 by Ray Bradbury. "The Toynbee Convector," from *The Ray Bradbury Chronicles: Volume One* (New York). Artwork courtesy of Byron Priese Visual Publications, 1992. Reprinted by permission; **229** Beers, S. and Lou Howell (2003) *Reading Strategies for Content Areas* – Chart, Book vii, (p. 388). Reprinted by permission. The Association for Supervision and Curriculum is an international education association for educators at all levels and of all subject matter, dedicated to the success of all learners. To learn more, visit ASCD at www.ascd.org; **242** (Q-Chart) Jan McLellan

Photos

1 Ryan McVay/Photodisc Red/Getty Images, inset top: Photodisc/Getty Images, inset bottom: Photolink/Photodisc Green/Getty Images; **3** left: Photodisc/Getty Images, right: Child Find Ontario; **9** © Corel; **11** © Corel; **12** Ryan McVay/Photodisc Green/Getty Images; **16** Fred Bruemmer/Peter Arnold Inc.; **19** Hans Strand/Photographers Choice/Getty Images; **22** Photolink/Photodisc Green/Getty Images; **24** Geostock/Photodisc Green/Getty Images; **39** © Royalty-free/Corbis, inset top: Don Tremain/Photodisc Green/Getty Images, inset bottom: Vicky Kasala/Photodisc Red/Getty Images; **41** © Royalty-Free/Corbis; **43** Kim Steele/Photodisc Green/Getty Images; **44** Reprinted with permission of *Fuel* Magazine; **46** top left: © Royalty-free/Corbis, right: Daniel Allan/Photodisc Red/Getty Images; **49** Don Tremain/Photodisc Green/Getty Images; **52** © Corel; **55** Kevin Bogetti-Smith; **58** Kevin Bogetti-Smith; **60** Vicky Kasala/Photodisc Red/Getty Images; **63** Reprinted with permission – TorStar Syndication Services; **66** Gaetan Charbonneau/Photographers Choice/Getty Images; **68** "Herbie" Carnegie, Sherbrooke Randies Quebec Sr. Hockey League, 1947; **72** Rim Light/Photolink/Photodisc Green/Getty Images; **77** Photolink/Photodisc Green/Getty Images; **81** And Images/Digital Vision/Getty Images, inset top: Olney Vasan/Stone/Getty Images, inset bottom: Lyle Stafford; **83** © Royalty-free/Corbis; **85** Olney Vasan/Stone/Getty Images; **93** Photodisc/Getty Images; **94** Lyle Stafford; **96** Efrem Lukatsky/AP Photo/CP Picture Archive; **99** Jules Frazier/Photodisc Green/Getty Images; **102** S. Alden/Photolink/Photodisc Green/Getty Images; **108** Royalty-Free/Corbis; **119** © J. Silver/Superstock, inset top: Photodisc/Getty Images, inset bottom: © Royalty-free/Corbis; **121** Royalty-Free/Corbis; **122** Photodisc/Getty Images; **125** Photodisc/Getty Images; **132** Bruce Heineman/Photodisc Green/Getty Images; **134** © Burstein Collection/Corbis; **139** Don Smetzer/Stone/Getty Images; **141** © Royalty-free/Corbis; **145** © Richard Hamilton-Smith/Corbis; **150** © Royalty-free/Corbis; **157** Ryan McVay/Photodisc Red/Getty Images, inset top: Shutterstock.com; inset bottom: © Corel; **159** Shutterstock.com; **161** (three images): *Fuel* Magazine; **163** Shannon Fagan/Photograher's Choice/Getty Images; **164** Ian McKinnell/Taxi/Getty Images; **168** © Corel; **170** © Corel; **173** Courtesy of Gina Gallant; **175** Spike Mafford/Photodisc Green/Getty Images; **176** Photodisc/Getty Images; **179** Kevin Frayer/CP Picture Archive; **180** Michael Jang/Stone/Getty Images; **182** Photodisc/Getty Images; **188** Claire Arnaud/Stock Image/Picture Quest; **195** Flatliner/Photodisc Green/Getty Images, inset top right: Flatliner/Photodisc Green/Getty Images; **197** Flatliner/Photodisc Green/Getty Images; **208** Reprinted with permission of *Faze* Magazine; **211** Photodisc/Getty Images; **231** Eyewire Images; **232** Jupiter Images; **239** Jupiter Images; **258** © Steve Skjold/Alamy; **277** © Royalty-free/Corbis; **282** C Squared Studios/Photodisc Green/Getty Images

Illustrations

26, 31 Cybèle; **86, 88, 90** Kathryn Adams; **104, 208** Jock MacRae; **114** Thom Sevalrud; **152** Kevin Ghiglione; **198** Carl Wiens; **203** Scott Chantler; **283** Cindy Jeftovic